ACCOMPLISHED
IN ALL
DEPARTMENTS
OF ART

ACCOMPLISHED IN ALL DEPARTMENTS OF ART

Hammatt Billings
of Boston, 1818–1874

James F. O'Gorman

UNIVERSITY OF MASSACHUSETTS PRESS

Amherst

Frontispiece. Hammatt Billings, 1856. Photograph by Whipple and Black (author's collection).

Printed in the United States of America
LC 97-46542
ISBN 1-55849-148-1

Designed by Dennis Anderson
Set in Centaur by Keystone Typesetting, Inc.
Printed and bound by Braun-Brumfield, Inc.

Library of Congress Cataloging-in-Publication Data

O'Gorman, James F.
Accomplished in all departments of art—Hammatt Billings of Boston,
1818–1874 / James F. O'Gorman.
p.   cm. — (Studies in print culture and the history of the book)
Includes bibliographical references and index.
ISBN 1-55849-148-1 (cloth : alk. paper)
1. Billings, Hammatt, 1818–1874. 2. Artists—United States—
Biography. I. Title. II. Series.
N6537.B525035   1998
709'.2—dc21
[B]   97-46542
CIP

This book is published with the support and cooperation of the
University of Massachusetts, Boston, and Wellesley College.

British Library Cataloguing in Publication data are available.

To the memory of
Lee Ann *Clements* Pralle
Wellesley College '78,
who introduced me to the work of
Hammatt Billings

AND

Margaret *Henderson* Floyd
Wellesley College, '53,
scholar of Boston architecture, student,
teacher, colleague, friend

Contents

Preface

WHO WAS Hammatt Billings? The short answer is, he was a designer who lived and worked in Boston during the middle of the nineteenth century, an artist-architect highly regarded in his own time and largely forgotten in ours. A longer answer will be found in the following chapters. The actual Billings lived, worked, died, and was forgotten. The Billings in this book is a re-creation based upon fragmentary evidence preserved through the accidents of time and retrieved through the fortunes of scholarship. This is the study of an artistic career of extraordinary range, from two- to three-dimensional design, from architecture to pyrotechnic display, from portraits to garden layout, from the illustration of books to the sketching of furniture. It was a career that rivaled the standard of versatility established in early nineteenth-century design by Billings's older English contemporary A. W. N. Pugin. This is a comparison of range and production, not of quality and influence, although the now invisible hand of Billings can be discerned by the scholar early in the works of better-known figures such as the artist Winslow Homer.

The following is an introductory study, not a definitive monograph. It recalls a professional life and is written close to the available sources, with speculative interpretation held to a minimum. I am astonished by the breadth of Billings's achievement—as were his contemporaries—rather than by the aesthetic quality of any one of his works, as fine as many of them are, so I have sought to give a broad historical overview of the most important branches of his art. I have separated the various categories in which he worked for the sake of this exposition, but it should be emphasized that his production was seamless. Work in illustration related to work in the design of sculpture; work in architecture informed work in illustration. There was rich diversity in Billings's professional life, but that life as a whole was a unit.

His output was so voluminous and so diverse that its parts cannot be treated exhaustively in one volume without tempting the reader to complain, as did Ambrose Bierce in the shortest review ever written, that "the covers of this book are too far apart." I have nevertheless sought to contextualize the work in general, and to supply a measure of depth by offering a more detailed analysis of some of his major, and diverse, accomplishments: the illustrations to *Uncle Tom's Cabin*, the design of Wellesley College, and the creation of the National Monument to the Forefathers at Plymouth.

A writer cannot completely divorce himself from his subject, but other than my necessary role in selecting what to emphasize, I have kept my intervention to a minimum. It seemed to me most useful to allow Billings's work and the assessment of his contemporaries to speak directly in this study, without the obfuscating gloss of currently fashionable theories.

Few personal papers seem to have survived. This book, therefore, is based primarily on the graphic evidence of his career as artist, architect, and designer collected into a series of scrapbooks, in some cases certainly, in others presumably, by his brother-in-law, the civil engineer Nathaniel T. Bartlett (ca. 1828–83?). I have fleshed out this information and some other primary documentation with gleanings from the journals, letters, and biographies of his patrons and clients, by citing contemporary accounts of his many activities to be found in the popular press, by collecting and cataloguing his illustrations for books and periodicals, and by reading recent histories of the culture, society, and politics of mid-nineteenth-century America. No one knows better than I how spotty my collecting has been. I fully expect much new information to emerge in coming years.

Why reintroduce Hammatt Billings now? Because in our age of highly specialized work, it might be inspirational to contemplate the career of a jack-of-all-designs. Because public art is a concern of the present, and the extent of his involvement with the public arts of Boston in the nineteenth century is, in the current word, awesome. No other artistic career can tell us so much about the cultural life of the city during the era in which it could truly be called the Hub. Because his talent was supported by, or illustrated the work of, or touched the lives of not only the urban patriciate but the hoi polloi as well. No other artist of his day was so completely interwoven into the public and private fabric of society. And because I want to make a point about the writing of history that can best be left to the afterword. The full meaning of Hammatt Billings's career will come only after an examination of its many parts, and that is best attempted after an introduction to the man himself.

THIS STUDY began many years ago when a student at Wellesley College chose to write her undergraduate thesis on the original College Hall, a building destroyed by fire early in this century. Lee Ann Clements discovered the name of the forgotten architect, Hammatt Billings, and she uncovered much documentary evidence, drawings, photographs, and written descriptions, that led to an imaginative re-creation of the building and its context in an exhibition at what was then called the Wellesley College Museum of Art (1978). Lee Ann died tragically early, and I have carried on the work, the sometimes exasperating work, in her honor. I have struggled to control the important but bewildering array of art and architecture produced by this tireless man for many reasons. Not the least of them was that I wanted one day to dedicate this study to the memory of this gifted young woman.

Two decades of interrupted research and writing have created an enormous debt to scholars, antiquarians, librarians, archivists, editors, curators, collectors, book sellers, artists, architects, designers, writers, photographers, administrators, critics, colleagues, friends, and relatives who have contributed to this book in every possible way from feeding me information or asking unanswerable questions to listening patiently while I told another tale of finding one more piece of the biographical puzzle. It would take a book-length manuscript to list them all. They know who they are, and they must be content to know that I could not have pulled this diverse study together without the assistance of each of them. I am delighted, however, specifically to thank the National Endowment for the Humanities for a summer stipend (1994) and a yearlong fellowship (1996) during the preparation of the manuscript, and I am also happy to acknowledge Wellesley College for a subvention in support of publication from the Class of '32 Humanities Fund.

I
"A Rare Man"

NEGLECTED AMONG the collections of the Pilgrim Society in Plymouth, Massachusetts, is a pedestal bearing the following inscription: Hammat Billings / Architect & Designer / of the / National Monument / Erected to . . . / the / Fore-fathers in Plymouth / Mass . . . He Was a Rare Man / with Genius Un-bounded / & / Accomplished in All Departments of Art (fig. 1). There are two points that should be noticed about this inscription. First, judging by the use of the past tense, it was written after the designer's death in 1874, although probably not long after. Nonetheless, even though it was a family name well known in Plymouth, his given name is misspelled. How quickly his presence dimmed![1] Second, the portrait bust that obviously once rested on this pedestal is missing. The story goes that it lasted into the 1960s when it was sent off to the town dump.[2] There it was rescued by one of the local citizens who placed it on his front lawn, from which it soon disappeared. How thoroughly our time has devalued the memory of a man once thought worthy of being placed on a pedestal. A "rare man," a "genius," and all but lost to history. We must wade through such forgotten, incomplete, and often inaccurate records in search of the man and his work.

What we know of the man himself comes more from secondary sources than from primary documents. While evidence of his professional life abounds in the form of existing works, design drawings, and written documents, knowledge of his private life remains patchy and is largely learned from a few letters, some obituary notices, and the reminiscences of people who knew him. It is characteristic of this evidence that the basic items of his biography, the date and place of his birth, have been variously reported as 1816, 1817, or 1818 at either Boston or Milton, Massachusetts. We can establish the correct date by citing Billings himself, for in a letter of 14 June 1841 he noted that the following day was to be his twenty-third birthday, a fact that places his birth at 15 June 1818.[3] The future designer's full name was Charles Howland Hammatt Billings, the "Howland" and "Hammatt" linking him to the earliest settlers of New England.[4] The family had run the Blue Hill

Fig. 1. Pedestal formerly holding a bust of Hammatt Billings (Pilgrim Society, Plymouth, Mass.).

Tavern in Milton since the seventeenth century.[5] Hammatt's father was Ebenezer Jr.; his mother, Mary Demale Janes.[6] They were married in Boston in September 1817. Hammatt was the oldest of six children.[7]

Whether born in Boston or not, Billings seems to have spent some of his earliest years in what is now suburban Milton; according to one obituary the family returned to the Hub when he was five; according to Stoddard, when he was ten.[8] Another obituary has him at about the latter age at the Mayhew School for boys near the family's home in the West End.[9] The school was then (1828–29) briefly under the supervision of the distinguished Harvard-trained educator Richard G. Parker (1798–1869), and it is reported that Billings had as classmates the future actor Edgar Loomis Davenport (1815–77) and the future sculptor Thomas Ridgeway Gould (1818–81).[10] Another sculptor, Thomas Ball (1819–1911), with whom Billings would on later occasions collaborate, also attended the school at this time. Ball remembered that he "detested" it, that Parker, the reading master, was "only severe," while a Mr. Holt, the writing master, "was at times brutal." Parker he describes as tall, austere, rather aristocratic, bespectacled, and "on the whole, kind-hearted." Holt was a "powerful, thickset man whose blows told." The boys wrote in the mornings and read in the afternoons. As was common in this period, the masters were assisted by monitors, older boys who drilled the younger. Ball remembered them as kind and helpful. He makes no mention of Billings in this connection, although he does relate a story about Davenport's reciting "Alexander's Feast" by John Dryden. Such was the stern elementary school training Billings and other Boston boys experienced in the 1820s.[11]

Despite a primary education largely devoted to words in the good Bostonian fashion, Billings early turned to images. He showed a precocious talent in the creation of shadow puppets as well as in the graphic arts. "When only ten," according to one later account, Charley, as he was then called,

> obtained some celebrity at the West end . . . by his wonderful skill in cutting minute figures of horsemen, animals and landscapes out of paper. We were ourselves boys with him . . . [and] recollect very well the wonder of delight it afforded us to see him with his little bits of scissors produce all the *dramatis persona[e]* of the ever-charming oriental play of the Forty Thieves . . . [which he performed] in a dark cellar behind a transparency made of a box and sheet or two of oiled paper. . . . Many of the parents . . . visited this exhibition of precocious genius, and went away prophesying that [he] . . . would become a great artist.[12]

This practice of scissors' graphics was perhaps inspired by something like the "Papyrotomia" of Master James Hubbard on view in Boston in the mid-1820s and described in the *Columbian Centinel* for 16 November 1825 as a "splendid collection of Cuttings in paper" by an artist "who possesses the peculiar faculty of delineating every object in Nature or Art with a pair of *common scissors*."[13] There is no mention of illuminated animations in this account, however; Billings may also have seen or heard of performances of *ombrés chinoises,* or shadow puppets, popular in Europe and the United States from the last quarter of the eighteenth century.[14]

Cutting paper seems to have been a passing fancy; graphic design became Billings's lifelong labor. Another account has him also at age ten receiving instruction from a "Mr. Grater."[15] This was, Franz Gräter, or Francis Graeter, that "eccentric German drawing-master" who had taught Longfellow's brother-in-law to be, Thomas Gold Appleton, at the Round Hill School in Northampton, Massachusetts, in 1827.[16] Shortly thereafter Graeter appeared in Boston, teaching drawing at Elizabeth Palmer Peabody's progressive school and giving private lessons to her sister, Sophia Peabody (later Mrs. Nathaniel Hawthorne).[17] In the early 1830s Graeter worked for Bronson Alcott at the Temple School, at which time Elizabeth Peabody described him as "a gentleman who probably possesses the spirit of Art more completely than any instructor who has ever taught in this country."[18] In the preface to *The Girls' Own Book*, which Graeter illustrated, Lydia Maria Child wrote that "to those who have been his pupils, nothing need be said in praise of his spirited and graceful sketching."[19] Graeter was a figure, landscape, and architectural artist, an illustrator of children's and other books, an author, and according to Sophia Peabody, something of an art critic. This range of graphic work and critical faculty presages Billings's own. Graeter set young Charley to drawing not from life but, in the custom of the day, from "studies of heads, casts, &c."[20] The youngster's parents must have believed in his talent to have footed the bill for private instruction from this solid teacher.

By 1831 Billings was at the English High School, one of the forty-six members of the class of 1834. The headmaster then was Harvard-trained Thomas Sherwin (1799–1869), a celebrated educator who held the post for thirty years.[21] Billings was to design a memorial tablet for him in 1870.[22] We know nothing about Billings's stay at English except that he did not graduate (nor did twenty-nine other members of the class).[23] English was a finishing school for boys whose parents could not afford to send them to college; the more fashionable Latin High then as now prepared its pupils for continuing education. English grounded its students in words and figures, subjects potentially useful in a commercial life. The curriculum, at least by the next decade, included composition, logic, geography, arithmetic, algebra, navigation, surveying, natural and moral philosophy, modern languages, and drawing. The mainstay of the prep school, the classics, were unknown.[24]

Billings's formal education, however truncated, was not without effect in his later life, for he was remembered in one obituary as a man whose "knowledge of English literature, and, through translation, of the great masters of other languages, was critical," and described by a contemporary as having "studied nature and art in all their various manifestations" and as "well versed in natural history, antiquities, history, [and] the botany of various countries."[25] In some of this he was probably self-taught, for a list of sixty-four titles he purchased at William D. Ticknor's bookstore between 1845 and 1858, in addition to publications on architecture and works obviously of use to a book illustrator interested in the latest production of London and continental artists, includes works on mathematics, music, marksmanship, English and American poetry, and other subjects (see appendix A). Despite the statement above that he read only English, in letters of May and June of 1842 he wrote of studying French in what must have been a course in conversation for he could already read the language: on 16 July 1841 he mentioned borrowing Charles Paul de Kock's *La jolie fille du Faubourg* (1840).[26] It would seem that the habits of disciplined reading he acquired at the Mayhew School and English High stayed with him for the rest of his life.

One other institution apparently influenced the young scholar. Charles F. Read wrote that Billings was during these years a Sunday school student at the Warren Street Chapel. Since this nonsectarian "free children's church" was not dedicated until 1836, he probably attended during his days as an apprentice after leaving the English High School, that is, as a late teenager. The chapel was devoted to the moral education of the young through religious, temperance, and other instruction. The institution began in the parlor of the reformer Dorothea L. Dix (1802–87) and was for many years under the supervision of the Reverend Charles F. Barnard.[27] Billings was to illustrate works devoted to the great moral questions of his day; perhaps his dedication to these reform issues was awakened at the chapel.[28] In any event, instruction there supplemented what he received as a scholar at the English High School and as an apprentice with Abel Bowen and Asher Benjamin, under whose tutelage he finished his education.

Billings may have left English early because of the founding of the Boston Bewick Company in 1833.[29] Accounts mention his youthful apprenticeship to one of the founders, Abel Bowen (1790–1850), a graphic artist and Boston's pioneer wood engraver, who had himself been trained by Alexander Anderson (America's first wood engraver) and begun his professional career in 1812.[30] Bowen has been characterized as a "conscientious craftsman" rather than a distinctive artist.[31] Nonetheless, from the 1820s on he produced a number of important illustrated books, chief among them Munroe and Francis's *Mother Goose's Quarto* (ca. 1825), *Bowen's Picture of Boston* (1829), *Mother Goose's Melodies* (1833), and the *American Magazine of Useful and Entertaining Knowl-*

edge (1834–37). Children's books, architectural views, and periodical illustration were all to figure prominently in Billings's career. He "had barely reached his teens when he went to learn the wood engraver's art," according to an 1859 account.[32] "We remember regretting that he did not take a higher starting-point," *Gleason's* editor wrote, "but perhaps it was for the best after all, and quite likely the knowledge thus obtained of that more mechanical branch was afterwards of material service when he became a designer on wood." Such an observation clearly defines the gap between the fine or private artist, like Boston's celebrated Washington Allston (1779–1843) or William Morris Hunt (1824–79), seeking rare beauty in a lonely studio, and the illustrator and designer who seeks popular communication and labors in the public eye. Although early on Billings aspired to the "higher" calling, his subsequent career exemplified the latter.[33]

We turn once again to the memoirs of Thomas Ball for a glimpse of apprentice life in Abel Bowen's shop. It occupied a large hall in Court Street. There were several pupils, "a jolly set of boys, harmlessly mischievous," who played the usual jokes on each other and anyone else who might fall their victim. "Those boys have mostly passed out of my sight," the sculptor wrote as an old man, "but not out of my memory. Hammatt Billings,—the handsome, blue-eyed one,—after making for himself an enviable reputation as an architect, died. Tom Deveroux *[sic]*—the dashing, musical one . . . Henry Brown—a delicate boy, . . . [and] George Miles. . . . The year was passing pleasantly enough; it could hardly be otherwise with such merry companions."[34] Other of Bowen's apprentices in wood engraving included Joseph Andrews (1806–73), Alonzo Hartwell (1805–73), and William Croome (1790–1860), some of whom were to carve Billings's illustrations in coming years. Hartwell's son, Henry, would become an apprentice in turn, in Billings's architectural office.

We know nothing specific about Billings's stay in Bowen's shop. We can guess that he learned not only how to engrave wood but to design as well, and the architectural bent of some of Bowen's work must have suggested to the apprentice another avenue for his restless talent.[35] Bowen had not only engraved views of buildings for his *Picture of Boston* and *American Magazine,* he had signed two copperplate engravings published by the architect Asher Benjamin in the sixth edition of his *American Builder's Companion* of 1827. And Billings is next to be found in Benjamin's drafting room as an apprentice. "When he was less than eighteen [i.e., before 1836] he went to Mr. Benjamin to learn architecture. . . . [and] remained two or three years."[36] Asher Benjamin (1772/3–1845) was one of the major neoclassical architects and the major publicist of Roman and Greek architectural forms in New England, if not the United States.[37] We know nothing about his office or his teaching methods; we can only guess that Billings got a thorough grounding in the classical orders from this prime force in the architectural development of early nineteenth-century New England.

Benjamin's younger rival Ammi Burnham Young (1798–1874), fresh from designing the Vermont State Capitol at Montpelier, won the competition for the federal Customs House in Boston in 1837. The domed cruciform building of Quincy granite in a Greco-Roman Doric style was erected over the next decade. Probably because he needed help in the Boston drafting room he established in 1838, Young hired Hammatt Billings away from Benjamin, who had been among the losing competitors.[38] Billings's graphic ability made him immediately useful. According to the obituary in *Old and New*, Billings "did not design the building; but all the drawings were made by him. He was with Mr. Young three years."[39] Such a claim seems too sweeping, as Young must have made some drawings in order to win the competition, but much of the surviving graphic material, in particular the presentation drawings and contract documents, may plausibly be given to Billings. In 1839 he exhibited a number of "very superior" drawings for the building.[40] These included a "truly beautiful" section that may or may not be that preserved in the National Archives.[41] In 1840 Young copyrighted an engraved view of the building that is certainly the east perspective dated 1840 and is among Billing's earliest published works (fig. 2).[42] A sheet of outline drawings of plans, elevations, section, and interior and exterior perspectives survives in the National Archives.[43] This shows the neoclassical graphic style of the fledgling draftsman.

If the chronology given by the obituary writer for *Old and New* is correct, Billings would have been ready to go out on his own about 1841. And indeed, on 11 August of that year he wrote that the day marked the end of two years and nine months in Ammi Young's office, and that "it may be very near the last day in which I shall serve anyone as a second officer of the ship, I cant [*sic*] bear it."[44] The fledgling was itching to try out his wings. In the event it took more than a month to make the break. On the nineteenth he wrote that he knew this would "be a great step and not without its dangers. I shall have no salary to depend upon." On the twenty-fourth he reported that he had offers for much work but was still undecided about his plans. By 30 September, however, he could happily write that "[my] business is becoming natural

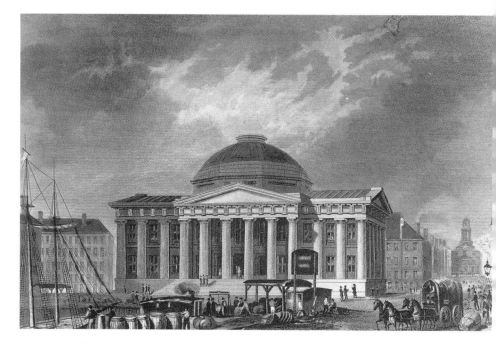

Fig. 2. Engraving by G. G. Smith after a drawing by Hammatt Billings, *New Custom House, Boston,* 1840. The architect was Ammi B. Young (author's collection).

to me and cannot fail in a pecuniary view to be agreeable." By 1842 he was listed in *Simpson's Boston Directory* as an independent architect, and by the following year he had added "designer" to his title. At this time he abandoned his full four-part name and assumed his professional persona as a crisp Hammatt Billings.

Hammatt's brother Joseph E. (ca. 1821–80), who seems also to have been trained by Young, joined him in architectural practice, both as a partner and as an independent, during the 1840s and again after the Civil War.[45] It would appear that Hammatt provided the designs while Joseph did the engineering. Their first commission was truly a plum: the Boston Museum on Tremont Street just north of King's Chapel, incorporating an exhibition space and a theater, of 1846. How these untried young architects managed to win this high-profile commission remains a mystery, but precocious as always, at the age of twenty-eight Hammatt there created one of the earliest Renaissance Revival buildings in the United States.

With and without his brother's help Hammatt in the next several years turned out Gothic churches, Italianate schools, clubs, and residences, a

Moorish arch over Tremont Street to celebrate the arrival of the public freshwater supply into the city in 1848, and a redesigned stair hall for E. C. Cabot's recently built Boston Athenaeum on Beacon Street. By the early 1850s he was an established architect and designer in the city (fig. 3). He was not only sought after by patrons but envied by his peers. Edward Cabot's brother Eliot, for example, wrote to Henry Lee in 1853 that "If the architects were all like Hammatt Billings I should most unconditionally knock under & say I knew nothing . . . , but as it is, I can do as well as any of them. Not a man jack here (except Billings) has done anything better than I can do as yet."[46] Nor, as we shall see, was this an isolated accolade.

The steady progress of his early professional career was paralleled by rough sledding in his personal life. One of his building activities during these early years apparently led to an economic disaster that was to plague his

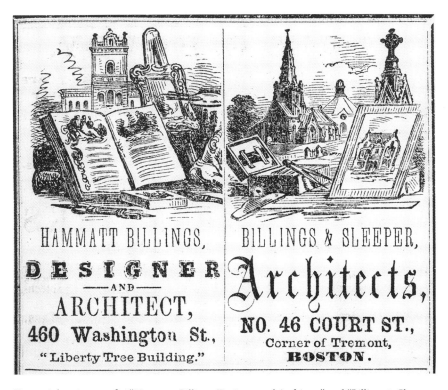

Fig. 3. Advertisement for "Hammatt Billings, Designer and Architect," and "Billings & Sleeper, Architects," *Boston Almanac for the Year 1854*. Both were presumably drawn by Hammatt, who illustrates the diversity of his services while limiting those of Joseph and his partner to architecture (author's collection).

financial condition for decades. He was precocious, but he also made mistakes. He not only designed the Church of the Saviour in Bedford Street in 1846 but agreed to build it as well. With the mason Benjamin G. Russell he contracted to erect the stone Gothic building for thirty-three thousand dollars.[47] Here apparently originated what seems to have been a lifelong struggle with money, for the cost of the completed structure is given as seventy thousand dollars, more than double the contract price, and in the next decade it was recorded that he "lost a great deal of money" on the venture.[48] One reading of what scanty personal documentary evidence exists is to see Billings's tireless efforts at universal design as a persistent scramble for money to meet his creditors. Nagging debt seems to have been his constant goad.

The early 1850s saw professional highlights in Billings's career, such as the original illustrations to *Uncle Tom's Cabin* and the design for the colossal National Monument to the Forefathers at Plymouth, but these years also saw the addition of personal grief to his financial woes. It was probably some time in 1843 that he married Sarah Mason in Roxbury.[49] In the absence of informative papers, only the barest suggestions of the sad end of this marriage come through to the present. Other than her name, what little is now known about Hammatt's first wife concerns her final years. In 1851 the architect's brother Joseph purchased what we would now call a "view lot" high above the meandering Charles River in Auburndale in the northwest corner of Newton, Massachusetts, a suburb of Boston.[50] In 1853 Joseph sold the lot and, judging by the sale price, a house, to Thomas Hall. The latter recalled in a note written long after the event, in 1915, but nonetheless generally in agreement with other known facts, that "Hammet [sic] Billings started building the house in 1852. He had the frame up and roof on when his wife was taken Insane & [went?] to the Hospital," perhaps the McLean Asylum, then in Somerville, Massachusetts.[51] The towered Italianate villa was finished and long occupied by Hall. In a letter to Charles Eliot Norton of 11 March 1852, Billings mentioned the "illness of Mrs. Billings," but her diagnosis and later fate remain unknown.[52]

Some time in the next few years, and probably about 1859, Billings married Phoebe A. Warren, who survived him by nine years.[53] He had no children by either spouse. We are left to wonder about Billings's relationship to his second wife, for the Boston directories show him after the mid-1860s boarding around town while Phoebe remained in residence at 59 Camden Street. Since no real estate is listed in Hammatt's probate records, whereas a lot and house at this address are listed in Phoebe's, it would seem that she was the sole owner.

Billings's apprenticeships with Asher Benjamin and Ammi Young did not lead him to concentrate his talents on architecture alone. His earlier artistic training with Francis Graeter and Abel Bowen also found ready outlet. During 1841–42, however, he oscillated between preferring one art form over the other. In July of 1841 a friend said to him that "Architecture is the Art of Arts" and he rejoiced in having his "own views confirmed." But a month earlier he had asked "Can I be a Painter?—Oh, can I give form & being to the visions that people my mind?" A month later he wrote that he had seen some engravings after Raphael. "Inspired and at the same time, down-hearted I turned away . . . to think of my doom, to model a door-cap ornament [for the Custom House]. . . . I am sick . . . that I cannot breathe the free air of high Art." And finally, when in early 1842 he began to draw at the Boston Artists' Association as a "commencement (at least I hope so) of a life in Art," he wrote that he "cannot give up this first love. . . . I . . . think how much I have turned away from my true faith." He was to reconcile this conflict by embracing both career options.[54]

The Boston Artists' Association founded in 1841 elected Billings to regular membership in November 1843. He joined Chester Harding, Isaiah Rogers, Fitz Hugh Lane, A. B. Young, Thomas Devereux, and other artists and architects in their professional and theoretical discussions. He also attended the drawing classes held in the association's rooms from life, and at the Athenaeum from casts.[55] Joseph soon joined. The brothers were active in the association until its demise early in the next decade, and Hammatt remained involved with its short-lived successor, the New England Art Union, and served as a director of *its* successor, the Massachusetts Academy of Fine Arts, which also "flourished 'its brief hour' " in the mid-1850s.[56] There is an architectural sketch by Billings of an Academy of Fine Arts that may relate to this organization.[57] Hammatt was still polishing his drafting skills as late as the 1860s, for in the winter of 1864 he was attending the Lowell Institute lectures given by William Rimmer. His sketches after Rimmer's blackboard drawings survive.[58]

Billings's work as book and periodical illustrator preceded his work as an architect. His earliest catalogued book illustration is the 1841 frontispiece to Jacob Abbott's *Rollo Code of Morals;* in 1842 he published two city views in the *Boston Miscellany of Literature and Fashion,* as well as views of Walter Scott's

Abbotsford and the obelisk of Luxor in Paris in Lydia Sigourney's *Pleasant Memories of Pleasant Lands* (see appendix B). Here and elsewhere in his career, he obviously worked from engraved sources. In 1845, with the many woodcuts drawn by Billings and engraved by Alonzo Hartwell in Munroe and Francis's *Chimes, Rhymes, and Jingles; or, Mother Goose's Songs,* Billings established himself as heir to Abel Bowen, as an important Boston illustrator of children's and other books and periodicals. By 1852 he was illustrating Harriet Beecher Stowe's *Uncle Tom's Cabin* and had begun a decade-long career as chief illustrator for *Gleason's* (later *Ballou's*) *Pictorial Drawing-Room Companion,* Boston's illustrated monthly magazine whose circulation reached over one hundred thousand by the middle of the decade.

Billings was a premier illustrator for many Boston publishers, major and minor, during that flowering of New England letters that has come to be called the American Renaissance. He drew illustrations for well over 250 titles during his career. They appeared largely as wood engravings, more rarely on steel, more rarely still as lithographs. He covered all the areas of current interest, as well as the literature of writers such as Oliver Wendell Homes, John Greenleaf Whittier, Nathaniel Hawthorne, Harriet Beecher Stowe, Louisa May Alcott, and English authors from Walter Scott to Oliver Goldsmith and Charles Dickens. Travel, gift books, history, readers, deportment, almanacs, religion, adventure: these and many other topics engaged his pencil. Children's books occupied the bulk of his time, however, and when he has been remembered in the modern literature, it has usually been for his work in this area.

His views for the *Boston Miscellany* and Mrs. Sigourney's *Pleasant Memories* combined his double-barreled talent as artist-architect, for here and in other work he acted as *vedutist,* or creator of urban architectural views, in the mode of his presentation drawing for A. B. Young's Customs House. Here he followed not only Bowen, who had produced the *Picture of Boston* in 1829, but the well-known architectural "composer" Alexander Jackson Davis. Davis (1803–92) was also an artist-architect of early accomplishment who turned out drawings for engraved architectural vignettes of New York and Boston in the 1820s.[59] Unlike Davis, however, who reconciled the internal conflict between artist and architect by concentrating his attention on architecture from the 1830s, Billings pursued a multifarious career. He designed buildings, and he continued to produce views of the major structures of his city (and New York) for book and periodical illustrations, framing prints, and sheet music covers through the middle of the nineteenth century.

As busy as he was as book and periodical illustrator, and as architect—not only of his own buildings but as (occasionally anonymous) designer for any number of other architects in the city, including S. S. Woodcock and G. F. Meacham, but especially the prolific Gridley J. F. Bryant—Billings turned out a bewildering variety of other work. This ranged from fireworks displays for the Common to a layout for the Boston Public Garden (unrealized), the composition of diplomas and certificates, the creation of private and public monuments, painted works in oil and watercolor, the design of sculpture as well as furniture and other decorative arts, the embellishment of public events stretching from the Water Arch of 1848 to the decorations for the reception at the Boston visit of the Prince of Wales in 1860.[60] He was, in short, everywhere in nineteenth-century Boston where the arts of design were called upon to celebrate, to commemorate, to mourn, to enhance the public and private activities of the people, the place, the era.

Financial worry as well as unbounded energy probably drove him to such diversity, and in the view of some of his contemporaries, he paid a price for spreading himself so thin. The uniqueness of his diverse talent was generally recognized in nineteenth-century Boston. There were those who were impressed by his range, and there were others who thought that rather than enhancing, it watered down his impact. On the one hand he was compared to Michelangelo for the richness of his talent, and a later critic, Montgomery Schuyler, saw this "draughtsman, painter, architect, illustrator, a[nd] person of exquisite artistic sensibilities" as "entirely anomalous and unprovided for in the general social and political scheme of . . . New England."[61] On the other hand friends such as Ednah Cheney had reservations. "He lacked the finer element of conscience which looks upon Art as a sacred calling," she remembered, and because of "pecuniary necessities" he "scattered his forces in many different and unworthy directions."[62] The writer of the obituary in *Old and New* thought that "had he devoted himself from the start to any one specialty, his life would have been one of greater accomplishment. He was always busy; but the element of caprice in the selection of department and subject, while it demonstrated his wonderfully varied accomplishments, prevented what should have been the full results of so much decided genius." These commentators not only disparaged his diversity, they emphasized the class distinction between the fine artist and the public servant.

In the 1850s Billings reached the summit of his career. He was firmly established in Boston as artist, illustrator, architect, and designer of note. We know what he looked like during this period from an occasional contemporary remark, and from a daguerreotype taken by Whipple and Black early in 1856 (see frontispiece) and published as a wood engraving in *Ballou's*.[63] He is shown at age thirty-eight with arms crossed over his chest, sporting long hair and a full beard, and the viewer quickly notices his steady gaze. He was described in the most useful obituary as having been a little above average in height, "with light hair and complexion," and "finely-cut features."[64] Here and elsewhere his eyes are called out for comment. Thomas Ball remembered the apprentice as handsome, and blue-eyed.[65] *Ballou's* in 1856 reported that "a stranger could hardly glance at his keen and penetrating eyes without deciding at once upon his profession." The author of the obituary in *Old and New* recalled "farseeing, deep-set gray eyes." A photograph of the older Billings shows a more somberly dressed, somewhat thinner figure with neatly trimmed hair, mustache and goatee, and the same, deeply shadowed gaze.[66] While these photographs confirm contemporary descriptions, it should also be noted that such remarks follow a pattern, that stressing an artist's eyes in descriptions and the equation of them with his profession were common in the United States at midcentury. Julian St. Cloud, the hero of Emerson Bennett's cheap thriller *The Artist's Bride* (1856), had for example "dark, full, dreamy eyes." This was also said of living artists, for example of Boston's premier early-century painter Washington Allston, whose eyes made him seem remarkable, made him look the painter in appearance.[67]

As contemporaries characterized him and associates remembered him, Billings seems to have been the most modest and sympathetic of individuals, although here again it should be made clear that there was a period style to the image of the artist in midcentury America, and the use of expected characteristics to delineate the individual puts something of a scrim between Billings and us.[68] *Old and New* described him as "kindly, but high-toned, and free from all petty jealousies," modest, self-possessed, ready to help younger artists with advice and assistance. Whether for modesty or other reasons, Billings rarely signed his many illustrations. Other commentators support and augment such praise. Another obituary remembered him as "noble and large-hearted . . . generous, even when he could ill afford it," while James Jackson Jarves wrote that "his own generous virtues and modest self-appreciation stand in the way of his worldly prosperity." *Harper's Weekly* called him frank and unselfish. Ednah Cheney reported that he was a "delightful talker," while John H. Thorndike described him in 1860 as "modest, unassuming, [and] industrious." Longfellow, finally, thought him a "charming fellow."[69]

We can penetrate the scrim of contemporary expectations, however, by quoting the young Billings on this subject. In July 1841 he described himself as a man "of grand ideas with puny execution" although he fought against this. "I wish to be first rate in my profession, to do all I can to advance a love of high & noble Art in our Country; the conventional distinctions of professional eminence I care nothing for, but the high truths & beauties of my art I would grasp and make my own."[70] Idealistic words from an aspiring youth, yes; but also confirmation of the modesty others saw in him.

The most common word used to characterize the man, as it was with so many other artists of the period, was "genius." "He looked the man of genius he was," according to *Old and New;* he was "a man of the rarest intelligence, almost amounting to genius," according to Ednah Cheney. William F. Gill paid tribute to Billings's "surpassing genius as an artist" in the dedication of his *Home Recreations* of 1875.[71] All of this referred to his capacity for imaginative work, his wizardry with a pencil, rather than to any analytical brilliancy. Agreement among so many observers must have some basis in truth. Certainly Billings had his detractors, but evidence that seriously contravenes these descriptions of this "rare man" has yet to come to light.

In the Whipple and Black daguerreotype the artist-architect wears a jacket with velvet collar and a flamboyant tie. His presentation was, then, artistic in the expectations of his day, and his attire, stylish. We know he was a regular customer of Hewins and Hollis, gentlemen's outfitters, who after 1843 clothed such leading Bostonians as Franklin Pierce, Edward Everett, George Ticknor, Josiah Quincy, Charles Sumner, Ralph Waldo Emerson, Henry F. Durant, David Sears, and countless others.[72] Billings was to work for many of these clients. In a democracy, even in Brahmin Boston, the architect and his patrons may buy their shirts at the same haberdashery. Although Billings had not, as had many of his patrons, attended Harvard College, it was these and other contacts through the network of Boston Brahmins who were to supply him with much of his patronage.

Billings descended from an old New England ancestry, but he was also a member of an economic class that could not afford to send him to Harvard. It must have been his intelligence, his talent, and probably, his personality that attracted many of the Boston patricians to him. Longfellow, Emerson, Richard Henry Dana Jr., Henry Fowle Durant (a lawyer and one of the founders of Wellesley College), the Cheneys (silk manufacturers of South Manchester, Connecticut), Harvard professor Charles Eliot Norton, Gov. William Claflin, Thomas Gold Appleton, these and many other Brahmins sought out not only his pencil but his critical faculties as well. As early as

1847 Longfellow called him the "best illustrator of books we have yet had in this country."[73] In a journal entry of 1863, Emerson thought of his native city as the home of great men and women, of "Franklin, Adams, . . . Horatio Greenough, of Wendell Phillips, of Edward Everett, of Allston, . . . of Daniel Webster, . . . of Billings the architect, of Mrs. Julia Howe, Margaret Fuller," and so on.[74] Heady company indeed! As architect of their houses, illustrator of their books, designer of their monuments, and critic of their taste, Billings served the design needs of the Boston establishment. As we shall see, the story of his winning of the commission for the design of the National Monument to the Forefathers, despite its allegorical subject, its colossal size, and his changing of the project from one to two structures, suggests the esteem in which he was held not only by the trustees of the Pilgrim Society, but the Massachusetts elite in general. He routed the original winner of the competition, and he exceeded the society's brief, both with the hearty approval of his patrons. The establishment needed him.

As did the populace in general. The people viewed his illustrations in the exploding number of children's books produced by the new high-speed presses for a growing literacy, monthly saw his work in the illustrated periodical press beginning in the 1840s, attended the patriotic fireworks displays he created for Fourth of July celebrations, mourned the death of Zachary Taylor with a public parade punctuated with a funeral car of Billings's design, sent its children to the public schools shaped by Hammatt and his brother, worshiped in churches he designed, bought the sheet music he embellished with Boston scenes and other vignettes, and received certificates he emblazoned. Readers cried at Harriet Beecher Stowe's description and Billings's depiction of the death of Little Eva in *Uncle Tom's Cabin*, or thrilled to his and Louisa May Alcott's visualizations of the exploits of the March girls in *Little Women*. Billings was omnipresent in the lives of mid-nineteenth-century Bostonians of the middle as well as the upper class. He was the designer who gave visible expression to personal as well as civic, patriotic, and other collective sentiments of his day.

Billings was an artist integrated into the society of his time, not marginalized or alienated. If his was not a household name, it was certainly broadly recognized in Boston. His Water Arch was a main feature of the parade held to celebrate the introduction of water into the city. His work was used as prototype for instruction in wood engraving at the New England School of Design for Women in the early 1850s.[75] He not only illustrated John Ross Dix's *Worth of the Worthless* in 1853, he appears in the text. John Bloker, the hero, contemplates the smoke rings from his pipe, and "the pictures therein framed became as distinct as if they had been drawn by the delicate pencil of Hammatt Billings."[76] He and his brother are casually mentioned as architects of the Church of the Saviour in a popular moral tract of 1856.[77] His name had recognition enough to be mentioned in real estate advertising, as when in 1857 a cottage on Dorr Street in Roxbury was proudly said to have been "designed by Billings" in the notice of sale.[78] And an "original pen-and-ink sketch by Billings" hangs next to works by Martin Johnson Heade and William Bradford in an economically furnished parlor in Harriet Beecher Stowe's *House and Home Papers* of 1865.[79] Such facts portray a familiar man about town—a designer integrated into the workaday world of Boston— rather than an aloof artist hidden in his garret. That such a noted player could so completely vanish from the stage of history is a wonder. Or rather, it says much about the class consciousness of traditional art-historical writing.

As an illustrator Billings placed his pencil in the service of the great issues of his time, especially the three most important moral issues: war, intemperance, and slavery. Any illustrator would find challenging the depiction of battle, and Billings gave visual form to great moments of the Mexican War and to generic struggles of the Civil War. Temperance literature was plentiful in an era of the Maine Law of 1851 and other attempts before and after midcentury to control or eliminate the sale and consumption of alcohol, and Billings found steady employment in that field. What he thought about these issues we do not know, but he seems to have been on the side of the abolitionists when it came to chattel slavery. In the wake of the Fugitive Slave Law he illustrated such literature as *Uncle Tom's Cabin* and John Whittier's *Sabbath Scene,* and he designed the third masthead for William Lloyd Garrison's Boston-based *Liberator*. Despite his financial problems, he donated his effort to Garrison, a drawing said to be worth twenty dollars.[80]

This contribution suggests a commitment to the antislavery movement, but other evidence produces a somewhat fuzzy picture of Billings's politics. A passing snide remark about "Young America" in a letter of 1854, although it refers to pushy financial practices rather than the political beliefs of the Democrats, as well as his following the lead of Daniel Webster, Edward Everett, and Rufus Choate in the iconography of the National Monument he designed for Plymouth in 1854, suggests Whiggish leanings, but he also called upon the xenophobia of the Know-Nothings to win the commission for the monument in 1855.[81] Perhaps that was mere, although effective, expediency, and perhaps it is not possible to be too precise in such matters relative to the 1850s, a time of political turmoil. Webster, Everett, and Choate were all compromising "Union-savers," who thought political disassembly worse than slavery, and in 1854 the *New York Tribune* reported that the "Know-Nothing Movement is in the hands of the Union-savers of 1850."[82] In any event, Billings was a man of public arts not of public policy.

He was honored and remembered for his "taste and skill." William Downes wrote that "his critical judgement in all things pertaining to the arts was admirable, and he had enriched a naturally artistic temperament by extensive reading." It was said that his "critical judgements of art were of the highest value." The same source reports that he was among the "first and most intelligent of Ruskin's admirers in America," and according to a notice of 1859, "his reading has been extensive, especially upon works of art, and in such matters we know of no one (if we except Ruskin) whose *dictum* we would so implicitly accept."[83] We know he owned in the 1850s Ruskin's *Modern Painters* and *Stones of Venice,* and it is recorded that he said the author of *The Seven Lamps of Architecture* "possessed a devil of a theory."[84]

But Billings's taste, like his art, was eclectic; he was as Francophile as Anglophile in his judgment. The most telling witness to his stature as an influence on the assessment of the art of his time occurs in Helen Knowlton's study of the Barbizon-inspired William Morris Hunt. In December 1859 Hunt's just-finished portrait of Judge Lemuel Shaw was exhibited at the gallery of Williams and Everett, and "while there excited more derision than any portrait that had ever been shown in Boston." Billings stopped by one morning to find a knot of artists "wondering if the portrait were not a joke." When one of the group asked his opinion, he on the contrary said he thought the work "the greatest portrait that was ever painted in this country." The crowd quickly did a critical about-face, its members remarking that they had made a mistake, "that here was a work of art which was quite above their comprehension. They walked away, and left Mr. Billings alone with the portrait." Obviously, the designer's well-formed opinions in artistic matters carried much weight with his peers. Obviously, "Mister" Billings was as respected as a critic as he was as man, artist, and architect.[85]

Billings spent nearly his entire life in and around Boston. His one recorded trip abroad remains something of a mystery. He was in England in the summer of 1865.[86] In a letter written from London in August, perhaps to the English painter and illustrator Henry James Townsend, he complains that he is "flat broke." He seems to be looking for work from the (Illustrated London?) "News," and has just received a book from Boston to illustrate. He might go to Paris and he is thinking about returning home in the autumn. He did return then. One can only guess that Billings was seeking to expand his horizons, his opportunities for work, by moving to England in the aftermath of the war. We can only wonder if troubles with Phoebe played a role in his departure.

The trip yielded some art. A small sketchbook preserves his jottings of urban street scenes and the compositions of old master paintings. Among the latter, for example, is a sketch of the right half of Veronese's *Presentation of Jesus in the Temple* (ca. 1555), which, since the original is in Dresden, he must have known from a print. One of the surviving scrapbooks of his work contains a watercolor produced on this trip. This is a picturesque wooded scene well north of London, a view of the Thorsgill beck in the Teesdale, at the extreme northern edge of what used to be called the North Riding of Yorkshire. The beck flows into the Tees just south of Barnard Castle in County Durham, and just below Eggleston Abbey, a Premonstratension house that was the site of a scene in Walter Scott's *Rokeby*.[87] Billings had illustrated some of the Waverley novels in the mid-1850s, although not apparently this one (see appendix B); perhaps he was drawn to the vicinity by its associations as well as such picturesque views as he was to record. Finally, Wellesley College once owned his oil, a *View on the Thames*, now unlocated.[88]

Billings may have visited England because work slowed somewhat during the Civil War. Fund-raising for the Forefathers Monument was on hold; architectural work declined, and so did book illustration. Joseph had been appointed civil engineer at the Boston Navy Yard in 1853. At war's end he rejoined Hammatt in architectural practice, which now took the bulk of Hammatt's attention (see appendix C). Work picked up dramatically, with major commissions from the Cheneys in South Manchester, Connecticut, for a library at Mt. Holyoke College, and for a new female seminary, now Wellesley College, in Massachusetts. There was commercial work in downtown Boston. There was work designing war memorials. He continued to illustrate books, but fashions had changed, and his postwar production was small compared to his heyday in the 1850s. *Ballou's* had ceased publication; periodical illustration had moved to New York, where the work of Winslow Homer, who as a tyro learned much from Billings, continued to enliven the pages of *Harper's*. The unbalance toward building design in his late years is reflected in his obituaries, some of which recalled him primarily as an architect.

Billings died at his brother Henry's house on West Fiftieth Street in New York (a site now occupied by Rockefeller Center) on 14 November 1874. He was just fifty-six years old, with his architectural career in high gear. The *Boston Post* noted that he had "not been in his usual health for some months, and a fortnight ago went to New York in the hope that the change might benefit him." He died intestate, and probate records show him to have had few financial resources.[89] In the final accounting of 1877 his personal estate was placed at $2,194.24. There was no detailed inventory, as he owned no real estate and apparently few other effects. The value of his estate was comprised of his well-stocked library, including books on art and architecture (more than $600), "Pictures, drawings, photographs[, and] Sketch books &c." (more than $1,300), artist's supplies (under $100), and copyrights on "Cabalistic" and perhaps other, unidentified cards (about $125). His interest as partner in the firm of Hammatt and Joseph E. Billings was "not susceptible of evaluation." It seems a sad accounting for thirty-five years of labor in all fields of design, but then, it did not take into account his grand contribution to popular culture.

2
"Unrivalled Skill in This Branch of Art"
Book Illustration

THE TENDENCY has been to think of worthy American book illustration as restricted to a "golden age" at the end of the nineteenth century, including the work of N. C. Wyeth, Edwin Austin Abbey, and Howard Pyle, or among those students and collectors who have penetrated that barrier, to the art of the previous generation, represented by artists such as Thomas Nast, Winslow Homer, and Harry Fenn. There was, however, still an earlier generation of native draftsmen who, however they have been ignored or condescendingly treated in the literature, laid the foundation of this popular art in the United States. This was a generation of workers born largely in the first quarter of the century whose early publications stem mainly from the 1840s. Augustus Hoppin, Benson J. Lossing, George T. Devereux, and John G. Chapman were part of the group whose leading figure was F. O. C. Darley, the one name that still brings recognition among even casual art historians and bibliophiles. Working in the shadow of the famous English and European illustrators of the first half of the century, and eclipsed by the brilliant color work at its end, these artists in black-and-white nonetheless contributed much to the history of book embellishment in the New World. Hammatt Billings was a member in good standing of that pioneer generation.[1]

Frank Weitenkamp has written that "book illustration in the United States first got into stride, in artistic and professional stature, in a comparably sudden outburst of production in the 1840s." Although the suddenness might be questioned, there did then appear a large group of illustrators, among whom were Darley, Hoppin, and Billings. The *Boston Almanac* for 1854 described Billings as possessing "unrivalled skill in this branch of art."[2] This may now seem an inflated estimate, especially as we judge Darley as the major

American illustrator of his generation, but it should be noted that the perceptive nineteenth-century art critic James Jackson Jarves placed Billings above Darley. After characterizing the latter as a "remarkable man," Jarves wrote that Billings

> has capacity of higher order. His taste is refined, talent versatile, fancy subtle, and imagination inventive. . . . In the lyrical grace, variety, and delicate beauty of his compositions, and sympathetic rendering of the text [Jarves refers here specifically to works by Keats, Tennyson, and the "most intellectually spiritual of the poets"] he has no superior in this country. His brain is a rich mine of aesthetic wealth. He does not so much translate poetry into pictorial art as recast it in exquisite shapes of his own invention.[3]

Billings joined Darley and others in establishing the book illustrator as a viable member of the artistic scene.[4]

Billings's was an eclectic style, drawing on a variety of imported and domestic precedents. In 1845 he acquired a copy of works by Goethe and Schiller illustrated with outline engravings after Moritz Retzsch.[5] This was a style he early emulated for both architectural and artistic work (see fig. 40). Among the books he purchased between 1845 and 1858 at Ticknor's bookstore at Washington and School Streets in Boston were works probably illustrated by Albrecht Dürer, Benjamin R. Haydon, Friedrich Overbeck, "Grandville" (Jean Ignace Isidore Gerard), Edward H. Wehnert, Fred M. Coffin, Gustave Doré, J. M. W. Turner, John Ruskin, Birket Foster, F. O. C. Darley, John Gilbert, and others (see appendix A). Somewhere he came across the work of William Blake. For his depiction of *Noche Triste*, the frontispiece to S. G. Goodrich's *Pictorial History of America* of 1849, he turned to the sublime style of John Martin. For the illustrations to P. J. Bailey's *Festus* (1853) and other works, he studied Thomas Cole (see fig. 9). His *Southwest Wind* in Ruskin's "King of the Golden River" (1856) was taken directly from Richard Doyle. John Gilbert inspired his title page to Joseph Jenks's anthology *The Rural Poetry of the English Language* of the same year. For a while in the 1860s he followed the lead of William Rimmer (see fig. 38). For some of the embellishments to Tennyson's *Last Tournament* (1872) he relied on Gustave Doré for motivation. His scratchy figures in H. B. Stowe's *Pink and White Tyranny* (1871) seem derived from Augustus Hoppin's work (see fig. 17). His frontispiece to William Morris's *Lovers of Gudrun* (1870) appropriately owes something to the Pre-Raphaelites.[6]

The artist's style was derived from a long list of distinct sources, then, but in its totality the work is particularly his own. Any perusal of English or French illustrations of the early or middle nineteenth century, or the work of older American contemporaries heavily influenced by the English, such as fellow Bostonian D. C. Johnston, reveals his innocence, his childlike grimness, his largely sober desire to get it right. Rarely does his work exhibit the bite of a Cruikshank or a Grandville, rarely any of their social or political parody. Only occasionally in his work for children's literature does he display an engaging sense of humor. Billings's figural work in general exhibits an interest in the heritage of the antique, and a classical decorum permeates his designs, which rarely show flashes of the romantic spirit. This is not to suggest, however, that his interpretations of texts were ineffectual. Far from it.

He was highly susceptible to earlier and contemporary illustrators, but Billings in turn had an impact, however short lived, on the next generation. Winslow Homer's first graphic work of the 1850s shows the presence of the established Billings, as, for example, Homer's sheet music cover "Minnie Clyde, Kitty Clyde's Sister" of 1857 owes much compositionally to Billings's frontispiece to A. B. Muzzey's *Young Maiden* of about 1850 (figs. 4–5). The impact was brief but certainly formative. Billings's characteristic compositional device for allegorical and emblematic work, the artistic narrative form in which a central circle or circle part surrounds vignettes, recurs in many a work by Thomas Nast (1840–1902). One example is Nast's *Emancipation of the Negroes,* published in *Harper's Weekly* on 24 January 1863.

Billings's work as book illustrator began in Boston in the 1840s. His earliest catalogued design in this "branch of art" is the frontispiece *(This is Benevolence)* to Jacob Abbott's *Rollo Code of Morals; or, the Rules of Duty for Children* (1841), engraved by O. Pelton after a design by C. H. H. Billings (see appendix B). It set the tone for the many illustrations to moralizing children's literature he was to create over a long career. By the end of the decade Billings had embellished a wide range of literature, including works by L. H. Sigourney, J. J. Jarves, S. G. Goodrich, O. W. Holmes, and J. G. Whittier. He had also provided architectural, landscape, and figural designs for gift books, travel literature, history, poetry, schoolbooks, and government that commenced the broad sweep of his talents as illustrator.

Hammatt's early work shows the impact of his first instructors, Francis Graeter and Abel Bowen. Graeter's illustrations to Lydia Maria Child's *The Hen-Coop* (1833) and Bowen's work for Munroe and Francis's *Mother Goose's Quarto* (ca. 1825) seem to underlie Billings's first major illustrated work, Munroe and Francis's *Chimes, Rhymes, and Jingles; or, Mother Goose's Songs* of 1845 (fig. 6).

Fig. 4. Lithograph by
J. H. Bufford after
Winslow Homer,
"Minnie Clyde, Kitty
Clyde's Sister," sheet
music cover published
by Oliver Ditson and
Co., Boston, 1857
(author's collection).

This contains some 135 large and small wood-engraved vignettes distributed throughout the text. They demonstrate a wide range of ability and a wide range of sources. It was not his finest work, but it did establish him as a worthy successor to Abel Bowen.

The 1850s saw U.S. book illustration come into its own. An article in the *Crayon* for 1857 noted that "Illustration . . . has progressed rapidly in this country within a period of three years; its kind and quality have both vastly improved. We do not now buy or steal *all* the designs that appear in American books. . . . We have now artists both as designers and engravers . . . who,

Fig. 5. Wood engraving
by S. A. Schoff after
Hammatt Billings, fron-
tispiece to A. B.
Muzzey, *The Young
Maiden*, Boston, 1850
(Special Collections,
Clapp Library,
Wellesley College).

in a degree, give to the public works that meet the standard of merit which
they pretend to."[7] In this decade Billings established himself as a mature
designer in great demand in "all departments of art," including book illustration. He began to work for the major publishers in Boston: Ticknor, Reed,
and Fields (later Ticknor and Fields); Little and Brown; Crosby and Nichols; Phillips, Sampson, and Co.; Benjamin B. Mussey; J. E. Tilton and Co.;
John P. Jewett; and lesser names, as well as the occasional house in New York
or Philadelphia. For Jewett he seems to have become a favorite illustrator in
the wake of his work on *Uncle Tom's Cabin* in 1852 and 1853. In the next decade
Billings added other, both emerging and established, publishers to his list of
clients: Lee and Shepard and Roberts Brothers, as well as other New York

Fig. 6. Wood engraving by Alonzo Hartwell after Hammatt Billings, "Mary Ester" (Little Miss Muffet), from *Chimes, Rhymes, and Jingles; or, Mother Goose's Songs*, Boston, [1845] (Special Collections, Clapp Library, Wellesley College).

establishments. He was present at the American Renaissance of letters, ornamenting books by "Grace Greenwood" (Sara J. C. Lippincott), Nathaniel Hawthorne, Harriet Beecher Stowe, Charles Sumner, John Greenleaf Whittier, Edward Everett, Lucy Larcom, and other, lesser lights. He also illustrated English authors, from Shakespeare to Walter Scott. Over the last fourteen years of his life Billings added "Oliver Optic" (William T. Adams), Alfred Lord Tennyson, Oliver Goldsmith, Jean Ingelow, Louisa May Alcott, William Morris, Charles Dickens, Walter Savage Landor, and "Gail Hamilton" (Mary A. Dodge) to the list of authors whose work he illustrated. His range continued to broaden. He embellished books on travel, history, adventure, architecture, poetry, religion, memorials, almanacs, manners, guidebooks, biography, fiction, and on and on. The reach was impressive, but juvenile literature formed the bulk of his work for the publishers.

What small reputation Billings has enjoyed in recent years has rested heavily on his work for children's books, including moral tracts, fairy tales, poetry, school texts, and novels.[8] His designs in this genre also began early, with his first catalogued work of 1841, carried through his early maturity in works for Hawthorne such as the original illustrations to *True Stories from History and Biography* and the *Wonder Book* (both 1851) and the *Tanglewood Tales* (1853), and lasted late, as with his embellishments to the first separate publication of Charles Dickens's *A Child's Dream of a Star* (1871; see fig. 16).[9] What is perhaps his finest work in this area came in the middle of his most accomplished years, including especially his designs for the anonymous *Curious Stories about Fairies, and Other Funny People* and Caroline C. Tappan's *Magician's Show Box, and Other Stories*, both published by Ticknor and Fields in 1856 (fig. 7). Some of these illustrations, such as *Southwest Wind* from Ruskin's "King of the Golden River" are derived from recognizable sources, but others show an imagination and a sense of humor that is not evident in Billings's work in other genre.

A sizable fraction of the works listed in appendix B are juveniles: small, thin volumes containing simple, usually moralistic stories that were the staple of childhood reading in the middle of the nineteenth century in middle-class America. Some of these appeared as single volumes, such as "Grace Greenwood's" *History of My Pets* (1851), *Tales from Catland* by an "Old Tabby" (1852), *A Happy Summer-Time; or, James and Jenny in the Country* (1861), and *A Kiss for a Blow; or, a Collection of Stories for Children; Showing Them How to Prevent Quarrelling* (1869) by Henry C. Wright.[10] Many were issued in series by authors who were often women and often favorites among young readers. These begin to show up in Billings's career in the mid-1850s, with titles such as Phoebe Phelps's *Home Stories* (1855) in four volumes, Ann Carter's *Great Rosy Diamond* (1856) in six volumes, *Mrs. Follen's Twilight Stories* (1856) in six volumes (with an additional six illustrated by Winslow Homer), Josephine Franklin's *Martin and Nelly Stories* (1859–65; some illustrations by J. N. Hyde) in twelve volumes, Caroline Guild's *Summer-House Series* (1859–65) in five volumes, "Madeline Leslie's" *Little Frankie* and *Robin Redbreast* series (1860), both in six volumes, and so on. Each of the volumes might contain just one vignette, a frontispiece perhaps, or several. Popular books reappeared in several editions.

A typical example of Billings's work for the juvenile trade is the *Fourteen Pet Goslings, and Other Pretty Stories of My Childhood*, by "Frank," otherwise unidentified, published in Boston by T. E. Tilton in 1858. This is a thin octodecimo volume containing eleven moralizing stories inspired by "Grace Greenwood's" *History of My Pets* of 1851 (see appendix B). It contains five full-page "Designs by Billings," according to the title page, engraved on wood by

Andrew-Filmer, with the frontispiece (illustrating the title story) repeated in stamped gilt on the red cover. There are also twelve small historiated initials (one a repeat at the foreword). Hammatt's illustration for the story of Pongo shows the pet "sitting in a chair just like anybody, smoking a cigar. . . . It made him very sick, and he never wanted to smoke again, which shows that mon-

Fig. 7. Wood engraving by John Andrew after Hammatt Billings, from [Caroline C. Tappan], *The Magician's Show Box*, Boston, 1856 (Special Collections, Clapp Library, Wellesley College).

Fig. 8. Wood engraving
by Andrew-Filmer after
Hammatt Billings, *Pongo
Smoking*, from *Fourteen Pet
Goslings*, Boston, [1858]
(Special Collections,
Clapp Library,
Wellesley College).

keys are more sensible than some people" (fig. 8). Hammatt's is a light-
hearted and effective characterization of the episode. Pongo's habit of im-
itating human activity, however, led to his sad end, for he cut his throat while
trying to shave. Hammatt's illuminated initial at this point avoids the blood-
shed by showing the preparation.

Billings's stature as a book illustrator in his own day also relied heavily on
his designs for works of poetry. James Jackson Jarves raved about his accomplishments in this field, but Jarves was hardly alone. The obituary in *Old and
New*, for instance, says "his illustrations of poetic subjects were in the very
spirit of the poetry from which they sprung *[sic]*. They were instinct with
grace. They did not servilely follow the author's words, but struck the very
centre of the genius which conceived them: so that the artist was a true co-
worker and designer with the poet." Billings's work in this genre covered most

Fig. 9. Steel engraving by C. E. Wagstaff and J. Andrews after Hammatt Billings, *Festus and the Angel*, from Philip James Bailey, *Festus*, Boston, 1853 (Special Collections, Clapp Library, Wellesley College).

of his career. It began (so far as we now know) in 1849 with volumes of poetry by Oliver Wendell Holmes and John Greenleaf Whittier. Whittier thought his illustrations to a later book, *A Sabbath Scene* of 1854, "the best of the kind I ever saw" (see fig. 13).[11] Billings went on to illustrate volumes by English poets such as Jean Ingelow, largely forgotten now but much read in her own day, *The Deserted Village* by Oliver Goldsmith (1866), *Rural Poems* by William Barnes (1869; see fig. 14), and several works by Tennyson: *Enoch Arden* (1865), *Poems* (1866), *The Last Tournament* (1872), and *Gems from Tennyson,* known only in a posthumous edition.[12] By this time, however, late in the 1860s and early in the 1870s, Billings's style of illustration was becoming dated. Of these late Tennyson embellishments James Yarnall has written, with something of the modern historian's slighting view of Billings and his audience, that "continuing support for conventional illustrations infers that the book-buying public remained content with, and perhaps even preferred, old-fashioned and less artistic illustrations."[13] That editions of Tennyson illustrated by Billings continued to be reissued did not mean that Billings's work continued to please everyone.

A characteristic volume of poetry embellished by Hammatt is *Festus* by the English poet Philip James Bailey (1816–1902), published in 1853 from the third London edition by Benjamin B. Mussey and Company, with title page and twelve full-page steel engravings by C. E. Wagstaff and J. Andrews after "Hammett" [*sic*] Billings. I doubt that *Festus* is much read now, but this must have proven a popular package in its own day, for there are later New York editions that retain the original illustrations. Binding options for this thick octavo volume included gilt-stamped cloth with historiated scenes on front and spine, and gilt edges. Billings's sources for these illustrations range from the School of Raphael to the works of the late Thomas Cole (fig. 9).

Juveniles and poetry joined other types of publications illustrated by Billings, and these include several works devoted to the burgeoning immigrant population of Boston. In Henry Dexter's *Street Thoughts* of 1859, the author's anti-Irish prejudice is tempered by Billings's rather objective depictions, which eschew the vicious apeman caricatures of contemporary illustration, and those later, more popular ones spewed forth by Thomas Nast (fig. 10).[14] His illustrations to Russell Conwell's *Why and How: Why the Chinese Emigrate, and the Means They Adopt for the Purpose of Reaching America,* published in 1871 by Lee and Shepard, on the other hand, offer more demeaning representations of the "heathen Chinee" during a decade of virulent antisinological feeling (fig. 11). As Sinclair Hamilton noted, however, the author claimed

Fig. 10. Wood
engraving by Andrew-
Filmer after Hammatt
Billings, *A Male Irishman*,
from Henry M. Dexter,
Street Thoughts, Boston,
1859 (Special
Collections, Clapp
Library, Wellesley
College).

authorship of the illustrations, despite the title-page credit to Billings, whose
additions to his drawings were "almost nothing."[15]

Although many of the books Billings illustrated are long forgotten, a
number of them dealt with the major New England preoccupations of the
mid-nineteenth century, moral issues brought to wide public attention by
Stowe, Whittier, Lowell, and other writers, Billings and other illustrators.
For example, the final pages of Emma Wellmont's 1853 temperance novel
Uncle Sam's Palace, a work embellished by Billings (see appendix B), contains "a
vision of the night" in which "three grim spectres" appeared to the author.
The first was of "boastful exterior" and listed "his mighty acts upon the *battle
field.* . . . He had slain his thousands . . . [and] sent desolation into many
innocent hearts." Upon his helmet was inscribed his name: War. The second

Fig. 11. Wood engraving after Hammatt Billings, Russell H. Conwell, or both, from Russell H. Conwell, *Why and How*, Boston, 1871 (Special Collections, Clapp Library, Wellesley College).

specter, "acknowledged by the historian as the great blot upon our national freedom, . . . stood before me with his *seared humanity*," our narrator continues. His crest bore golden characters forming the word Slavery. But the third seemed to Wellmont the worst of all, for he claimed that "the other spectres may boast of having slain or carried terror and dismay to the heart of thousands, but I have slain my *ten thousands*." This was "the triumphant king"; this was Intemperance. Emma Wellmont sought, at the crest of the movement against the consumption of alcohol that culminated in the Maine Law of 1851, to accomplish for temperance what Harriet Beecher Stowe had accomplished for abolition in the wake of the Fugitive Slave Law of 1850. Her present obscurity proves her lack of lasting literary success, but Wellmont's apocalyptic vision brought forth the three great moral issues of her day, issues as fraught for her time as atomic energy, abortion, and illegal drugs have been in ours. These were issues that preoccupied politicians, reformers, and the public at large. In consequence they concerned the writers and artists as well.

    For the New England reformers, war, slavery, and intemperance were varying aspects of the same social malaise. Pacifism was a plank in the platform of William Lloyd Garrison years before he began the *Liberator*. As early as 1828 he was editing the *National Philanthropist,* the goals of which were peace, temperance, and emancipation.[16] For James Russell Lowell and others the Mexican War of 1846–48 was an immoral attempt to extend slavery into new territories.[17] As that unpopular contest came and went, and the clouds of civil strife began to gather on the southern horizon of the 1860s, the specter of war could not have been very far from the popular imagination.

Billings's pencil described battles of the French and Indian War, the Revolution, the War of 1812, the Mexican War, and the Civil War, and these views appeared in many different formats, but the controversial Mexican War looms largest in his work because interest in it carried through his heyday in the 1850s. Although it was not a popular engagement in Boston, Billings and other illustrators were called upon to create scenes of the conflict for books of poetry and history. As early as 1848 Billings made drawings for Benjamin Mussey's edition of Whittier's *Poems* that appeared in the next year with eight steel engravings after the artist's designs, among them the *Angels of Buena Vista,* celebrating the women who ministered to the dying after that battle. The many small cuts in the text of S. G. Goodrich's *History of America* of 1849, for which we know Billings provided the design of the Martinesque frontispiece and the title page, must come from a variety of sources, but those illustrating the Mexican War can be assigned to him on the basis of comparison with other work. For *Ballou's* he provided several views of the war during the next decade. As late as 1869, for John Abbott's *Lives of the Presidents,* he produced variations on the scenes of battles he had begun to illustrate twenty years earlier.

As there is no record that he took part in the engagements, he must have drawn heavily upon eyewitness accounts and published views of these momentous events. We know he owned George W. Kendall's *War between the United States and Mexico* of 1851, a large folio containing panoramic color lithographs of the battles after drawings by Carl Nebel (see appendix B). There are in two private collections three spirited drawings by Billings showing the battles of Palo Alto (fig. 12), Vera Cruz, and Chapultepec. A fourth, *The Battle of Buena Vista,* is known only from a print. The drawings were certainly intended to be and were, with the *Buena Vista,* reproduced in a series of engravings by James Duthie published by S. Walker of Boston, New York, and Philadelphia.[18] The *Buena Vista* was in turn reused in John Abbott's *Lives of the Presidents,* where it is deceivingly labeled as "prepared expressly" for that publication.[19] Billings's views of the battles of Palo Alto and Vera Cruz seem only very slightly influenced by Carl Nebel's renderings, if at all, but his

Fig. 12. Wash drawing by Hammatt Billings, *The Battle of Palo Alto*, ca. 1850 (author's collection).

Chapultepec was almost certainly based on Nebel's *Storming of Chapultepec—Pillow's Attack*, as published in Kendall. He leaves out the main block of the fortress, reconstructs the details of the uphill charge, and produces a more dramatic rendering, but these are clearly related views.

That would date at least this drawing to 1852 at the earliest, but Billings must have already worked on this series, because a version of his *Battle of Buena Vista* first appeared in S. G. Goodrich's *Pictorial History of America*.[20] Billings is not credited with the wood-engraved illustration, but he either drew it or he copied it for his similar rendering engraved by Duthie and published by Walker. In this version he adapted the earlier figure grouping and combined it with the setting depicted in Nebel's view for Kendall.[21] For a version of the battle he drew for *Ballou's* in 1856, he again adapted the Nebel setting to yet another grouping of the same equestrian officers.[22] All this suggests that the series was created over a period of time. The war continued to provide him with employment, and he continued to vary his depictions of it.

While most of Billings's views of battle remain rather static, suggesting little of the tumult of conflict, especially when compared to Winslow Homer's animated evocations of the Civil War, his one view of that conflict, a generic battle piece he designed for sculptural relief on the unexecuted Boston Soldiers and Sailors' Monument of 1866, shows he was capable of capturing something of the sweep of the charge (see fig. 80). That Billings apparently produced no other major drawings of the later war suggests the beginning of the decline of his reputation.

The charge he drew for Boston was not the first time Billings had designed a battle scene in conjunction with a proposal for a monument. One of the reliefs on his 1859 design for a colossal monument to the opening skirmish of the Revolution showed Lexington town green on 19 April 1775. This reappeared on a certificate of the Lexington Monument Association in 1860 (see fig. 90) and again as the frontispiece to Charles Hudson's *History of the Town of Lexington* in 1868 (see appendix B). Billings was an economical designer; similar or identical works by him can show up in various branches of art. This view stems from Ralph Earl's famous sketch, made shortly after the fight, or more likely from Amos Doolittle's engraving after it, but with important differences. Whereas Earl accurately showed the scattering Americans offering little resistance to the disciplined British line, Billings transformed the Americans into a monumental foreground wall of patriots standing their ground while the British are reduced to background incidents. It was all part of the filiopietism of the turbulent fifties and a forerunner to the Colonial Revival reinvention of the preindustrial past that was to dominate the latter part of the century.[23]

The second of Emma Wellmont's specters, slavery, also commanded Billings's attention. He worked for the abolitionists by contributing a masthead to Garrison's *Liberator* in 1850 and by providing designs for both the first and the illustrated editions of *Uncle Tom's Cabin* of 1852 and 1853. These credentials got him other commissions as well, including the new, illustrated edition of Richard Hildreth's *White Slave* of 1852, one of many publications dealing with various forms of slavery that appeared overnight in the early 1850s, and a new edition of Charles Sumner's *White Slavery in the Barbary States,* which appeared in the following year. Other than *Uncle Tom's Cabin,* however, Hammatt's best antislavery work appeared in Whittier's *Sabbath Scene.* John P. Jewett published it in 1854 in a slim volume of twenty-nine pages printed on one side of each leaf, with a wood-engraved vignette and two stanzas of poetry occupying each recto (fig. 13). Written in emotional reaction to the Fugitive Slave Act of 1850, the poem tells of a runaway black woman who

I saw the parson tie the knots,
　　The while his flock addressing,
The Scriptural claims of slavery
　　With text on text impressing.

" Although," said he, " on Sabbath day,
　　All secular occupations
Are deadly sins, we must fulfil
　　Our moral obligations :

Fig. 13. Wood engraving by Baker, Smith, and Andrew after Hammatt Billings, "I saw the parson tie the knots," from John Greenleaf Whittier, *A Sabbath Scene*, Boston, 1854 (Special Collections, Clapp Library, Wellesley College).

seeks refuge in a white man's church. She is immediately bound by the congregation, with the preacher himself tying the knots while defending slavery on the Bible. Although the author cries out against this injustice, he is shouted down. In scene after little scene Billings's pencil effectively envisions the sordid action, as the black woman is roughly handled by white men carrying buggy whips and assisted by the parson. Whittier's indictment of religion's support of slavery is strengthened by Billings's illustrations, and as we have seen the poet was delighted with them.

As Emma Wellmont made clear in her dark vision, war and slavery were serious symptoms of national malaise, but for many New Englanders at midcentury, intemperance was the most pressing moral problem of the day. We do not know whether Billings was a "cold-water man" himself, but he did frequently lend, or more likely sell, his pencil to the cause. Some of his most characteristic mature works appear in this genre, including the illustrations to *Uncle Sam's Palace,* John Dix's *Passages from the History of a Wasted Life* and his *Worth of the Worthless,* 1853 and 1854 respectively, the latter published by the Sons of Temperance, and E. W. Reynolds's *Records of the Bubbleton Parish,* 1854. Lee and Shepard of Boston issued George M. Baker's *An Old Man's Prayer* in 1868 with nine designs by Billings engraved by S. S. Kilburn. This is a temperance equivalent to Whittier's *Sabbath Scene,* even in its design, for here, too, the poem is printed on one side of each leaf.

Billings's heyday as a book illustrator lasted through the 1850s and into the aftermath of the Civil War. His tireless production suggests that he was one of the most sought-after illustrators of his generation in the Boston area. Yet by the time of his death in 1874, he had been largely by-passed as a graphic artist of consequence. The handwriting appeared on the wall perhaps as early as 1869, when he was paid less for more work on the same project, Roberts Brothers' publication of William Barnes's *Rural Poems,* than was his erstwhile protégé, Winslow Homer. While Homer received $120 for six designs, Billings earned just $95 for seven, plus a cover device.[24] Changing taste is clear from the illustrations as well, in the contrast between the heavy, plodding figures of Billings versus the lithe, light, and linear forms of Homer (figs. 14–15).

Billings's fluttering reputation is perhaps also evident in the reception given his work in Charles Dickens's *A Child's Dream of a Star* copyrighted by Field, Osgood, and Co. in 1870. This, the first edition of the tale in book form, is a thin duodecimo volume containing eleven full-page illustrations engraved on wood by W. J. Linton. It was intended as a "gift book" for the

Fig. 14. Wood
engraving by W. J.
Pierce after Hammatt
Billings, "Now you have
whack'd my jug," from
William Barnes, *Rural
Poems*, Boston, 1869
(Special Collections,
Clapp Library,
Wellesley College).

" Now you have whack'd my jug ;
Now you have crack'd my jug."

Christmas season of 1870, with each illustration facing the text printed on
one side of the leaf and surrounded by a red line border. Billings is credited
with his full name (correctly spelled) not only on the title page but in gold
stamp on the cover as well (fig. 16). This is rare indeed. In general the reviews
were complimentary, and it was somewhat unusual for a nineteenth-century
American reviewer to comment on illustrations, but there was a decidedly
unfavorable undertone, at least to one of them. *Literary World* of 1 January 1871
thought this "one of the most touching little sketches that Dickens ever
wrote," and that it had been a "felicitous idea to make it the subject of
illustrations, especially such as Hammatt Billings would be likely to give it."
The *World*, then, recognized Hammatt's long career as distinguished illustrator. William Dean Howells in *Atlantic Monthly* for February of the same year,
however, found the pictures "such as children will love, full of sympathy and
a quaint fidelity to the text. . . . The first five are singularly sweet and touching."[25] While the nineteenth century could use such adjectives less cynically

Fig. 15. Wood engraving by W. J. Pierce after Winslow Homer, "With comely steps, up hill she rose," from William Barnes, *Rural Poems*, Boston, 1869 (Special Collections, Clapp Library, Wellesley College).

" As there, with comely steps, up hill
She rose by elm-trees, all in ranks."

than we might today, there is a slight note of condescension in Howells's voice, a note that signals the beginning of the end of Billings's prominence as an artist. This is especially true since this same article has more complimentary things to say about the illustrations of Harry Fenn, Casimir Griswold, Sol Eytinge, and Winslow Homer.

Hammatt's waning reputation can be measured by the number of times he was replaced as illustrator of new editions of books his work had once adorned, as for example, when *Little Women* reappeared in 1880 with new engravings after Frank Thayer Merrill. It is often these "secondary" illustrations that are reused in modern editions, and that replacement further buries Billings's contribution to the history of the book. A dramatic demonstration of his fading presence occurs in a series of editions of Adeline D. T. Whit-

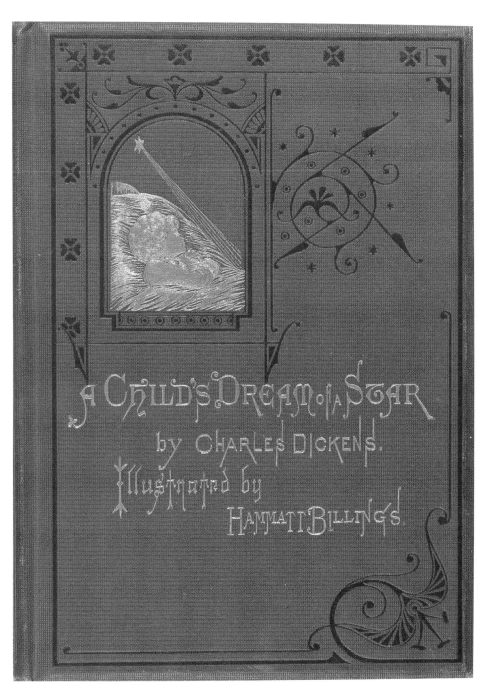

Fig. 16. Gilt-stamped cover for Charles Dickens, *A Child's Dream of a Star*, Boston, 1871 (Special Collections, Clapp Library, Wellesley College).

PINK AND WHITE TYRANNY.

———◇———

CHAPTER I.

FALLING IN LOVE.

LILLIE.

"WHO *is* that beautiful creature?" said John
Seymour, as a light, sylph-like form tripped

1

Fig. 17. Wood engraving by Morse after Hammatt Billings, *Lillie,* from Harriet Beecher Stowe, *Pink and White Tyranny,* Boston, 1871 (Special Collections, Clapp Library, Wellesley College).

ney's *Mother Goose for Grown Folks*. The original (New York: Rudd and Carleton, 1860) contains a frontispiece credited to Billings on the title page, a
situation that survives several reprintings in the next decade. A "new, revised,
and enlarged" edition by a new publisher (Boston: Loring, 1870) moves
Hammatt's frontispiece to the engraved title page and adds a new frontispiece and several illustrations by Augustus Hoppin. Both artists are credited
on the title page. Hoppin (1828–96) was a near contemporary of Billings,
but his scratchy, lighter style suited the new era better than Hammatt's
ponderous manner. Billings, in fact, sought to appropriate Hoppin's elegant
line at least once at just this time, for his illustrations to Harriet Beecher
Stowe's society novel *Pink and White Tyranny*, issued by Roberts Brothers in
1871 (fig. 17). A later edition of the *Mother Goose* (Boston: Houghton, Mifflin,
1891) retains the work of both artists, but only Hoppin is mentioned on the
title page. In this instance, at least, Billings has been stricken from the record
of graphic history.

But in fact Billings's reputation as a book illustrator has survived somewhat better than his reputation as a whole. When histories of American
illustrated books have been written he has usually found a small place, and in
some recent cases, a place of some significance. It is true that at his death and
early on in the literature he was remembered more for his buildings than his
books.[26] As late as the 1920s the authors of *The American Spirit in Art* characteristically wrote that he possessed "a rather feeble and sentimental talent,
but . . . had the distinction of being about the only imaginative illustrator in
America in his day. He was an architect by profession."[27] Of late Billings has
found some fame, among the cognoscenti at least, as the illustrator of *Uncle
Tom's Cabin* and of children's books in general.[28] The pioneering work of
Sinclair Hamilton, finally, placed him as an important member of his generation.[29] Especially with the destruction of so many of his major buildings, his
illustrations now carry the standard of his reputation.

3

"The Power of the Pencil Adds Much to the Power of the Pen"

Evangeline, Uncle Tom's Cabin, and Little Women

THE HISTORIES of Hammatt Billings's associations with the first editions of three of the most popular works of nineteenth-century American fiction, one from the mid-1840s, one from the early 1850s, and one from the late 1860s, provide detailed case studies of his role as book illustrator during the three principal decades of his career. It is part of the story that he did not illustrate them all. Both the first edition (1852) and the first illustrated edition (1853) of Harriet Beecher Stowe's *Uncle Tom's Cabin* contain his work, the latter in profusion, but only the second part of Louisa May Alcott's *Little Women* (1869) is enhanced by "cuts" after his drawings, while Henry Wadsworth Longfellow's *Evangeline* (1847) never appeared embellished by his pencil. These histories reveal failure as well as accomplishment, and they explicate Hammatt's relationship to the larger world of illustration, as well as to authors, publishers, and texts.

The tale of Billings and *Evangeline* is a story of lost opportunity, perhaps caused by procrastination on his part, perhaps caused by the presumed superiority of English over American illustrators in the 1840s, perhaps both.[1] Longfellow (1807–82) had been unhappy with the results of earlier efforts to illustrate his books. For his *Poets and Poetry of Europe* of 1845, the publishers Carey and Hart of Philadelphia had used a steel-engraved title page that bore no relation to the book's contents. The poet felt "bound to protest" the "very bad" plate; had he seen it in advance he would "never have consented to its going in." He had in an earlier letter established his opinion that "engravings

44

which have no connection with the subjects in the book—would be to me a deformity and not a beauty." Abraham Hart's reply to the poet made it clear, however, that the anthologizer had no say in the selection of plates in the books published by his firm. Neither did the author. For Longfellow's *Poems,* which Carey and Hart published in the same year, the firm chose Daniel Huntington (1816–1906) as visualizer. The quality of Huntington's work was better than that Hart had used in the anthology, but Longfellow was still unhappy. Huntington had made his designs in Europe, and the washed-up maiden of "The Wreck of the Hesperus" looked to Longfellow "too like a Roman peasant," while the fisherman bore no relationship to "a Marble-head fellow."[2] Indeed, the maiden descended from an ancient Ariadne by way of Giorgione's Dresden Venus. This experience taught the poet that he wanted control over the illustrations in his books, and he thought he wanted American subjects illustrated by American artists.

As early as the winter of 1844–45 Longfellow was thinking of using Billings as illustrator for a new edition of his *Hyperion.* "There is a young artist by the name of Billings in Boston," he wrote to his Philadelphia publishers, "who has the talent for such designs."[3] By the end of 1845, however, this project was abandoned as he was hard at work on what was to become *Evangeline,* and by early 1847 he was contemplating its published appearance. In January he went to Boston to see Billings "about illustrating 'Evange-line.['] I want to have an illustrated edition at the same time with a cheaper one," he noted.[4] In his journal, and presumably to Billings as well, he briefly outlined his ideas for embellishing the work: "I shall have margins from American subjects such as Indian corn, hops, muscadine vines, amid festoons of evergreens and mournful pines." He wanted American subjects to enrich his American saga, not classical Ariadnes sprawled on North Shore granite.

Billings quickly followed Longfellow's visit with visits to Craigie House, the poet's home in Cambridge. On the eleventh of January he announced his desire to collaborate, "and enters warmly into the plan." And, Longfellow adds to his journal, he is a "charming fellow . . . and altogether the best illustrator of books we have yet had in the country." The following week Billings is again at Craigie House, where he must have felt privileged to hear the poet read "some passages in Evangeline, previous to making designs."[5] This seems a promising beginning but it was in fact the end. A month later Longfellow is disappointed to find no work done on the illustrations, and no edition ever appeared with Billings's designs. There is, however, an epilogue to the tale. The artist did make at least one drawing for the poem, an original soft pencil sketch of "the forest primeval" that occurs on the opening page of the unillustrated edition in a copy datable to May 1848. This was either detached musing or the artist thought he still had the commission at that late date.[6]

In November 1849 Longfellow rejoiced to a correspondent that an illustrated edition of the poem was in press in England, even though it was a pirated edition not enhanced by his countryman.[7] He had no hand in picking the illustrators, who were Jane E. Benham, Birket Foster, and John Gilbert, the last two at least at the top of the profession in Britain. Longfellow was not pleased with Benham's depiction of his heroine, but he judged the landscapes "very beautiful."[8] This comes as a surprise. How could the man who once thought to embellish his American epic with American flora drawn by an American draftsman accept Foster's view of the lowly Ozarks as snow-capped Alpine peaks, or his transformation of Philadelphia into a medieval English village? These illustrations had no more place in *Evangeline* than did the title page of his *Poets and Poetry* belong in it. Certainly these cuts fit his earlier criteria for engravings that, in relation to the text, were a "deformity and not a beauty." It would seem that Longfellow's Anglophilia got the best of him and that the established English illustrators were esteemed far above their emerging American counterparts, even when their work stood an arm's length from the text.

In the 1840s Billings and the profession of book illustration in the United States were alike at the beginning of an uphill battle against the presence and assumed superiority of British and European artists. This perception survives in a modern study of the Boston publishers Roberts Brothers, where it is said that as late as the 1860s "there were few illustrators in America to match the galaxy of Britishers. . . . [O]ur illustrated books did lack the sparkle of real talent."[9] As we have seen, Billings seemed to have decided that, if he could not beat these British and European heavyweights, he should join them. His eclectic output often follows the lead of many an English or Continental illustrator, but with his work on *Uncle Tom's Cabin*, he apparently attempted something different.

Although many a Billings book illustration of the 1840s and 1850s (and later) follows closely the work of his favorite British illustrators, in his work for *Uncle Tom's Cabin*, at least, he put some distance between himself and his foreign sources. This was perhaps inspired by the novel's inherently American subject, and it is best demonstrated briefly by contrasting Billings's work with that of one of the foremost English draftsmen of the day, George Cruikshank, who also produced early illustrations for the novel.[10] Longfellow's original desire to have an American artist embellish his American tale with American ornaments to a certain extent was fulfilled by Billings's work for Harriet Beecher Stowe.

Uncle Tom's Cabin first appeared in book form as a two-volume work published by John P. Jewett (1814–89) in Boston in March of 1852. (The details have been discussed in many books on Stowe and her novel.) In an oft-quoted passage in a letter of 1851 from the author to Gamaliel Bailey, editor of the *National Era* in which the text was first serialized (without illustrations), Stowe (1811–96) wrote that her "vocation is simply that of a *painter,* and my object . . . to hold up in the most lifelike and graphic manner possible Slavery. . . . There is no arguing with *pictures,* and everyone is impressed with them, whether they mean to be or not."[11] Stowe was, of course, referring to verbal depictions, and critics have long remarked upon the graphic character of her language in tracing the opposing strands of her tale: the northward flight and ultimate freedom of George Harris and his family, and the southward drift and ultimate death of Uncle Tom. Yet Jewett—and it was probably the publisher rather than the author who engaged Hammatt Billings to provide the first edition with "six elegant designs" (plus title-page vignette)—must have thought that illustrations would enhance the book's sale. And when it was on its way to becoming a runaway best seller, Jewett again called upon Billings to provide designs for more than a hundred new cuts for the illustrated edition dated 1853 but ready for the Christmas trade in 1852. Billings is credited with the seven illustrations in the original edition in Jewett's advertising, but not in the book; his name does appear in the illustrated edition. The seven "designs" of the first edition are the earliest graphic depictions of some of Stowe's scenes and characters, Eliza, George Harris, Little Eva, Tom, and Cassy, but that is the last completely unquestionable statement to be made about the chronological relationships among Billings's scenes and the many other illustrations that appeared as rapidly as did new editions and translations of the novel.[12]

There is no document explaining the choice of illustrator. Billings was locally available and had by the early 1850s gained his place as one of the region's leading graphic artists, but it may have been his sympathy with the abolitionist cause that got him the job. We know, for example, that he designed the third masthead of William Lloyd Garrison's Boston-based *Liberator* in 1850 and that he donated his effort, despite what were probably his

OUR COUNTRY IS THE WORLD—OUR COUNTRYMEN ARE ALL MANKIND.

BOSTON, MASS., FRIDAY, JUNE 14, 1850.

Fig. 18. Wood engraving after Hammatt Billings, masthead to the *Liberator*, 1850 (author's collection).

straitened economic circumstances.[13] This suggests he was an adherent to the cause of emancipation. He was to illustrate other antislavery literature as well. John Greenleaf Whittier's *Sabbath Scene* first appeared in an edition with Billings's effective illustrations in 1854. Like *Uncle Tom's Cabin*, it had been written as a heated reaction to the Fugitive Slave Act of 1850. Although it might be generally true, as Bernard Reilly has recently observed, that "the artists . . . tended to occupy a much humbler . . . position [than the orators within the antislavery movement, and] their work [was] usually subordinate to the rhetorical center of abolition," Billings's illustrations to Stowe's text contributed significantly to the polemic.[14]

For Garrison's *Liberator*, Billings reworked the second masthead designed by the Boston-based illustrator David Claypoole Johnston (1799–1865). He retained the view of the slave auction and the vision of emancipation, but gave the design more legibility by creating scenes of greater cohesion and giving the entire composition more focus (fig. 18). The latter he achieved by his characteristic narrative composition: a central (allegorical) circle flanked by (realistic) vignettes. The masthead was engraved by Alonzo Hartwell, Billings's former fellow apprentice at Abel Bowen's shop.

Both Johnston and Billings drew on the left an auction at which slaves, horses, and cattle are indiscriminately knocked down to the highest bidders. In Billings's revision the sale is organized into "lots to suit the purchaser," and all this takes place beneath the aegis of the national flag and within full view of the U.S. Capitol whose dome supports the standard of "Slavery." Such a juxtaposition of slaves, slave auction, and seat of government was then old in the iconography of the abolitionist movement.[15] On the right Billings redrew the scene of impending freedom to depict a group of black people tumbling out of a hovel and catching sight not only of the Capitol, now flying the flag of "Freedom," but also the flag-bearing gateway of "Emancipation" leading to it.

These scenes of, respectively, reality and hope are separated by a roundel showing the risen Christ "come to break the bonds of the oppressor." He stands between an unshackled black man who kneels before him and a fleeing former slavemaster. A ribbon admonishes all to Love Thy Neighbor. Billings here adds the impress of evangelical religion to the standard emancipation iconography, the image of the kneeling and supplicating black asking "Am I not a Man and a Brother?" This had been created for the late eighteenth-century seal of the English Committee for Affecting the Abolishment of the Slave Trade and appropriated by the Massachusetts Anti-Slavery Society.[16] It was an iconographical dimension that would prove even more effective when applied to *Uncle Tom's Cabin*. There is a clear visual relationship between the masthead and some illustrations in the book: the scenes Billings created for Garrison's newspaper were to reappear, more or less reworked, in Stowe's novel.

The vignette repeated on each title page of the original two-volume edition (and as a gilt stamp on the cloth covers) is the first illustration of *Uncle Tom's Cabin* (fig. 19). It is a variation on the right side of the *Liberator* masthead. The hovel has now become Uncle Tom's "small log building" with Tom, his wife, and their children depicted as a domestic unit. Billings pruned back the "large scarlet begonia and . . . native multiflora rose" of Stowe's description, which "left scarce a vestige of the rough logs to be seen," but this is nonetheless a felicitous frontispiece, for it depicts a home, however humble, and a family, however "lowly," and domestic relationships and their disruption by the "peculiar institution" of chattel slavery form a central thread in Stowe's narrative. It would clarify the study of mid-nineteenth-century book illustration if we knew who picked the scenes to be illustrated, but no document is known that would answer that question.

Six other vignettes enrich the two volumes; they are horizontal wood engravings on tipped-in plates placed on end in the book. These are the archetypes for all later depictions of similar scenes, whether in later editions

UNCLE TOM'S CABIN;

OR,

LIFE AMONG THE LOWLY.

BY

HARRIET BEECHER STOWE.

VOL. II.

TWENTIETH THOUSAND.

BOSTON:
JOHN P. JEWETT & COMPANY.

CLEVELAND, OHIO:
JEWETT, PROCTOR & WORTHINGTON.

1852.

Fig. 19. Wood engraving by W. J. Baker after Hammatt Billings, title page to Harriet Beecher Stowe, *Uncle Tom's Cabin*, Boston, 1852 (Special Collections, Clapp Library, Wellesley College).

Fig. 20. Wood engraving by W. J. Baker after Hammatt Billings, *Little Eva Reading the Bible to Uncle Tom in the Arbor,* from Harriet Beecher Stowe, *Uncle Tom's Cabin,* 1852 (Special Collections, Clapp Library, Wellesley College).

of the novel or in other media. The first of the three in volume one again places us at the cabin door, as "Eliza comes to tell Uncle Tom that he is sold, and that she is running away to save her child." Thus the opposed journeys and fates of Uncle Tom and the Harrises are visually introduced. The second scene, *The Auction Sale,* adapted from the *Liberator* masthead, was to have a long and lasting influence on other illustrators and publishers, appearing over and over again reengraved as Billings created it or redesigned by later artists. It was repeated line for line in English editions, for instance, and copied in oil by a painter surnamed Taylor in his *American Slave Market* (ca. 1852) now in the Chicago Historical Society.[17] The third of Billings's designs in the first volume depicts the freeman's defense, in which George Harris takes his fate into his own hands by shooting and wounding a pursuing slave trader.

Volume two contains *Little Eva Reading the Bible to Uncle Tom in the Arbor,* without doubt the most important image of the first edition (fig. 20); *Cassy Ministering to Uncle Tom after his Whipping;* and the Harrises giving thanks for their safe arrival in Canada. The last two visually sum up the results of the opposing journeys of Tom and the Harrises. Except for *The Freeman's Defense,* which is itself rather static, these are not scenes of action. In both content and style Billings's work here as elsewhere is unemotional and quiet.

Uncle Tom's Cabin, as everyone knows, was a phenomenally successful book, with three of the five thousand copies of the initial printing sold on the day of publication, and some three hundred thousand copies in circulation in this country alone by the end of the year. By then Jewett had himself published a one-volume illustrated edition in several styles of binding (some historiated), and with 116 small wood-engraved vignettes designed by Billings and engraved by Baker, Smith, and Andrew of Boston. All are credited on the title page. Billings must have produced the second set of designs during the summer and/or autumn of 1852. Faced with the production of so many sketches, and pressed for space in a single volume, he composed his vignettes as groups of figures with little suggestion of ambience, and the printer locked the engraved blocks into the text. Each chapter has a half-page headpiece, a historiated initial, one or more scenes, and a small tailpiece. For his illustrations of the freeman's defense, Eva reading the Bible to Tom, and the Harrises in a free land, Billings reworked his drawings from the first edition. For the Eva and Tom of the illustrated edition, for example, he truncated the vista to the left to fit the scene to the vertical page, reworked the foliage, repositioned both hats, and shifted Eva's feet from under her. But the bulk of the images were newly invented for this presentation; here again it must be assumed that Billings had no prototypes at his disposal, as did later illustrators. Here we first see Eliza and Harry cross the frozen Ohio River, Uncle Tom save Little Eva from Mississippi waters, Topsy cavort in Miss Ophelia's clothes, the ghost appear to Legree. Some of these events demand at least a weak show of action, but an overall calm pervades the little wood-engraved scenes, which are mostly depictions of figures at rest. These bunched, statuesque people seem to anticipate the soon-to-be-popular "Rogers Groups" of plaster parlor figurines.[18]

John P. Jewett milked Stowe's narrative for all it was worth. With the first and illustrated editions, he simultaneously published *Pictures and Stories from Uncle Tom's Cabin,* a soft-cover, thirty-two-page booklet "designed to adapt Mrs. Stowe's touching narrative to the understanding of the youngest readers," according to the foreword. The preface is dated January 1853. This contains ten full-page wood engravings carved by M. Jackson after an unnamed artist who was *not* Hammatt Billings (fig. 21). Each image is a framed event set within a border, with four lines of poetry beneath. The main scene takes place within an archway whose spandrels are filled with ancillary action. The contrast with Billings's work for either of Jewett's editions of the novel is marked not only by composition but content as well.

Fig. 21. Wood engraving by M. Jackson after unknown artist, *Eva Putting a Wreath of Flowers Round Tom's Neck,* from *Pictures and Stories from Uncle Tom's Cabin,* Boston, 1853 (author's collection).

Some of the Billings illustrations commissioned by Jewett were more popular than others. Depictions of Eva and Tom became among the most reproduced vignettes from the novel, and three of them demand special notice. One illustrates a scene in chapter 22 in which the two sit "on a little mossy seat, in an arbor, at the foot of the garden" of Augustine St. Clare's "East Indian cottage" in Louisiana (see fig. 20). It is sunset, "which kindles the whole horizon into one blaze of glory, and makes the water another sky." Eva is reading her Bible to Tom when she encounters a passage that suggests the sunset. She fancies she sees in the evening clouds the New Jerusalem— "great gates of pearl . . . and . . . beyond them . . . gold"—and, resting her left hand on his right (which in turn rests on his knee), tells Tom that she will soon be going there in a foreshadowing of her melodramatic death four chapters later. It would be difficult for the reader to overlook the fact that Little Eva is depicted by Billings with a wasp waist and developed breasts. Nor would the reader in the 1850s fail to remark Tom's attractive features and fine clothing. Billings emphasized the equality between child and man in this intimate moment. He drew it for the first edition, and reworked it for the illustrated edition. His version was repeated over and over again for framing prints, sheet music covers, and other ephemera.[19] It was reworked in oil by artists such as Robert Stuart Duncanson, and clearly recalled in the mannered figuration of Miguel Covarrubias for the Limited Editions Club version of the novel published as late as 1938. It also inspired Cruikshank.

Some later artists reworked this image, however, robbing it of its intimacy and Tom of his dignity. Early on, for example, Nathaniel Currier, in his undated lithograph of Uncle Tom and Little Eva, which is clearly dependent on Billing's rendition, physically separated the two, made Eva appear superior and schoolmarmish, and dressed Tom in poorer clothing and gave him a dull visage. Thus began the transformation of the Stowe-Billings characterization of a shared humanity between the races into the white supremacist stereotype common in later decades.

Currier actually based his lithograph on a scene in an earlier chapter (16), a scene in which Eva and Tom were shown at play in the courtyard of St. Clare's house, with Eva hanging a garland of roses around Tom's neck. This picture first appears in the illustrated edition; in it Billings drew the two alone and closely entwined on a stone garden bench (fig. 22). Eva, who seems to have lost some but not all of the anatomical maturity she possessed in the 1852 illustration, sits on Tom's knee and throws arms and flowers around his neck. How must the segregationists, north or south, have recoiled from this image of biracial, cross-generational, physical intimacy illustrating a novel reeking of miscegenation! Stowe in fact seems to have had a knee-jerk reaction in mind when she wrote this scene, for she set it to entrap Miss Ophelia, who is from New England. Southerner St. Clare has been pointing out the hypocrisy of northern attitudes toward blacks when this vignette comes into view. "How can you let her?" asks Ophelia, and this bigoted exclamation gives St. Clare the opportunity to point out that "personal prejudice" is stronger north than south of the Mason-Dixon line.

Alternate versions of the scene in the St. Clare courtyard were created by other artists, such as Nathaniel Currier, probably to avoid the problem posed by showing an embrace between a delicate white girl and a "large,

Fig. 22.   Wood engraving by Baker and Smith after Hammatt Billings, *Little Eva and Uncle Tom in a Garden,* from Harriet Beecher Stowe, *Uncle Tom's Cabin,* Boston, 1853 (Special Collections, Clapp Library, Wellesley College).

broad-chested, powerfully-made man" of a "full glossy black" color, the father, we remember, of many small children, as Stowe describes Tom in various places. Some illustrators, such as the anonymous designer of Jewett's *Pictures and Stories,* show an earlier and less intimate moment in the narrative, with slave and child parted and the pair clearly chaperoned by Ophelia and St. Clare (see fig. 21). Later, as the separation of the races became more complete under Jim Crow laws and other forms of radical racism, it became common to soften the sexual overtones of the moment by eliminating such scenes altogether or presenting Tom as a dull-witted, harmless old man with white wool fringing a balding head.[20] Thus was he visually transformed from Stowe's and Billings's virile father into the benign "old uncle" who has bedeviled twentieth-century criticism.

Fig. 23. Wood engraving by Baker and Smith after Hammatt Billings, *Tom Saves Eva from the Mississippi,* from Harriet Beecher Stowe, *Uncle Tom's Cabin,* Boston, 1853 (Special Collections, Clapp Library, Wellesley College).

Other of Billings's images for *Uncle Tom's Cabin* suggest another reading. According to the critic Elizabeth Ammons, Stowe deliberately feminized Tom in the novel. She gave him the stereotypical nineteenth-century female attributes of piety, purity, noncompetitiveness, unselfishness, emotionality, domesticity, and outward submissiveness. But if this version made Tom sexually harmless it also made him spiritually potent. Stowe cast Tom and Eva, still according to Ammons, as two halves of the "feminine-Christ principle."[21] That the artist visually reinforced the author's presentation of the pair as possessed of sanctified characteristics is demonstrated by a third vignette, which first appears in chapter 14 of the illustrated edition (fig. 23). In Billings's small composition showing Tom saving Eva from the Mississippi, the disembodied arms and unattached poles of the rescuers on board the steamboat assume a radiant pattern emanating from the single triangle formed by black slave and white child. The association of that emanation with a sanctifying aureole, or nimbus, is difficult to avoid. In this one reduced vignette, Billings encapsulated much of Stowe's message.

The observations made in the last paragraphs are contradictory. Billings's images have been characterized as possessing both erotic and sacred connotations. This is a contradiction that must stand as representative of the complexity of both Stowe's text and Billings's illustrations. Piety and sexuality can coexist in life as in literature, if not in homiletics. Whether the relationship between Eva and Tom is seen as sexual or pious, or both, however, Billings's images suggest an equality between them that was difficult to accept in the middle of the nineteenth century, north or south. It was the less intimate scene presented by artists such as the anonymous designer who illustrated Jewett's *Pictures and Stories* that found the most imitators. This was the one copied, for example, by Nathaniel Currier in this country and Adolphe Bayot in Paris, and it inspired Cruikshank and others in England.

The first English edition of *Uncle Tom's Cabin* was apparently unillustrated, but eight different illustrated printings appeared before the end of 1852. The edition published by John Cassell has an introduction dated December, but the work was first issued in the autumn in weekly tuppenny parts, of which there were eventually thirteen, each containing two full-page wood engravings on plate paper. At least eight different engravers signed the illustrations, and that would seem to indicate a publisher in a hurry. The artist was George Cruikshank (1792–1878), whose name appears on the title page in type double the size of that which identifies the author. He was then in the second half of a long and distinguished career as graphic artist. Billings, near the beginning of his career as illustrator, developed his scenes in reaction to Stowe's text; Cruikshank applied to the text his mature graphic style. Comparison reveals that the American's placid vignettes are the more sympathetic to the author's intentions, however more the Englishman's animated line might appeal to the modern collector.

Assuming that Cruikshank began work for John Cassell in the late summer of 1852, only Billings's seven scenes from the first edition could possibly have been available as prototypes, plus whatever other English illustrations then existed (if any). Cruikshank did study the illustrations first drawn by his American counterpart, but his handling of them differed significantly. His Eva and Tom in the arbor is clearly indebted to Billings's version (the process of copying results in the reversed engraved image), although he has reworked the original. His setting is less rustic, the enframement more architectural, and the figures more prim. They do not touch. The depictions of

Cassy attending to Tom after his beating are also distant cousins, with Billings's version being the more concentrated composition and, uncharacteristically, the more dramatic rendering. With *The Freeman's Defense* the connection seems more distant: Cruikshank picked the climax of the action, while Billings's figures are, as usual, relatively inactive.

With the need to create some twenty-one illustrations more than Billings had for the first edition, Cruikshank was forced to originate scenes. It seems impossible that he could have known Billings's second series of vignettes, but it is useful to keep them in mind as we look at some of the Englishman's remaining images. Billings's are basically different from Cruikshank's in that they are constrained vignettes interspersed with the text, whereas Cruikshank had a full page on which to develop his visual events. Comparison of selected subjects reveals Billings's penchant for quiet decorum and Cruikshank's for enlivening caricature. This is true even in scenes of repose, such as Shelby and Haley discussing the sale of little Harry, or Uncle Tom at home. In the latter, Cruikshank shows blacks with stereotypical bulging eyes and thick lips cavorting like children, whereas Billings depicts George Shelby quietly (and illegally) teaching Tom how to write. Since Stowe sought to portray a common humanity among all her characters, Billings has clearly captured her intention here. Cruikshank was capable of adjusting his characterization, as in his *Prayer Meeting*, where Tom and others possess a dignity befitting the event, but he seems to have been more comfortable, more characteristically "Cruikshankian," where he could give free reign to his comic genius, as in the figures depicted with appropriate abandon in *Andy and Sam's Trick* and other high-spirited episodes. It is fair to say that Billings's work here and elsewhere is largely humorless.

Cruikshank's full-page scenes are explicit and anecdotal; Billings's vignettes, emblematic. Contrast, for example, the draftsmen's approaches to *Tom Saving Eva from a Watery Grave* (cf. figs. 23 and 24). The Englishman "explains" how Tom and Eva were pulled from the water with the help of fellow passengers in a "graphic" depiction that was found to be a suitably literal source for this episode by the artist of the *Classic Illustrated* comic book version of the novel published in the 1940s. The same event, as we have seen, gave Billings the opportunity to move beyond what "happened" to signify the conjoined sanctity of child and slave implicit in the text.

In general, Billings used few strokes to capture the essence of a scene, and in so doing increased the impact of the text for the American audience (cf. figs. 25 and 26). Thus in chapter 30, in his depiction of the public sale of the

Fig. 24. Wood engraving by T. Williams after George Cruikshank, *Tom Saves Eva from the Mississippi*, from Harriet Beecher Stowe, *Uncle Tom's Cabin*, London, 1852 (author's collection).

pale mulatto, Emmeline, he sketched just four main characters: auctioneer, two competing bidders, and the vulnerable "goods" dressed in timeless, classicizing garb. But he squeezed maximum effect from this simple composition, for his Emmeline is a vested version of Hiram Powers's naked *Greek Slave*, a sculpture finished in 1843 and widely exhibited in the years just before publication of Stowe's narrative, and so he makes demure allusion to an equation currently popular among American reformers, that of chattel slavery and female exploitation. Cruikshank, product of a very different political and cultural milieu, achieved less appropriate results in his more elaborate depiction of the slave auction. He outfitted Emmeline in plain contemporary dress, placed her in the midst of an animated crowd of bidders and bystanders, and drove home the irony of the action by placing it in a vast hall ornamented with pilasters and niches. Although slaves were sold beneath the

Fig. 25. Wood engraving by Baker and Smith after Hammatt Billings, *Slave Auction*, from Harriet Beecher Stowe, *Uncle Tom's Cabin*, Boston, 1853 (Special Collections, Clapp Library, Wellesley College).

Fig. 26. Wood engraving after George Cruikshank, *Slave Auction,* from Harriet Beecher Stowe, *Uncle Tom's Cabin,* London, 1852 (author's collection).

neoclassical dome of the St. Charles Hotel in New Orleans, Cruikshank's inclusion of allegorical figures of Justice, Freedom (who holds a liberty cap and the Declaration of Independence), and Christianity is a bit much. Here we have more bombast, but less effect.

While both Billings (elsewhere) and Cruikshank were at home in the use of classical allegory, only the American was as adept at limning angels and Christ. The headpiece of chapter 33 of Jewett's illustrated edition, for instance, a chapter in which Jesus appears to Tom and fills him with Christian endurance in the face of evil and oppression, depicts a black slave kneeling before his thorn-crowned, radiant, and white, Lord. This is an image as completely in keeping with the evangelical sentiment of the text as Cruikshank's classical iconography is alien to it. It descends, of course, from Billings's design for the masthead of Garrison's *Liberator*. Thomas Ball, Billings's childhood friend and erstwhile collaborator, was to appropriate and transform it in his statue of Lincoln as the emancipator (1872).

Which of these two illustrators, the famous Cruikshank or the emerging Billings, created the more effective illustrations to Stowe's text? Cruikshank may have been the more sophisticated graphic talent, but Billings more closely captured the complexity and thrust of Stowe's polemic. His illustrations are more than apt graphic translations of Stowe's characterizations, more than sympathetic visual interpretations of her verbal pictures, more than mere textual decorations: they are quiet but effective reinforcements for her impassioned attack on slavery and consequent plea for social change. As one reviewer wrote of Jewett's illustrated edition, "the power of the [artist's] pencil adds much to the power of the [author's] pen."[22] Like Birket Foster's earlier work on *Evangeline*, Cruikshank's for *Uncle Tom's Cabin* kept the text at some distance.

Uncle Tom's Cabin is certainly the best-known book for which Billings provided the first illustrations; only part two of Louisa May Alcott's *Little Women* gives it competition. When in 1868 Roberts Brothers of Boston issued the first part of the history of the March girls it contained wood engravings after drawings by Louisa's sister Abigail May Alcott (1840–79).[23] Her work was roundly condemned, however. A reviewer writing for the *Nation* called the scenes "indifferently executed illustrations, in which Miss [Abigail] May Alcott betrays not only a want of anatomical knowledge, and that indifference to or nonrecognition of the subtle beauty of the lines of the female figure which so generally makes women artists, but also the fact that she has not closely studied the text which she illustrates."[24] Louisa May Alcott (1832–88) must have suggested her "Amy" to illustrate the book, for Thomas Niles Jr. of Roberts Brothers, the publishers, had written asking her to "recommend a designer for 4 or 6 cuts." He went on to propose that the Pickwick Club's voting of membership to Sam Weller (that is, Laurie) in chapter 10, with the members in costume, should be one of the illustrations. This is a rare document relating to the selection of scenes to be illustrated in a novel, but nothing came of it.[25]

Not even a loving sibling could find much to praise in Abigail May's flaccid efforts, and it was obvious that a professional artist should be chosen to illustrate the second volume. As early as 1864 Louisa May had written to the abolitionist Boston publisher James Redpath that she would like Billings to illustrate her fairy tales, although she also noted that another illustrator, Elizabeth Greene, had "a delicate fancy & if she would let me see her designs before engraved I could tell her how to make them suit me better."[26] Louisa May it seems had strong opinions about illustration, and this was to make itself known to Billings when he was chosen to produce four drawings for the second part of *Little Women,* which appeared in 1869. His efforts were not without criticism; the commission was not without its problems. His first attempt at the frontispiece was roundly condemned by the author for the same lack of attention to text that had been assigned to her sister Abigail May. In a letter of 1 April 1869 to Elizabeth Greene she wrote: "Oh, Betsey! such trials as I have had with that Billings no mortal creter knows! He went & drew Amy a fat girl with a pug of hair, sitting among weedy shrubbery with a light-house under her nose, & a mile or two off a scrubby little boy on his stomach in the grass looking cross, towzly, & about 14 years old! It was a blow, for that picture was to be the gem of the lot."[27]

Louisa May wrote "Oh, please change em!" on the proof of the first attempt and returned it to Niles at Roberts Brothers, who "set Billings to work again." The author thought the artist's second attempt was better but still not perfect (fig 32). "[T]he man followed my directions & made (or tried to) Laurie 'a mixture of Apollo, Byron, Tito & Will Greene,'" continued her diatribe to Betsey. "Such a baa Lamb! hair parted in the middle, big eyes, sweet nose, lovely moustache & cunning hands; straight out of a bandbox & no more like the real Teddy than Ben Franklin. I wailed but let go for the girls are clamoring & the book can't be delayed. Amy is pretty & the scenery is good but—my Teddy, oh my Teddy!"[28]

Louisa May could be hard on illustrators and was perhaps more tolerant of Billings than of others. She ripped out the cuts in a copy of the 1870 edition of her *Moods* (they were apparently not after Billings's designs), and she was to have unkind things to say about the work of her friend Betsey Greene as well.[29] We have no record that she ever mutilated a copy of the second part of *Little Women,* and in fact, she seems actually to have been happy with Billings's work, as we learn from another letter from Thomas Niles written just three days after her outburst to Betsey. "I am glad the 2d part pleases you," he wrote, and added that he liked "all the pictures but one— Beth & Jo on the Sea Shore, which is rather a failure." As pleased as Louisa

Fig. 27. Wood engraving by John Andrew or Mathews after Hammatt Billings, *Amy and Laurie,* frontispiece to Louisa May Alcott, *Little Women, Part Two,* Boston, 1869 (Special Collections, Clapp Library, Wellesley College).

May was, finally, with Hammatt's efforts, she seems to have been even happier with the new illustrations by Frank Thayer Merrill that adorned the new edition of 1880.[30]

Billings provided four designs for *Little Women:* the frontispiece of Amy and Laurie, *Jo in a Vortex, The Professor and Tina,* and *Jo and Beth.* Niles was right to single out the sisters on the seashore as the weakest of the lot. The frontispiece of Amy sketching and Laurie lounging in the French countryside is adequate if not inspired (fig. 27). In a design that captures the intended gemütlichkeit, Professor Baehr swings little Tina around his study while a tabby rubs familiarly against his ankle. Billings depicted the professor the way Louisa May described him, his advanced age suggested by his full beard. Actors cast for this part in later movies have considerably lowered his age, and thus changed the character of Jo's marriage.

Jo in a Vortex is a superb illustration, capturing all the energy and focus of the accompanying description (fig. 28). This is a study in concentration. Dressed in her "scribbling suit" ("a black pinafore on which she could wipe her pen at will"), Jo leans into her writing before a window in a room strewn

with rejected pages. In Billings's illustration, genius does seem to burn on her face. This is the perfect visualization of aspiring intelligence at creative work. Here Billings made up for his earlier inattention to Louisa May's words. Nowhere in his mature book work—or that of many of his peers—is there an illustration that better encapsulates a text; only in *Uncle Tom's Cabin* did he occasionally equal this.

The histories of Billings's work—or lack of work—on *Evangeline, Uncle Tom's Cabin,* and *Little Women* illuminate his relationship to midcentury book illustration in general and the development of his own mature strengths in particular. There were failures and triumphs. In his work, and that of his pioneering contemporaries, American book illustration established a beachhead from which it was to capture the high ground of its full potential in the following generation. This was true not only of his generation's work in books but in periodicals as well.

4

"His Pencil Has Been in Constant Demand"

Periodical Illustration

B Y THE 1840s the profuse illustration of popular journals and newspapers had become a fact of the publishing world. The *Illustrated London News*, which first appeared in 1842, set the standard for subsequent mass-distributed publications in Europe and America. After spotty beginnings in this decade, during the next the illustrated press became a common feature of American popular culture. *Gleason's* (later *Ballou's*) *Pictorial Drawing-Room Companion*, published in Boston from May 1851 until December 1859, became the first important lavishly illustrated newspaper in the United States.[1] Although it dominated the 1850s, *Gleason's / Ballou's* did not survive long after the appearance in New York of the more widely distributed *Frank Leslie's Illustrated Newspaper* in 1855 or, in 1857, of *Harper's Weekly*, the best-known of these periodicals, which lasted well into the twentieth century.[2]

In an article published in 1855, *Gleason's / Ballou's* noted that the "taste for a pictorial literature has greatly increased within a few years. . . . [T]here has been a great demand for an illustrated literature of all kinds, religious and secular, solid and light."[3] Hammatt Billings was not the only illustrator working for *Gleason's / Ballou's*, but he was among the principal artists for the journal. In 1856 it informed its readers that "his pencil has been in constant demand," and indeed, as we shall see, an extraordinarily large number of sizable (some double-page) wood engravings after his designs appeared in this journal during the decade. But his work for the illustrated periodicals began earlier, and it continued later.

At the beginning of his career Billings was called upon to supply pictures for the fledgling, and short-lived, illustrated journals of the 1840s. The *Boston Miscellany of Literature and Fashion*, edited first by Nathan Hale Jr. and then briefly by Henry T. Tuckerman, lasted only from January 1842 through February 1843.[4] Billings, who was still signing work as C. H. H. Billings, designed the etched border of flora and fauna surrounding the engraving after George Miller that appears as the frontispiece of volume 1. His full-page *Bunker Hill Monument* formed the frontispiece to the number for August 1842, and his *Boston Common*, likewise full page, fronted the issue for December. Both were engraved on steel by J. A. Rolph.[5] The view of the Common is framed by the State House on the left and Park Street Church on the right and centered on the "symmetrical beauty" of the Old Elm, the senior of New England trees.[6] These were, as we will see, examples of his depictions of urban vistas. Billings was twenty-four in 1842, so he was as precocious as an illustrator as he was as an architect; these are prominently displayed works for such a tyro.

In their "Introductory Address," the editors of the *Pictorial National Library*, published at Boston during 1848 and 1849, considered the pictorial not the least important aspect of their journal.[7] "Pictures," they wrote, "are often more intelligible, instructive and inviting than words. . . . They attract the child, they allure the listless and unthinking, they speak to the wise and serious. . . . They improve the taste, instruct the eye, assist the perceptive faculties, strengthen the memory, please the fancy, and often touch the heart when words would be powerless." The portrait of Daniel Webster that appeared in the first volume was probably just one of many drawings Billings sent to this short-lived journal. We know for certain that the cover (or wrapper) and the "ornamental title on the first page" were also his. This masthead, the earliest of several he was to design, is composed of a central cartouche with side vignettes, a narrative format we have come to recognize as typical of him. Within the cartouche is a view of a characteristic mid-nineteenth-century library, with bookshelves forming alcoves, presided over by a standing figure of what appears to be Athena / Minerva within a Palladian niche. The design seems to have been generally inspired by the second-floor reading room of the Boston Athenaeum, known from a photograph by Southworth and Hawes of 1853.[8] The vignettes to left and right depict a single young woman reading by lamp light and an elderly gentleman reading to what appear to be his spouse, his grandchild, and a dog. Thus did Billings suggest that the "wise and serious" of all generations would find the *National* improving. We know the editors were most happy with his work, because they noted that his "fertile and graceful pencil is its own sufficient praise."[9] This was an early example of the many contemporary compliments bestowed on his drawings for the illustrated periodicals.

Gleason's / Ballou's was not the only illustrated magazine to which Billings contributed during the next decade. The *Bulletin of the New England Art Union*, which appeared in Boston in 1852 and then vanished (as did the union itself), contained Billings's design for the seal of the organization (a tondo housing a draped female representing the arts) and his illustrations to Longfellow's "Skeleton in Armour."[10] The poet was a vice-president of the union. Billings's vignette, which according to the editors "shows what rapid progress the art of design is making here" in America, illustrated two scenes: "Far in the Northern land / . . . I . . . / tamed the ger-falcon," and "Oft to his frozen lair / Tracked I the grisly bear—" (fig. 29). The engraver was William Jay Baker. Sometime prior to September 1847 Billings borrowed the poet's copy of Esaias Tegner's *Frithiof's Saga* while working on these illustrations. In February 1851 he wrote to the poet asking permission to have his drawings engraved for a gift book he hoped Ticknor would publish in 1852. This apparently never appeared, and only this vignette survives from this project.

In 1853 Billings created the allegorical title page to P. T. Barnum's *Illustrated News,* another short-lived publication, edited by Rufus W. Griswold (see chap. 9; see fig. 89).[11] He also continued to design mastheads. One certainly by him topped William Lloyd Garrison's *Liberator* (see fig. 18), and one that may be plausibly attributed to him graced, for at least a decade, the *Youth's Companion,* edited and published in Boston from the 1820s by Nathaniel Willis and his successors.[12] Billings frequently illustrated children's books and magazines. There is in the author's collection a horizontal pencil study for a masthead for the *Youth's Companion.* The vignette shows a man rowing a boat with a woman seated astern and reading a newspaper, certainly the *Companion* (fig. 30). Although this particular scene never appeared in the *Youth's Companion,* perhaps because the people in the rowboat were older than the paper's target market, this sketch establishes the fact that Billings at one point studied the design.

The journal in fact displayed a new, wood-engraved masthead on the first issue of volume 31 (1857), and this has all the characteristics of a Billings composition (fig. 31). Within a centered half-circle sits a couple visibly younger than the pair in the boat in the pencil study. (We are told in the description that the youngsters are brother and sister.) They read the *Companion* with the approval of a dog at their feet. To their left is an upholstered chair and straw hat suggesting, according to the editors, that the girl has just returned from the post office with the paper; to their right, a vista of lake and hills. Beyond the half-circle, to the left, is a vignette of even younger children

8   BULLETIN OF THE NEW ENGLAND ART UNION.

" Far in the Northern land,
    By the wild Baltic's strand,
    I, with my childish hand,
        Tamed the ger-falcon ;
    And with my skates fast bound,
    Skimmed the half-frozen Sound,
    That the poor whimpering hound,
        Trembled to walk on.

    Oft to his frozen lair
    Tracked I the grisly bear,
    While from my path the hare
        Fled like a shadow ;
    Oft through the forest dark
    Followed the were-wolf's bark,
    Until the soaring lark
        Sang from the meadow."

ILLUSTRATION OF PROFESSOR LONGFELLOW'S SKELETON IN ARMOUR.

Fig. 29. Wood engraving by William Jay Baker after Hammatt Billings, illustration to H. W. Longfellow, *Skeleton in Armour*, from the *Bulletin of the New England Art Union*, 1852 (author's collection).

Fig. 30. Graphite drawing by Hammatt Billings for a masthead of the *Youth's Companion*, early 1850s? (author's collection).

reading the newspaper while a baby sleeps in its crib; to the right, a young shepherd and his dog watch the flock. The shepherd too reads his *Companion*. "The Designer who drew the plan, has given it a very airy, graceful aspect," wrote the editors, who also noted its intent: "These figures seem to indicate our duty to instruct, amuse, and caution our young readers, which we shall endeavor to do."[13] This masthead was replaced with a variant by J. N. Hyde beginning in the issue of 27 December 1866.

Billings's work for the popular press continued through the 1860s. Only one illustration by him can be firmly identified in *Harper's Weekly*, the pedestrian *Launch of the United States Gun-Boat* Maniton *at the Boston Navy-Yard, August 25, 1866*, which appeared in volume 10, although at least two others reflect his influence.[14] The allegorical representations of the state of Mississippi and Alabama in the same volume follow those Billings designed for *Ballou's*, nearly a decade earlier.[15] He also drew for juvenile magazines. Volumes 3 and 4 (1868) of the *Nursery: A Magazine for Youngest Readers*, published at Boston by John L. Shorey with Fanny P. Seavers as editor, contain at least fourteen cuts after Billings's designs for various items, including a story by "Cousin Fanny" and poems by Emily Carter.[16] His work also appears in *Our Young Folks*; for example, he embellished a series of articles on gardening in 1869. This Boston-based *Illustrated Magazine for Boys and Girls* published from 1865 an impressive list of authors and illustrators, including Thomas Bailey Aldrich, Edward Everett Hale, and Lucy Larcom, as well as F. O. C. Darley, Augustus Hoppin, and W. L. Champney. Billings is also listed as one of the illustrators of *Oliver Optic's Magazine* in the late 1860s, although no specific works by him have been identified.[17]

In some cases these periodicals reused illustrations Billings had drawn as

Fig. 31. Wood engraving after Hammatt Billings (?), masthead of the *Youth's Companion*, 1857 (author's collection).

embellishments in books, either to illustrate articles or to enhance publishers' ads. This spread his work far afield, although anonymously, since he is rarely credited with such graphics, and without profit, since it is doubtful he received any payment for such added exposure.

His periodical work carried into his final decade. *Every Saturday*, issued at Boston in the late 1860s and early 1870s under the editorship of Thomas Bailey Aldrich, was illustrated only during 1870 and 1871 when many of its pictures were electrotypes from the London *Graphic*. There was, however, also much work from the hands of Darley, Hoppin, Waud, Homer, and others, including at least one large engraving after Billings: *Remembering the Parson,— Thanksgiving in the Olden Time.*[18] The celebration of Thanksgiving was not unknown in New England, but as a national day of remembrance it was relatively new in 1870, as it had been established during the Civil War by President Lincoln. In Billings's view, a countryman on a chilly day brings the parson and his family pumpkins, apples, fowl, and perhaps, a barrel of cider. He shows the event not as a seventeenth-century occurrence; his "olden time" is, perhaps more appropriately, well within the nineteenth century. This is, then, related to the group of scenes he had drawn from American history, the bulk of which appeared in *Ballou's*.

All of this miscellaneous magazine work from the decades before and after the 1850s, which was no doubt greater than is here recalled, pales before the illustrations "from the pencil of Billings" that appeared during that decade in *Gleason / Ballou's*.[19] These range from graphic reportage to flights of allegorical fancy, from the "solid" to the "light." They fall into a number of types: depictions of current events such as the visit of the Hungarian patriot Louis Kossuth to Boston in 1852, or the inauguration of the statue of Benjamin Franklin in Boston in 1856; allegorical representations of the hemispheres; a plate devoted to "Gods & Goddesses of the Grecian Mythology";

urban vistas; regional vignettes; allegories of holidays such as May Day, the Fourth of July, Christmas, or New Year's; emblematical representations of the states; and visualizations of suggestive events in American history. The last two categories have great significance for the fraught decade in which they were produced, the years leading to the Civil War.

Most of these illustrations appeared as folio-size wood engravings. With a circulation of more than one hundred thousand by 1856, the magazine aspired to a presence "on the center table of every parlor in America," and some of its wood engravings might have found their way into frames and adorned the walls of even the most modest of those parlors.[20] These illustrations represent an extraordinary outlay of creative labor and should be viewed as a major component of Billings's busy life. Through them his pencil reached well beyond the confines of Boston or New England. In them he achieved some of his finest graphic work, and some of the finest popular graphic work of his era.

Billings's "allegorical and emblematical representations of the hemispheres," occupying a two-page spread in *Ballou's* for 19 December 1855, exemplify his multifigured, allegorical compositions, of which he created many for the press (fig. 32). The angle of vision is Euro-American; these plates and the accompanying text embody the attitude of superiority assumed by the West vis-à-vis the rest of the world. A circle segment centers both compositions, that in *The Eastern Hemisphere* containing "a group strongly characteristic of the gorgeous East," including a camel, an elephant, and Arabs; that in *The Western Hemisphere* encompassing Indian horsemen on the prairie. "Europe . . . a female sovereign of exquisite and commanding loveliness" presides over the eastern half of the world, as indeed she then did through her colonial powers. She is flanked by personifications of Africa and Asia, the latter "a favorite sultana, attired in rich barbaric finery, and seated in a car drawn by a lion and a tiger." The lower corners are occupied by stereotypes of the Chinese and the Turks; at the bottom is a scene from the Crimean War! The text looks upon this strange Eastern composite as representative of the "other." It is less "an integral portion of the common heritage of humanity than as another world . . . another planet, as it were."

In Billings's "equally beautiful and characteristic" *Western Hemisphere* the narrative's principal figure is, of course, (American) Liberty holding "the shield of our Union." At her feet "crouches an Indian, the type of that gallant but fated race," fading before the march of civilization depicted in the vignettes to her left and right showing the "semi-civilization" of Mexico and

Fig. 32. Wood engravings after Hammatt Billings, *The Eastern Hemisphere* and *The Western Hemisphere*, from *Ballou's Pictorial Drawing-Room Companion*, December 1855 (author's collection).

the "clearing, settling, &c." of a party of immigrants. The lower corners balance Inuit kayaks with "a keel boat loaded with produce and rowed by blacks." The contrast between East and West reinforces the contemporary belief that "westward moves the course of empire," and the editors make clear who will lead the migration: "To the Anglo-Saxon alone, we believe, is reserved the triumph of civilizing and commanding the Western hemisphere." Billings's pencil is here fully engaged in visually interpreting current atti-

tudes. In his work for the popular press he gave allegorical expression to popular opinion.[21]

His pencil drew a wide range of other topics as well. There are half a dozen allegories of holidays attributed to Billings in the pages of *Gleason's /Ballou's*, three of them representing New Year's. The earliest appeared on the first day of 1853 and was immediately acclaimed by the editors of *Dodge's Literary Museum*. They found *Gleason's* a "brilliantly-illuminated weekly jour-

nal," and selected for particular praise "among a large number of most beautiful and artistic engravings," the "fine allegorical picture, by Billings, of the
incoming New Year." Billings alone of the illustrators is mentioned by name.
An article in Ballou's for 1856 was to call him "without rival in this country"
and rivaled only by John Gilbert in England.[22] The comparison is apt, although Billings was more a sometime follower than the equal of the chief
artist for the Illustrated London News.[23] Gilbert practiced a belated Baroque
style in which "statuesque men and beautiful women" appeared in allegories
where "lofty sentiment and patriotism could be expressed through mytho-
logical deities" floating among the clouds.[24] In his New Year's of 1853 Billings
follows Gilbert's manner closely.[25] He shows the Christ Child as the New
Year carried in the arms of Winter who floats through the air above a chilly
landscape accompanied by allegorical figures representing the other seasons.
"The old years flee before him, while Cupids scatter flowers in his pathway,"
according to the text.

The representation of Christmas that Billings had supplied the journal
the previous month is probably best described as Dickensian rather than
Gilbertian (fig. 33). Billings's graphic work varied according to his task. This
is a composition the editors told the readership that is "graceful, full of
significance, and tells a story fluently, at first sight," an essential characteristic
for an illustration in a magazine reaching for mass appeal. Billings balances a
"Merry Christmas" with a "Dismal Christmas." In the former, children and
young lovers dance to gay music coming from the orchestral gallery within a
bough-bedecked interior; in the latter, a lonely figure trudges through the
snow outside Boston's Park Street Church. Between is a vignette of the first
Christmas and, in the exact center of the composition, a scene right out of
A Christmas Carol (1843) bearing the admonition to "Remember the Poor."
Above, Old Father Christmas presides over all, with his "savory bowl of hot
stuff (soup, perhaps), symbolic of good cheer."[26] "Soup, perhaps," because
temperance feelings still ran high.

The drawings Billings contributed to Ballou's as tributes to the states
outnumber any of his other illustrations. Each appeared as a wood engraving
occupying half of the front page of an issue. The series commenced in
January 1855 with the emblem of Maine, and this was quickly followed by
Pennsylvania, Florida, Iowa, Arkansas, North Carolina, New Hampshire,
Virginia, Missouri, Connecticut, and California. Although the draftsman of
these early emblems is unnamed, they can be attributed to Billings on the
basis of the following designs that are assigned to him in the text: Georgia,

Fig. 33. Wood engraving after Hammatt Billings, *An Allegorical Picture of Christmas,* from *Gleason's Pictorial Drawing-Room Companion,* December 1852 (author's collection).

Texas, Louisiana, New York, Illinois, Michigan, Maryland, South Carolina, Delaware, New Jersey, Rhode Island, Wisconsin, Indiana, Kentucky, Mississippi, Tennessee, and Alabama. These plates represented all sections of the country: New England, the mid-Atlantic, the South, the old Northwest, the Southwest, and the West.

The series must be seen against the backdrop of the political turmoil of the 1850s, part of which concerned the struggle for balance of power between the Union and the states. It was a struggle that preoccupied not only politicians but artists as well. Historian David Reynolds has recently shown, for example, that Walt Whitman's impulse in writing *Leaves of Grass* (original edition, 1855) was the poet's despair at the political upheavals of the decade. He sought a cultural solution to the turmoil that was tearing the country apart. In "Song of Myself," the narrator envisions himself as one of "an average unending procession" of individually named states and cities representing the four corners of the Union, an image which, according to Rey-

nolds, "purposely imposes comradely unity on a highly disunified country."
At the moment Whitman was composing the first of the *Leaves*, Billings was
designing his own (vastly different) appeal for national unity, the Monument
to the Forefathers at Plymouth, Massachusetts. And six months before the
publication of the *Leaves, Ballou's* began the series of states' emblems, Billings's
visual rather than Whitman's "rhetorical intermingling of North, South,
East, and West."[27] There may or may not have been a causal relationship
between Billings's emblems and Whitman's listing, but the coincidence in the
appearance of these inventories strengthens the connection between Billings's designs and the boiling struggle between the nation and the states.

Maine, Pennsylvania, Florida, and Iowa were the first states to be illustrated, so the series of emblems immediately knitted the country together
north to south, east to west. The arrangement contains its own subliminal
message, the accompanying texts (probably written by the editors, not the
artist) occasionally obliquely refer to current events, and some of the images
contain less than subtle references to the contemporary national debate.
Illinois for example (19 April 1856) displays its arms with a banner reading
"State Sovereignty—National Union." The text describing South Carolina
(21 June 1856) says she is "prompt to assert her State[s'] rights, and ready to
defend them, [but] she has nevertheless never been backward in pouring out
blood or treasure when the national good demanded them." Native Americans dominate the pictorial vignettes, perhaps partly because they were—at
least for the moment—as an issue politically neutral, but in the emblems
representing Georgia, Louisiana, South Carolina, Mississippi, Tennessee,
and Alabama (ranging from October 1855 to May 1857) the South's economic
basis in slavery is prominently represented by Billings (although, with the
exception of Louisiana, more or less skirted by the author of the accompanying texts). In these emblems, black slaves working at cotton or cane are
depicted as dutiful laborers. Billings neither caricatures them nor renders
them woeful; they share the common humanity he gave "the lowly" in *Uncle
Tom's Cabin*.

The format of each design is similar to the others, and highly characteristic of Billings's compositional strategy for devices of this kind. In each the
center is occupied by the state seal flanked by or superimposed upon telling
vignettes of local history, industry, or commerce. In most cases (Illinois is an
exception) the Native Americans occupy the left (sinister) flank (the engravings are reversed from Billings's drawing, but he certainly had this in mind),
yet they, too, are treated by Billings with dignity. Of course, in so doing, he

Fig. 34. Wood engraving after Hammatt Billings (?), *Connecticut*, from *Ballou's Pictorial Drawing-Room Companion*, August 1855 (author's collection).

applies to them, as he did to the blacks, Anglo-American virtue, which robs them of their special identity. But how else from the point of view of his time could he humanize them? In some cases they are pacific, occupied in characteristic pursuits or posed allegorically; rarely do they appear as menacing. An exception is the depiction of Connecticut, in which a Puritan on the way to church with his family does not suspect that "a Pequot warrior is dodging [*sic*] his footsteps, and that on his return from divine service he will find his home desolate" (fig. 34). This is a scene George Henry Boughton was to recreate so memorably in his *Pilgrims on Their Way to Meeting* of 1867. Billings (unlike Boughton) shows the warrior hiding in ambush, tomahawk in hand, but the text also contains a measured assessment of the aftermath: "Fearful was the vengeance often inflicted upon the 'bloody heathen,' the destruction of whom was justified by quotation from Holy Writ." This seems mildly to reflect the sympathetic attitudes of some New Englanders toward the Indians, an attitude expressed in the writings of Lydia Maria Child, Catharine Sedgwick, and others.

Some of these images are variations on themes Billings was working on elsewhere. Scenes of encounters between Europeans and natives, one version of which he had just designed for the Forefathers Monument, appear in his *Georgia*, where a mounted De Soto confronts the standing inhabitants, and in his *Illinois*, where Lasalle and his party encounter the chief of the Illinois. In the latter the two emblems of conquest are much in evidence: the "foreigners" are heavily armed with harquebuses and include a Roman Catholic priest "with cross and rosary." "The rude arms of the Indians, their war clubs and spears, contrast with the more perfect appointment of their visitors." The chief offers the calumet, while his young tobacco-bearer carries a "plentiful supply of the vile weed." Another encounter is shown in the emblem of Mississippi.

Billings's *Massachusetts* (February 1856) balances to left and right of the state seal the landing of the Pilgrims, in which a native watches the arrival at Plymouth, with the Minute-Call, in which a plowman is summoned to take up arms "in defense of his country" (fig. 35). The artist was also studying these scenes as part of his current monumental designs. The bottom vignette shows the industrial present, with its "tokens of peaceful industry and prosperity." These are appropriate enough as emblematic of the Commonwealth, but the Commonwealth saw itself, and many others saw it, as the cornerstone of the nation, and it would seem that here Billings extends the program of his Forefathers Monument: here he again enlists a shared pictorial heritage in the discovery of the New World and the creation of a new nation in the service of contemporary attempts to preserve the bonds of union. This agenda carries over to the series of emblems as a whole and to the several historical scenes he drew for *Gleason's / Ballou's* during these same, anxious years.

History headed the hierarchy of categories of painting in the academic theories of Sir Joshua Reynolds and others in the eighteenth century because it dealt with universal themes of human grandeur and patriotic sacrifice. Although Americans were slow to accept history painting, it had achieved great popularity by the 1840s and 1850s, during, that is, "an era marked both by optimistic nationalism and by ultimately disastrous sectionalism."[28] By the early 1850s history painting was being called on this side of the Atlantic "the noblest and most comprehensive branch of art," holding "the most exalted rank in the various departments of art," and collections of it were exhibited to enthusiastic audiences in Boston (1852) and elsewhere.[29] American history was of course a favorite. According to the *American Whig Review* for 1846, "the connoisseur will be likely to prefer subjects of our own history . . . because they cherish love of country and respect for our ancestors." This

Fig. 35. Wood engraving after Hammatt Billings, *Massachusetts, the Bay State,* from *Ballou's Pictorial Drawing-Room Companion,* February 1856 (author's collection).

Whiggish sentiment also fueled Billings's work in the next decade on the National Monument to the Forefathers.

Nationalistic, patriotic themes came to dominate American history painting at midcentury; Emanuel Leutze executed the best known of these, for example the huge *Washington Crossing the Delaware* painted in 1850–51. In the eighteenth century the Frenchman Denis Diderot labeled such vast, multi-figured canvases "les grands machines"; Billings and other illustrators for the popular press harnessed these vast engines for domestic consumption by reducing them to journalistic scale. They democratized history painting in the 1850s by transposing it into a graphic format for mass distribution.

Billings's historical scenes begin to appear in *Gleason's/Ballou's* during mid-1855, at about the same time as his emblems of the states.[30] The editors considered them not "as mere ornaments" but "as a means of education." "Vivid representations of striking scenes of history serve to fix events indelibly upon the memory," they wrote. "Here the pencil aids the pen and perfects

Fig. 36. Wood engraving after Hammatt Billings, *Pocahontas Saving the Life of Captain Smith*, from *Ballou's Pictorial Drawing-Room Companion*, January 1857 (author's collection).

the images of the past."[31] The editors of *Gleason's / Ballou's*, with a distribution that was national in scope, avoided taking a firm stand on the issues that divided the country in the 1850s (as we have noted in discussing Billings's representations of the states). They devoted themselves to expressions of cohesion, "to the image of the great American Union," according to historian Sally Pierce.[32]

The first history piece from Billings's pencil to appear in the journal (July 1855) depicts the defeat of General Braddock during the French and Indian War. Others represent Pocahontas saving John Smith and Columbus discovering America (figs. 36 and 37), which, like the remaining scenes, represent common legends of the nation. The remainder are concerned with events surrounding the Revolution (*Franklin Presented at the French Court*, *The Boston Tea Party*, *Washington at Valley Forge*, and *The Battle of the Cowpens*); the War of 1812 (*Battle of New Orleans* and a scene of the engagement of the *Constitution* and the *Guerriere*); or the Mexican War (General Scott's entry into Mexico and the *Battle of Buena Vista*); concerned, then, with creating, sustaining, and expand-

BALLOU'S PICTORIAL DRAWING-ROOM COMPANION.

COLUMBUS DISCOVERING AMERICA.

Fig. 37. Wood engraving after Hammatt Billings, *Columbus Discovers America*, from *Ballou's Pictorial Drawing-Room Companion*, February 1857 (Boston Athenaeum).

ing the United States.[33] In Billings's depictions of the War for Independence he was following in the footsteps of Benson Lossing, whose *Pictorial Field-Book of the Revolution* appeared in two volumes in 1851. Lossing sought to create descriptive rather than artistic illustrations; Billings's work seems to walk a fine line between the two.

Billings's tiny London sketchbook, with its copies of compositions by Veronese and others, evinces an interest in the old masters he had followed since early in his career.[34] His multifigured compositions for *Ballou's*, the reliefs on the National Monument to the Forefathers, and related works descend from the art of the Italian High Renaissance reinvigorated by the French and English neoclassicists. They are axially balanced, theatrical groupings of clustered figures with central focus and closed sides descending from the Vatican *stanze* of Raphael and his school through the more recent works of Jacques Louis David and Benjamin West and their schools.[35] As a composer of figural works, Billings like his contemporaries was anything but innovative. His historical drawings, like his designs for low relief sculpture, are built of quotations and paraphrases from any number of familiar sources.

The composition of his *Pocahontas* originates with a central triangle of figures that radiates out to the edges (see fig. 36), and in this it recalls West's *Death of General Wolfe* of 1770. The composition of the *Battle of the Cowpens* forms a great V of which the figures to the right seem to have drifted over from a battle piece by Copley or Trumbull. The groups of men flanking Columbus enclose him as if in parentheses; they seem lifted out of a Raphael or Giulio Romano (see fig. 37). If Billings's compositional formula is traditional, however, his representations often stand apart from typical contemporary renditions of the event. For example, he shows Columbus still aboard ship espying the New World. In this his view is markedly different from most contemporary representations of the event, which, like Trumbull's monumental depiction of the landing (1839–46), show Columbus triumphantly ashore.[36]

There was a special reason for Billings's use of traditional compositional and figural sources for his historical works, for they produce in *Gleason's / Ballou's*, as in the works of the High Renaissance or the English or French neoclassicists, immediately legible images. This borrowing from familiar models resulted in figures that are stiff and postured but created overall clarity. To paraphrase what the editors of the journal said of such historical scenes, the artist's classical composition "perfects the images of the past" "to fix . . . [them] indelibly upon the memory."[37] Billings presented these readable images of the memorable events of the union's past in the middle of a decade of accelerating disintegration to a public that greatly outnumbered that reached by Trumbull or any other history painter. It is nothing short of surprising that, in an era of antielitist art history, his work and the works of others laboring for the popular press have been largely overlooked.

Billings's large illustrations for *Gleason's / Ballou's*, as do his other graphic works and his architectural and monumental designs, demonstrate that he was a master of the historical composition, the patriotic emblem, and the allegorical vision. They also represent an enormous amount of work, especially when we remember that he was during this decade, the 1850s, busy as well in other "departments of art," including other graphic work, but most notably book illustration and architectural design.

5

"Draws So Many Things So Well"

Graphic and Other Art

IN A DISCUSSION of the economical means of furnishing a domestic interior in her *House and Home Papers* of 1865, Harriet Beecher Stowe (writing as Christopher Crowfield) has her male protagonist inventory the artistic treasures in his modestly furnished parlor. The survey ranges across the popular artists, imagery, and media of the day. It includes a cast of the Venus di Milo, a German lithograph of Raphael's Sistine Madonna, a sketch of a twilight scene by Martin Johnson Heade, some "sea-photographs" by William Bradford, and "an original pen-and-ink sketch by Billings."[1] Stowe had been familiar with Hammatt Billings's graphic art at least since he illustrated her *Uncle Tom's Cabin* in 1852 and 1853, and she must also have known that his works, as one of his obituarists put it, "adorn[ed] the walls of the residences of many Boston families."[2] Mrs. William Claflin, wife of the governor and patron of Billings, for example, owned his *Enchanted Monk* in sepia, "a notable drawing," and *The Presentment*, a pen drawing of 1865, was among his works in the collection of Wellesley College after 1875.[3]

When he is remembered at all, Billings is remembered as a graphic artist in public service, the products of whose pen, pencil, or brush became illustrations for books and periodicals as well as architecture and other three-dimensional design, but he also produced finished graphics: drawings, designs for framing prints, watercolors, and oils for both public and private collections. These ranged across a wide spectrum of media and subject matter, from portraits to poetry, religious imagery to architectural views. As a writer for *Ballou's* put it in 1856, he "draws so many things so well."[4]

Hammatt's artistic training derived from eighteenth-century graphic methods. For figure study this meant sketching from copies of the old masters and casts of antique sculpture. He began the process with Francis Graeter in the late 1820s and continued to follow the method well into the 1840s, when, as a member of the Boston Artists' Association, he joined other artists and architects in drawing casts at the Athenaeum, and in the study of the live model (whether draped or undraped we do not know).[5] In his forties he was still adding to his knowledge of anatomy and honing his skills at figure drawing by attending in 1864 the Lowell Institute lectures of the eccentric Boston anatomist and sculptor William Rimmer and by copying in 1865 the works of the old masters in whole or in part. A collection of drawings by Billings and others survives, which contains his copies of Rimmer's blackboard sketches based upon antique figures and Renaissance paintings.[6] In the author's collection of miscellaneous graphic work by Billings is also a drawing of a dragon holding a figure in its mouth that was clearly influenced by Rimmer (fig. 38). A sketchbook in the Boston Museum of Fine Arts contains studies after Veronese and other Italian masters. Billings's contemporaries thought of him as skilled in the "drawing and grouping of the human figure." All his figures, it was said, had "a naturalness and correctness" and were "always effective."[7] Natural, correct, and effective: that is, serviceable, if not brilliant.

Figures joined landscapes in Billings's repertory, a category perhaps begun under Francis Graeter and stimulated by the works of Thomas Cole and the Hudson River School. (A number of landscape drawings by Billings survive from the 1830s and early 1840s.)[8] He also drew architectural scenes, first under the tutelage of the German-American master, further stimulated by the Boston work of A. J. Davis, and developed during his apprenticeships to Abel Bowen and Asher Benjamin. Billings was also influenced by any number of illustrators at home and abroad. By the 1840s he was skilled in a variety of graphic genres suitable for exhibition on their own or reproduction in either books or periodicals. His grounding had been broad and sound, and he was well prepared for his career as graphic artist in many guises.

Billings's work as portraitist ranged from drawings for wood and steel engravings to lithographed sheet music covers and, perhaps, oils as well. Among the earliest of these is the portrait of Daniel Decatur Emmett (1815–1904) that adorns the 1844 cover for "Old Dan Emmit's Original Banjo Melodies" (second series) issued by Keith's Publishing House in Boston.[9] Songwriter and stage performer, Emmett was one of the originators of the blackface minstrel shows and author of such popular nineteenth-century songs as "Old Dan Tucker" and "Dixie." The awkwardness of this early work was avoided in engraved portraits such as those of Daniel Webster or Isaiah

Fig. 38. Graphite drawing by Hammatt Billings (?), *Ship Attacked by a Dragon*, ca. 1860s (?); presumably drawn under the influence of William Rimmer (author's collection).

Thomas published as illustrations later in the decade. The head and shoulders of Webster appeared as a wood engraving in the *Pictorial National Library* in 1848.[10] Billings's source seems to have been Chester Harding's likeness of about 1847–48 now in the Shelburne Museum in Vermont (which was itself based on daguerreotypes by John Adams Whipple).[11] It was in fact the most widely copied and circulated of all Webster portraits. The likeness of Isaiah Thomas (1749–1831), printer, historian, and founder of the American Antiquarian Society at Worcester, appeared as a superb steel-engraved frontispiece to the first volume of Joseph Buckingham's *Specimens of Newspaper Literature* of 1850 (fig. 39).[12]

Only slightly removed from this category of work is the tiny, idealized likeness of George Washington that appears on souvenirs of Mount Vernon dated 1859. These are two-inch diameter paper circles called in one contem-

Fig. 39. Steel engraving by S. A. Schoff after Hammatt Billings, *Isaiah Thomas,* frontispiece to Joseph T. Buckingham, *Specimens of Newspaper Literature,* Boston, 1850 (from a restrike in the American Antiquarian Society, Worcester, Mass.).

porary account "Mount Vernon Gems."[13] They were designed by Billings, copyrighted by Horace Barnes, engraved by the American Bank Note Company, and framed in wood grown at Mount Vernon and purchased by one J. Cruchett. The central tondo with classical profile of Washington is surrounded by a draped female figure of Liberty holding a spear and wearing a Phrygian cap, and views of the villa and Washington's grave. The Mount Vernon Ladies' Association, incorporated in 1857 to preserve the president's home, apparently received a tenth of the proceeds from the sale of these small mementos.[14] How Billings came by this commission remains a mystery, although we can guess that he owed it to Edward Everett who was often his supporter during this decade. Everett's barn-storming lectures on Washington at the end of the 1850s provided major funding for the purchase of the villa by the association.[15]

That Billings may have been a portraitist in the usual meaning of the term, that is, a painter of likenesses in oil on canvas, is suggested by two works in the Hood Museum of Art at Dartmouth College. Both sitters were associated with the Dartmouth Medical School. Albert Smith (1801–78) graduated from the college in 1825 and received his medical degree in 1833. He taught in the school of medicine during the third quarter of the century. Edward Elisha Phelps (1803–ca. 1880) taught at the school from the 1840s onward. Both men are shown in somber head-and-shoulder portraits; both are exemplars of the keen medical professorate; both are professional if not inspired likenesses. Although his name appears on the reverse of each (in what appears to be another hand), these works represent something of an anomaly in Billings's far-flung career, and one hesitates to assign them unequivocally to his hand.[16] The portrait specialist E. T. Billings (1824–93) was a contemporary of Hammatt, and the two can be easily confused in contemporary references to paintings when those references are simply to "Billings."

Although Hammatt Billings was and is primarily known as a graphic artist, he did paint in oils, and hence the portraits at Dartmouth cannot be dismissed out of hand. The Wellesley College art historian Elizabeth Denio listed some of his works in this medium: *Sir Galahad, Italian Mother and Child, New England Scene in Winter, View on the Thames,* and *Happy Hunting Ground.*[17] An undated catalogue of works for auction by Samuel Hatch of Boston includes pictures by Thomas Moran, William Bradford, Elihu Vedder, George Fuller, A. T. Bricher, and other painters, as well as two *(Interior* and *Cattle)* by Billings. Perhaps these too were oils.[18] They are not now known. And we hear of a "painting" of the landing of the Pilgrims of 1855 while Billings was busy with the National Monument to the Forefathers.[19] There were certainly other canvases as well, although none are known but the Dartmouth portraits that can be associated with Hammatt Billings.

We may know something about the appearance of one of the oils mentioned by Denio, however, for there is at the Massachusetts Historical Society an ink drawing on buff cardboard labeled on the reverse: "Sketch of / Dying Indian Chief / by / Hammet [sic] Billings."[20] It can be dated by a letter affixed to the reverse of the drawing, a letter from Eliza S. Quincy to Charles Deane of 17 October 1849: "Billings . . . made a beautiful sketch some years ago of the death of an Indian Chief—with a vision of the Indians Paradise in the distance." This description exactly fits the drawing (fig. 40). Billings here used an outline graphic style he could have learned from any number of European sources or the work of his countryman and contemporary F. O. C. Darley, but certainly knew firsthand from his own copy of

Umrisse zu Goethe's Faust and *Umrisse zu Schiller's Lied von der Glocke* illustrated in line by Moritz Retzsch and published in 1837–43 (see appendix A). Especially comparable is the lessening of the weight of the line to suggest atmospheric perspective or different realms of actual and posthumous existence.[21] We have in this drawing a graphic version of the *Happy Hunting*

Fig. 40. Graphite drawing by Hammatt Billings, *Dying Indian Chief* or *Happy Hunting Ground*, ca. 1848 (Massachusetts Historical Society).

Ground mentioned by Denio, one that shows the dying chief tucked into the lower right corner while his family and dog mourn his passing and his anthropomorphic spirit rises toward a celestial landscape.

The artist was a prolific illustrator of juvenile literature. Thirteen small, undated pen-and-ink drawings for "Who Killed Cock Robin?" were once owned by the Boston Public Library.[22] They cannot now be located, but there is in a private collection in New Jersey a series of nine pen-and-ink drawings for "The House That Jack Built" that have been traditionally assigned to Billings's hand.[23] If they are by Billings they would seem to be early, probably stemming from the 1840s when he was working on his Mother Goose (see appendix B). The architectural, animal, figural, and other drawings relating to the fairy tale seem intended for wood engraving.

Billings produced several series of drawings for religious and other subjects, some of which may have been destined for book illustrations, although others seem to have been finished products or designed for works other than illustrations. Some are known only by brief references, and some are known because they were described in detail during his lifetime, or survive in part or in whole. We have, for example, record of an undated series of watercolors on the life of Joseph, and another, unfinished, on the life of Moses.[24] The finished works have disappeared but a small preliminary pencil sketch of the finding of Moses survives in a collection of miscellaneous drawings that also contains a watercolor depicting Joseph or Moses before pharaoh (fig. 41).[25] In the latter a youth stands in front of the ruler's chair in an airy room, more templar than palatial and formed by huge lotus columns. The handling of the color washes over a graphite base, thin and almost monochromatic for the surroundings, varied and deeply hued on the seated Pharaoh and his attendants, focuses the viewer's attention on the center of the narrative. Such a survivor attests to the watercolor work for which Billings received much praise during his career.

Religious and biblical scenes occupied much of Billings's graphic time. Isaac Danforth Farnsworth (1810–86), early benefactor of Wellesley College and boyhood friend of its founder, Henry Fowle Durant, in 1880 presented the school with "a beautiful & valuable collection of fifty-four drawings in India ink illustrating the book of Revelation by the late Hamet [*sic*] Billings."[26] According to one obituarist Billings executed these "on order for a panorama."[27] If that is correct, they were intended as studies for a painted continuous canvas that would have been unrolled before a public and probably paying audience while a speaker read or commented upon the biblical

Fig. 41.   Watercolor by Hammatt Billings, Joseph or Moses before pharaoh, undated (author's collection).

passages depicted, but they were also distributed through engraved copies. The rather large, brushed originals of this series are now lost, perhaps in the fire that destroyed Wellesley's College Hall in 1914, but twenty-three of them are known from photographic reproduction, and at least one of these also survives in an engraving. The Boston Public Library owns a bound volume inscribed "Illustrations of the Book of Revelation—Designed by Hammatt Billings" on the top of each leaf. The name J. C. Crosman (or J. G. Grosman) appears on the first page, whose reverse bears this note: "There are but two other copies of these magnificent Illustrations extant—and the negatives from which they were made were immediately destroyed."[28] The engraving *The Woman Standing on the Moon, Clothed with the Sun, and the Dragon* (Rev. 12:1, 3) is tipped into an edition of Joseph Priest, *The Anti-Universalist,* now in the Wellesley College Library.[29] The caption accompanying the engraving reads: "this extraordinary exhibition . . . was produced . . . by that most eminent Artist, Hammatt Billings, esq., whose brilliant conceptions of the Visions of Saint John have borne out the statement . . . by . . . Albert Barnes . . . that these 'visions would make the finest drawings in the world.'" The engraving must date from the early 1850s, so the entire series of drawings probably dates circa 1850.[30]

Judging from surviving images of the Revelation series (fig. 42), this was an ambitious project; judging from comments such as those quoted above, it earned Billings much praise. "Beyond any other of his designs, they have the stamp of artistic power," according to *Old and New*. "They give grand expression to the terrible, the sublime, and the beautiful in the heavenly and earthly scenes they represent." In our secular and cynical age, in which their religious content may be as distant to some as Zoroastrianism is to most, we tend to wonder at the plaudits garnered by such works, but these drawings—like all Billings's diverse designs—must be assessed in context. They were the products of an age in which a writer like John Greenleaf Whittier could praise bad poetry because it contained inspirational religious sentiment. The drawings themselves, or at least what we can know of them from what is photographically preserved, for once evince a great deal of energy. They were large, animated, multifigured compositions, in which Billings seems to have attempted to create the effect of aquatint (or, ultimately, oils) with his brush and washes. They were inspired by some of Billings's most important sources: Italian masters such as Raphael, Englishmen such as William Blake

Fig. 42. Photograph of an India ink drawing by Hammatt Billings, "And I saw a woman sitting on a scarlet-covered beast" (Rev. 17:3), undated (Fine Arts Department, Boston Public Library, courtesy of the Trustees of the Boston Public Library).

and John "Pandemonium" Martin, and the American Thomas Cole. They once more demonstrate the eclecticism that is the hallmark of Billings's work as a graphic artist.

Nineteenth-century sources mention a number of other drawings for which Billings received much praise in his own lifetime. None are now to be located. Elizabeth Denio listed the following (in addition to other works mentioned elsewhere in this chapter): *St. Agnes's Eve, Sleeping Palace, The Lady of Shalott, The Angel of Death, God's Acre, The Supplication, The Ministering Angel, Titania in Love,* and *Sympathy.* Some of these were broadly known in nineteenth-century Boston. The obituary in *Old and New* mentions the *Sleeping Palace,* the *Lady of Shalott,* and the *Eve of St. Agnes* with a fourth work called *Delusion.* James Jackson Jarves mentions two of them in the short list of Billings's works he published in *The Art-Idea* of 1864: *St. Agnes's Eve* and *Sleeping Palace,* plus two others, presumably drawings: *Marguerite* and *Sister of Charity.* One of these, *The Sleeping Palace,* was exhibited at the Boston Athenaeum in 1859 as the property of one H. Woodman.[31] The range of sources, at least of those that can be identified from these titles, is representative of the mid-nineteenth century in general and of Hammatt Billings in particular: Keats, Tennyson, Wordsworth, Martin Tupper, Shakespeare, the Bible, and other religious texts. Since these were works owned by private and public collections there can be no doubt they were created as finished works of art.

James Jackson Jarves (1818–88), whose pioneering collection of Italian "primitives" is now in the Yale University Art Museum and whose *Art-Idea* was among the most perceptive works of criticism to come out of the mid-century in the United States, mentions Billings's drawings in the context of a comparison of his work with that of Thomas Cole and F. O. C. Darley. He contrasts the "sweetness, variety, delicacy, and fertility, the fine taste, imagination, fancy, and pure feeling displayed by Billings's designs . . . with the dramatic vigor and obtrusive individualism of Darley's drawings." Billings's self-effacing artistic persona appealed to him. Both drew in a "masterly manner," he continues, "but on what different keys of design! Grace guides one pencil, force the other."[32] Whether or not we would still agree with the distinction, this contemporary comparison itself puts Billings's work on a par with the production of a draftsman we now think of as the leader of the generation.

Billings designed an unknown number of images that, when engraved, were probably thought suitable for independent display. These remain for the most part known only from literary sources. As early as 1849 he copyrighted an engraving entitled *The Mother's Appeal.* No impression has yet surfaced, and nothing more is known of it.[33] On 11 October 1858 he received another copyright for a print of *Delusion.* The subject was inspired by the poem "Of To-morrow" in Martin Tupper's *Proverbial Philosophy,* the two parts of which appeared in London in 1838 and 1842, with a handsome Boston edition containing both parts that came out in 1852.[34] Tupper's *Proverbial Philosophy* may be forgotten now, but Walt Whitman thought highly of it, and it eventually sold more than three hundred thousand copies.[35] Billings was here clearly climbing aboard a popular bandwagon in hopes of a marketable product. The first stanza of the poem envisions the future as an island to which we are attracted by a siren whose "eyes are bright with invitation." But there Delusion also lurks, "laughing with seductive lips." "Often, the precious present is wasted in visions of the future, / And coy To-morrow cometh not with prophecies fulfilled." No examples of this print have yet come to light; we are left to wonder how Billings embodied this vision. Its moralizing content was typical of the work he illustrated.

No examples have yet been found, either, of his *Confidence,* a chromolithograph of 1872. It is described, however, in some detail in *Old and New* in December of that year. In this issue Edward Everett Hale (1822–1909), the editor of the magazine who was well acquainted with the artist's work, published a story with this title illustrated "with a chromolith, by H. Billings."[36] This was apparently not to be bound with the magazine but distributed separately.

In the story, Janet, the little heroine, instills a sense of trust in a small bird and in turn displays trust in her father. She jumps from the hayloft into his waiting arms "because he told her to, and she loved and trusted him." Her confidence created confidence in everyone and every creature on the farm. Billings's work is described in the story as representing both sides: "she trusted the birds, and the birds trusted her." Billings, however, represented her as a grown girl, and when she is married (by the Reverend Hale) to John Wildair in the story, the artist sends the picture to him, and it is hung "above the mantle in the dining room."[37]

The rear cover of this issue of *Old and New* is completely taken up by an advertisement for this "beautiful picture," which has been "Chromolithed, in the first style of the art" for new subscribers to the magazine or those who renew their subscriptions before the first of the year. This representation of *Confidence,* worth five dollars at retail we are told, could not be purchased, but it could be had in a number of gilt or black walnut frames of different widths for a graduated series of additional sums.[38] No copies of this print have surfaced, and it has been suggested that it may not have been issued.[39] According to Elizabeth Denio, however, there did once exist an undated drawing of the subject by Billings.[40]

By the middle of the nineteenth century John Bunyan's *Pilgrim's Progress*, a moralizing tale of the choices between good and evil, had become the second most read book (after the Bible) in the English language. Illustrations to this parlous story of Christian's journey among the pitfalls of life were accordingly numerous, and not only as book illustrations. Edward Harrison May's panorama, for example, with contributions by F. O. C. Darley, Frederic Church, and others, toured the American cities as entertainment in the early 1850s.[41] In 1853 Daniel Wight Jr., as "author," received copyright for an engraving of *Bunyan's Pilgrim*.[42] This is an impressive plate (24″ x 30″) whose list of credits runs almost as long as that of a recent film. The sheet names the following multitude of contributors: engraved (on steel) by J. Andrews, etched by E. A. Fowle, designed by the Reverend Daniel Wight, drawn by Hammatt Billings, printed by Wilson and Daniels (Liberty Tree Building, Boston), and published by John P. Jewett, Cornhill (fig. 43).[43] It was said to have taken Andrews five years to execute, so Billings's drawing must have been made around 1848.[44] With such an investment of time and talent, Jewett certainly expected this to become a moneymaker.[45]

Billing's *Pilgrim's Progress*, with its many sequential scenes, seems as cinematic as its long list of credits. It was, more cogently, clearly affected by his study of the art of the recently deceased Thomas Cole (1801–48), and his contemporaries were not blind to that fact. Cole's late and unfinished project, the series of paintings collectively called *The Cross and the World* (1846–47), was especially important for Billings. It has been pointed out for example that the arrangement of the figures in Cole's *Two Youths Enter Upon a Pilgrimage* Billings repeated in the lower center of his plate.[46] In the eyes of some critics, however, his achievement fell rather short of Cole's. The writer for *Dodge's Literary Museum* pronounced one of the first impressions from the plate a "sublime failure" in comparison to an engraving after Cole's *Youth* from his series on the voyage of life. But, the writer went on to say, "we have since seen impressions from the revised plate," containing changes suggested by Edward Everett (who, we are coming to realize, was apparently in close contact with Billings at least through the 1850s, both criticizing and boosting his work) that seem to have improved it. These changes have "rendered the upper third of the picture 'striking, and satisfactory as a work of art,'" but our critic also

Fig. 43. Steel engraving by Joseph Andrews with etching by E. A. Fowle, after a design by Daniel Wight drawn by Hammatt Billings, *Bunyan's Pilgrim*, ca. 1848–53 (American Antiquarian Society, Worcester, Mass.).

lamented the lack of evidence of an artist skilled "in linear and aerial perspective, and chiaroscuro." In his view this resulted in the lower two-thirds of the plate seeming pinched, distorted, and lacking in "all breadth of effect, without which no picture can be a successful work of art."[47]

Dodge's critic was of course justified in his reservations, for the plate does spot discontinuous figural vignettes through a rather oriental-looking landscape that rises to rather than recedes from the mundane world to the celestial city. Achieving a coherent and effective image of the many incidents of Christian's episodic tale while compressing it into one plate, however grand, seems to have been beyond Billings's reach in the middle of the 1840s. Still, the print was apparently popular, for many impressions are now in public and private collections.

Billings was an architect, and he had also apprenticed to the wood engraver and author Abel Bowen, who had produced *Bowen's Picture of Boston* in 1820 (2d ed., 1833). This was a guide to the city with numerous views of important buildings, and Billings must have known it well. Especially early in his career he too produced a number of urban views, what the Italians call *vedute*. In this he connected with an old English topographical tradition, but in the short run he followed not only on the heels of his mentor but the example of A. J. Davis as well. Davis was an architect who had in the 1820s and 1830s executed views of important monuments in New York and Boston. Billing's *vedute* appeared as engravings and lithographs in books and magazines, on sheet music covers and other ephemera, and as framing prints.

His earliest architectural views were of rising or recently completed buildings in Boston and New York. An 1840 engraving by J. Archer of Ammi Young's federal Custom House in Boston, a project Billings worked on as draftsman for the architect, was meant to introduce a major public work just then under construction rather than to record an existing landmark (see fig. 2). A new building is shown in his delineation of the New York Merchant's Exchange, a work of 1836–42 by Isaiah Rogers, engraved by J. Archer and published in Boston by S. Walker about 1843.[48] G. J. F. Bryant's new Suffolk County Jail in Boston, finished in 1851, appears in a tinted lithograph of 1848 by J. H. Bufford.[49] Billings's perspective of the Revere House shows a hotel erected in 1847 in Bowdoin Square in Boston for "a company of gentlemen connected with the [Massachusetts] Charitable Mechanic Association," of which the artist was a member.[50] This view had a varied and extended life as an engraving by George G. Smith. It occurs as a framing print, on hand bills, and as a sheet music cover, and, reduced, as an illustration in *King's Handbook of Boston* (and thus it eventually returned to something like its origins in Bowen's guidebook).[51] It may have had its widest distribution as a steel engraving adorning the cover of Charles Mueller's "Revere Polka and Redowa," published in Boston by G. P. Reed.[52] Any number of views of other prominent Boston landmarks issued from Billings's pencil and found their way into books and magazines: the Bunker Hill Monument, the McLean Asylum, the residence of David Sears, the Faneuil Hall Market, the Massachusetts State House, the Boston Common, and so on.[53] Urban vistas formed an important aspect of his early career and must have generated a certain income for the artist.

At the 1841 exhibition of the Massachusetts Charitable Mechanic Association, Billings showed twelve drawings and won a silver medal. According to the judges one of his sepia designs for a certificate "is all that can be

Fig. 44. Graphite drawing by Hammatt Billings, presumed certificate design for the Massachusetts Charitable Fire Association, undated (author's collection).

desired in this branch of art."[54] This may have been the "outline sketch" for the diploma of the Knights Templar that Billings gave to a friend in November.[55] Certificates of membership in various organizations, of award for contributions or prizes, or diplomas signifying one achievement or another also occupied Billings's busy pencil over an extended period. He must have paid many a bill with income from this steady work. There is enough evidence of this activity to allow us to trace the evolution of certificate design from preliminary sketch to finished product.

A small undated pencil study that appears to be for a vignette for a certificate, bearing the name of the Massachusetts Charitable Fire Association, survives in a collection of miscellaneous Billings sketches (fig. 44).[56] In it a winged allegorical female holding a jug (for water?) sits atop a central half-circle flanked by groups of figures. Those to the left obviously represent the victims of a fire that has left their city in ruins, but those to the right are not easily identified.[57] The format of circle or half-circle flanked by historiated vignettes is one we encounter frequently in Billings's allegorical work.

In the collection of the Library of Congress are two more advanced studies for a different vignette and an example of the finished product on the diploma of the Massachusetts Charitable Mechanic Association itself

Fig. 45. Engraving after Hammatt Billings, certificate for the Massachusetts Charitable Mechanic Association, 1856 (Prints and Photographs Division, Library of Congress).

(fig. 45). This can be dated with some accuracy, for Billings showed the association's "New Diploma" at its exhibition in September 1856.[58] In the finished design a group of three figures is centered within a half-circle with groups of other figures to left and right. The first drawing, sepia wash, graphite, and red ink on off-white Bristol board, is a study for the left and central groupings without the final setting. The second, brown wash and ink over graphite on the same type of board, is a finished study showing the entire vignette. The ultimate diploma was engraved by Stephen Alonzo Schoff and printed by J. H. Daniels. According to the exhibition catalogue the central figures are Pallas (Minerva) holding a wreath and a shield bearing the insignia of the Commonwealth of Massachusetts, Justice to her left who points out those worthy of the diploma, and a scribe to her right who records their names. To the right of the central group "a procession of artisans approach, with specimens of their handicraft, as candidates for the prizes," while to the left are figures representing the arts. The setting is described as an exhibition hall, and it will be immediately recognized as inspired by the Crystal Palace erected in New York in 1853.[59]

At about the same period (ca. 1855) Billings designed the large rococo cartouche displayed on the lithographed certificate of the U.S. Agricultural Society of Washington, D.C. A car filled with allegorical figures, drawn by oxen led by farmers and accompanied by swirling celestial deities (the whole inspired by the work of the English illustrator John Gilbert) surmounts the cartouche. It is flanked by representations of Plenty and Flora. At the bottom, flower and vegetable growers frame a view of Mount Vernon, then, as we have seen, the subject of efforts to preserve it.[60] They represent the yeoman traditionally thought to have been the backbone of American democracy.

These diplomas and certificates draw upon the classical tradition for their style and imagery, but Billings the graphic artist like Billings the architect could call upon the Middle Ages for inspiration as well. He apparently thought the Gothic style for architectural enframement especially suited masonic commissions. The Museum of Our National Heritage in Lexington, Massachusetts, has a large collection—fourteen at preliminary count—of such certificates from lodges within the Commonwealth. All of these were designed by Billings and engraved by George G. Smith. An especially impressive example comes, however, from copies in the collections at Wellesley College and the American Antiquarian Society. This is an undated engraving by Smith, Knight, and Tappan of a certificate delineated by Billings for the Grand Lodge of Massachusetts (fig. 46).[61] The text is contained within an elaborate ecclesiastical Gothic frame surmounted by the figure of Charity and flanked by Faith and Hope. For the Boston encampment of the Knights Templar in 1858 Billings created an even more ornamental example of certificate Gothic.[62]

The mechanics and masons might have looked to the classical or Gothic traditions for their certificates, but other, Protestant, organizations were content with less pretentious display. For the Massachusetts Sabbath School Society, Billings embellished a certificate of life membership with a more appropriate, simple rectangular scene engraved by O. Pelton sometime before 1850.[63] Within the plain interior of a meeting house segregated and well-chaperoned groups of boys and girls listen to Bible readings. Books are much in evidence in this representation because such societies published moralizing tracts for children. Billings is presumed to have illustrated some, but none can be firmly identified. Here the Book, the Bible, presides over all.

Fig. 46. Engraving by Smith, Knight, and Tappan after a drawing by Hammatt Billings, certificate of the Grand Lodge of Massachusetts, undated (American Antiquarian Society, Worcester, Mass.).

Among the many other things Billings drew so well were the quotidian tasks of a hired pencil such as business cards, advertisements, stationery, book plates, and other ephemera. This was decidedly workaday art, although one that occupied much time at the printshops of the city. No discussion of Billings's far-flung labor would be complete without at least brief recognition of this area of his income. It can probably be assumed that he designed the advertisement for his own wares that appeared in the *Boston Almanac* during the 1850s (see fig. 3). It is probably safe to assume, too, that the popular and trade journals of midcentury are loaded with anonymous exam-

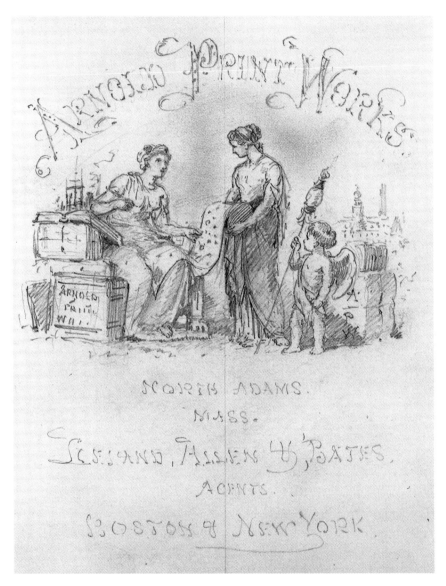

Fig. 47. Graphite design by Hammatt Billings for an advertisement for the Arnold Print Works of North Adams, Mass., undated (author's collection).

Fig. 48. Graphite design by Hammatt Billings for a decorative gift book plate, undated (author's collection).

ples of his work such as the unsigned "cuts" of the bookstore and the tea shop of Alexander Williams that we know he drew.[64] The collection of miscellaneous graphics already mentioned contains a number of sketches of work of this kind. There is the graphite drawing on laid paper for an ad or business card for the Arnold Print Works in North Adams, Massachusetts, a firm devoted to printing and dying raw cotton (its former factory is now part of the Massachusetts Museum of Contemporary Art) (fig. 47). There is an unfinished pencil sketch for a business card for Burrage, Cole, and Tucker, woolens, 49 Franklin Street, Boston. There is another for the Cutler Brothers of Boston, wholesale druggists and importers.

There are examples of artistic tasks related to books that did not produce text illustrations. There is, for example, the pencil draft of what looks like one of those decorative plates, often in the nineteenth century printed in gift books especially, on which the names of the presenter and presentee might be inscribed. This shows a picturesquely designed home (and hence this design is probably dateable to the late 1860s) within an upper half-circle, and empty bottom circles, presumably for small portraits, labeled "the Giver" and "the Receiver" (fig. 48). Billings in such designs gave visual form to the gift-giving passion of Victorian middle-class society. Another design of the same type contains two domestic scenes: an interior of a parlor with the family gathered around the reading of a book prominently labeled "Bible," and an exterior showing a croquette match between couples. The artist frequently depicted such scenes of familial bliss, of the cult of domesticity.

Billings's pencil, then, produced a wide variety of finished work, far more, it seems, than has been preserved. As we have seen, his contemporaries knew him also if not primarily as an illustrator of books and periodicals. They also knew him as a designer of monuments, buildings, furniture, and a variety of other useful things. In many of the business cards, certificates, and especially urban views, he depicted existing buildings, but the design of new buildings formed a major part of his efforts. Billings was one of the leading architects of mid-nineteenth-century Boston.

6
"Has Shown Himself a Master"

Architecture

DESPITE HAMMATT BILLINGS'S enormous output and signal successes as a graphic artist, one who turned his talent to drawings and other graphic arts, book and periodical illustration, watercolors and oils, there were those who thought of architecture as "his real profession."[1] Indeed, he had a long and productive career as architectural designer, one that stretched from the 1840s into the 1870s and embraced building types ranging from theaters and churches to social clubs, houses, commercial buildings, libraries, stables, schools, and railroad stations (see appendix C). He built for the urban patriciate, the political, commercial, financial, and intellectual elite: governors, mayors, authors, businessmen, philanthropists, men of the cloth, and any number of other Boston blue bloods. According to a building committee that included at least one of this elite, Ralph Waldo Emerson, Billings was considered "an architect eminent for taste and skill."[2]

Billings's birth in June 1818 came within months of Charles Bulfinch's departure from Boston to take up his first full-time architectural position as superintendent of the Capitol in Washington. Bulfinch (1763–1844) left behind in his design for the Massachusetts General Hospital (1818) the seeds of the "Boston Granite Style," the local variation on the Greek Revival, itself a subset of international late neoclassicism.[3] Billings's death in November 1874 occurred a few months after H. H. Richardson's return to the Boston area after professional education in Paris and architectural practice in New York City. At Trinity Church on Copley Square (1872–77), Richardson (1838–86) established a "disciplined picturesque," the Richardsonian Romanesque, as his personal variation on the eclecticism of his day. It was a conservative, "quiet and massive" architecture that built upon the basic granite block of local tradition.[4] Hammatt Billings's career as an architect spanned between these two poles: from classicism to eclecticism.[5]

When Bulfinch decamped, Boston was a town of some fifty thousand inhabitants served by a handful of architects. When Billings died the city could boast of a newly diversified population approaching three hundred thousand, served by more than one hundred architects.[6] The career of Hammatt (and of his erstwhile partner, his brother Joseph E.) Billings unfolded during this era of growth and change. The brothers matured in the course of the Greek Revival, connecting with it at its tail end as draftsmen in the office of Ammi B. Young at the federal Customs House. The granite block that distinguished the local Greek work also gave special character to churches erected in the "Gothick" style in the 1830s, such as the Bowdoin Street Meeting House (1831–33) attributed to Solomon Willard.[7] As H. and J. E. Billings entered practice in the mid-1840s, Italianate forms began to replace Greek ones in classical work, as in E. C. Cabot's winning design for the Athenaeum (1845–49); a more articulated, less blocky Gothic came to be used in ecclesiastical design, as for example at St. Paul's, Brookline (1848–51) by Richard Upjohn; and other historical forms occasionally appeared. The works of the brothers, as of their contemporaries, were to reflect these waves of fashion in mid-nineteenth-century Boston architecture, beginning with the classic-Gothic debate of the 1840s, touching the exotic (Hammatt's moorish Water Arch of 1848; see fig. 93), embracing the French Second Empire (Boston City Hall, 1861–65, by Bryant and Gilman) as well as the English Victorian (Memorial Hall, Harvard, 1865–78, by Ware and Van Brunt), and ending in the 1870s with the picturesque Anglo-French eclecticism of post–Civil War America (the Billingses' own College Hall, Wellesley, 1871–75; see fig. 63). As we shall see, however, often even the most progressive of the brothers' late work was rooted in their classical beginnings under Asher Benjamin and Ammi Young.

In 1845 Hammatt Billings was listed as one of eighteen architects working in Boston.[8] He had, of course, cut his teeth as architectural draftsman in the previous decade as apprentice to Benjamin and assistant to Young (see fig. 2). He exhibited his drawings for both Young's federal Customs House in Boston (1837–47) and for Young's lost 1838 proposal for the University of Michigan.[9] By 1845 he was illustrating William Bailey Lang's *Views . . . of the Highland Cottages at Roxbury* (see appendix B) with fully developed perspectives that represent the earliest influence in Boston of Andrew Jackson Downing's *Cottage Residences* (1842), with its rendered presentations by A. J. Davis of houses nestled in nature. In the views lithographed by J. H. Bufford for Lang's book, Billings broke with the dry graphic style Boston had inherited from Bulfinch.[10] He, then, came to architecture from his background as a graphic artist, and he seems to have relied upon his brother, whose interest appears to have been in civil engineering, or other of his several collaborators for technical expertise.

Billings's colleagues took a variety of different routes into the emerging profession. Some were "originally carpenters or masons," and some were "without the disagreeable formality of previous study."[11] The older Edward Shaw (1784–1855?) jumped from the building trades.[12] The younger Arthur Gilman (1821–82) attended Trinity College, Hartford, traveled abroad, established himself as a lecturer and writer, then opened an architectural office in the mid-1840s. Where he learned to draw and build remains a question. Most architects of midcentury, including Hammatt and Joseph Billings, acquired their skills in apprenticeship to established practitioners. What little we know about the Billings office suggests a changing educational situation: Henry W. Hartwell (1833–1919) entered his office "to study architecture" in 1851.[13] He was the son of Hammatt's colleague at Bowen's, the engraver Alonzo Hartwell, and later a principal in the firm of Hartwell and Richardson. Charles F. Read joined the office in the 1870s after attending MIT.[14] The first School of Architecture in the United States opened its doors at the Massachusetts Institute of Technology in the mid-1860s.[15] As architecture grew into a professional practice during the century (Hammatt Billings was among the nine architects who met in the office of Nathaniel J. Bradlee on 15 May 1867 to initiate the Boston Society of Architects),[16] a period at university combined with some office practice became the educational rule.

Although Hammatt billed himself as an architect as early as 1842, it is not until 1845 that we hear of independent projects in collaboration with Joseph.[17] In that and the following year the Billingses received commissions for two major buildings, the Boston Museum and the Church of the Saviour, neither of which survives.[18] By what means these two untried if not unknown designers, the older of whom was a mere twenty-eight, managed to land the commission for the Boston Museum, a most conspicuous building erected on fashionable Tremont Street between King's Chapel and the Tremont House hotel, remains a mystery. Nor do we know how Hammatt received the commission for the Church of Saviour on Bedford Street. All we can say for certain is that his golden connections to the upper levels of patronage in Boston began surprisingly early.

The Boston Museum once stood on the east side of Tremont on a site acquired by the promoter David Kimball from the Athenaeum in December 1845. Earlier that year the Athenaeum, a Brahmin proprietary library, had sponsored a competition for the design of a building of its own for the ground.[19] The winning project by George M. Dexter (1802–72) showed a three-story Italianate facade probably inspired by Charles Barry's recent London clubs, which were known in the United States through publications such as W. H. Leeds's *Travellers' Club House* (1839), and by direct knowledge by architects such as Arthur Gilman, who had recently returned from study abroad and was championing the Renaissance style in articles and lectures. Within, Dexter proposed a vaulted central stair hall with colossal Corinthian columns. The scheme proved too expensive, and the Athenaeum abandoned the project and sold the site to Kimball. The following year it called for new proposals for a new site on Beacon Street. Entries were received from Billings and others, including Edward Clark Cabot (with his brother, James), whose winning Palladian palazzo facade still graces the Beacon Hill site.[20] Meanwhile, Moses Kimball, David's brother who managed the Boston Museum, engaged Hammatt and Joseph to design the new building for the museum on the Tremont Street site abandoned by the Athenaeum.[21] The Kimballs acquired the lot no later than December 1845, did not get clear title, apparently, until May 1846, and the building opened to the public on 2 November of that year. There is thus reason to date the Hammatt Billings design to late 1845, and this suggests that it was adapted from his unknown and unsuccessful competition entry for the Athenaeum building on the same site. This is pure speculation, of course, but perhaps Kimball admired that drawing and sought to appropriate the architects and their design, at least of the facade, for his very different building. This might explain the choice of a pair of tyros.

The Boston Museum was actually two buildings in one. It masked its primary function as a playhouse, still a dubious venue for some Bostonians, behind a name suggesting education and culture. As the English publisher William Chambers wrote, the building was "tolerated under the name of a 'Museum.' To invest it with this illusory character, its spacious vestibule was environed with cases of dried snakes, stuffed birds, and other curiosities, which nobody . . . took the trouble to look at."[22] No plan or other drawings have yet come to light, but the building was a long rectangle divided length-wise into entrance hall—museum in the front and theater behind. An authoritative 1847 description of the building tells us that

> it is arranged in two main portions with an area between for light and air, one communicating with the other at either end by a wide passage. . . . [T]he front . . . is of [dressed Quincy] Granite in a chaste and beautiful style of Venetian [Renaissance] Architecture, with three spacious balconies running the entire length of the building, [which] contains on the first story, five commodious stores, and the entrance to the Museum. Above this story, the whole front building to the eaves, three stories, is occupied as a grand Corinthian Hall . . . containing the collection. The galleries . . . are supported by twenty stately columns rising from the floor. . . . A spacious staircase and passage-way leads to the Exhibition Hall [i.e., theater] in the rear building . . . capable of accommodating nearly two thousand persons.[23]

The historically important architectural features of the building were parts of the Tremont Street moiety: Corinthian Hall and the facade (figs. 49–50). Little is known about the theater proper (a view of which has yet to come to light), although William Chambers reported that it was "fitted up with a hanging-gallery, and pews as like a church as possible."[24] The hall contained curiosities of natural history and art ranging from the "Feejee mermaid" to Thomas Sully's monumental *Passage of the Delaware* (1819) on the landing of the grand staircase (and now in the stair hall of the west wing at the Museum of Fine Arts). This was unquestionably among the most dramatic interiors of mid-nineteenth-century Boston. Its design may owe something to Dexter's projected stair hall in the first Athenaeum competition, but it was grander in proportion and more glittering in effect. It had its own progeny in Charles Kirby's Boston Public Library of 1854–58 and, by some stretch of the imagination and some stylistic permutation, Billings's own "Centre" at Wellesley College.

Until its destruction in 1903, the long, horizontal, Tremont Street facade was one of the Italianate glories of public Boston. For their first important urban building Hammatt and Joseph followed Dexter and Gilman in selecting a Renaissance model. The ground-floor shops carried the commerce of the street across the width of the exhibition hall—theater. This combination of uses in one building was apparently introduced to Boston by Billings's former mentor, Asher Benjamin, in his 1839 Fifth Universalist Church on Warren Street.[25] It is also a feature Louis Kahn, for example, was to appropriate in his Yale Center for British Art in New Haven more than a century later. The broad, dressed granite plane above the shops was interrupted by three layers of identical round-arched openings outlined by crisp moldings and topped by a modillion cornice. Cast-iron balconies and gaslight fixtures stood out from the stonework. In August 1846 this seemed to several news-

Fig. 49. H. and J. E. Billings, Boston Museum, 1845–46, Tremont Street facade (The Bostonian Society/Old State House).

Fig. 50. H. and J. E. Billings, Boston Museum, 1845–46, Corinthian Hall (The Bostonian Society/Old State House).

paper correspondents a daring or incorrect innovation. The novelty of the Italianate details is clearly apparent in this otherwise murky exchange, in which Arthur Gilman defended the choice of style and called the building "beautiful."[26]

He was seconded by the *Christian Examiner,* which thought what it called "the Roman palatial style" "better adapted to the wants of our city architecture than any other."[27] The facade was in fact a round-arched variation on the Boston granite style, an update of the granite Greco-Roman mode that Hammatt and Joseph had learned at firsthand under Ammi Young at the Custom House, which was just being completed as they began work on the museum. The facade was not only a fine early example of the Renaissance Revival in America (John Notman's Athenaeum of Philadelphia, usually called the first use of the style, predated the museum by just a few months), it was an important link in the chain of stringent lithic design in Boston that culminated in H. H. Richardson's mature work. All in all, then, the Boston Museum was an impressive achievement for a pair of architects still in their twenties.

The museum was the major but not the only Italianate design by H. and J. E. Billings during midcentury. If for the museum facade they looked to the north Italian works of Sanmichele or Sansovino, for the Temple Club in West Street (1849–50) they followed Dexter's lead in studying Raphael's Palazzo Pandolfini at Florence through Barry's London interpretations. In fact, on 11 July 1846 Hammatt bought at Ticknor's bookstore at Washington and School Streets a copy of Leeds's *Travellers' Club House*.[28] For the facade of the Temple Club the architects relied on Leeds for general inspiration only, developing their narrow vertical plane in three levels: a base composed of a classical arcade divided from the upper floors by a heavy balustrade surmounted by paired, rectangular bays opened by double, round-arched windows (what the Italians call *bifore*) topped by grouped, triple, linteled openings at the third story, the whole framed by quoins and a bracketed cornice.[29]

Other works in the Italianate style included several outlying residences, built and projected. For Josiah Quincy Jr., the second Boston mayor of that name, Billings designed a foursquare house at Wollaston, south of the city, in 1848.[30] It does not survive. For Richard Henry Dana Jr. (1815–82), author of *Two Years before the Mast* (1840), he created in 1851 the Italianate house with bracketed gables that still stands at 4 Berkeley Street in Cambridge.[31] In 1854 Dana wrote to Hammatt to say that he had "been so much pleased with the house you planned for me" that he was recommending his friend Dwight Foster (1828–84) of Worcester, a lawyer who was to be the attorney general of Massachusetts during the Civil War, to consult with the architect about his new residence. "I hope you will . . . aid him in refreshing the rather questionable taste of Worcester in domestic architecture," Dana wrote.[32] As late as 1871 Dana would still regard Billings's work for him as "a beautiful home—and in such good taste."[33] (Whether Billings also designed the Italianate Dana house at Manchester, Massachusetts, on Boston's North Shore, remains a question; he did, however, produce a view of it for G. P. Putnam's *Homes of American Authors* of 1852.)[34] Billings also in 1852 produced a stone summer house at Newport for Dana's Cambridge friends the Nortons. It was planned for Prof. Andrews Norton and his wife, Catherine, but at Andrews's untimely death finished by their son, Charles Eliot Norton (1827–1908), a friend and correspondent of Ruskin who was to teach at Harvard the country's first courses in the history of art.[35] The house was enlarged and "mansarded" in the 1870s. Although no early views have yet come to light, it was undoubtedly of Italianate design. Hammatt began for himself or his brother a towered Italianate villa in Auburndale, a section of suburban Newton, between 1851, when Joseph purchased the lot, and 1853, when he sold it with the house unfinished to a Thomas Hall, who completed it.[36] It, too, survives.

Billings planned more Italian projects than he built. The scrapbook of his architectural sketches now in the Stowe-Day Library at Hartford contains many drawings after Italian models and for Italianate projects, not all of them residential and not all of them as yet identified. One sheaf of drawings, for example, is a presentation package dated 7 February 1850 for a Perkins house. This is a large, elaborate, towered Tuscan villa (fig. 51), not unlike that Hammatt used to illustrate Emma Wellmont's temperance novel, *Uncle Sam's Palace*, published in 1853.[37] Although the present text neatly separates his work into categories, Hammatt moved simultaneously among the various departments of art.

Some Protestant thinkers might have disagreed, but according to the midcentury architectural theory of associationism, Italian classicism was appropriate for civic buildings and country houses, but ecclesiastical design called for the medieval styles, and especially the Gothic. Billings was ready to answer the call. As early as 1841 he was dreaming of the pointed arch as suitable for Christian architecture. In a letter of 3 August he wrote passionately that he wanted above all to build a Gothic cathedral.

> The Church in this country must be suitably entombed, and how more fitting[ly] than in such a mausoleum.—When I think of what might be done in the embodiment of the whole sublime worship of Christianity in such a building; of the vast materials lying before the designer—the works and experience of all who have gone before, I feel the faith and genius of the olden time stir within me.—I see the armies of the saints & martyrs in long procession thro' the vaulted nave of Time, and in the Choir of Eternity I hear heavenly voices chaunting and stimulating me onward.[38]

Such was his romantic mood as he embarked on his own Gothic quest. Cathedrals eluded him, but he did design several Gothic churches.

By May 1842 he had visited Richard Upjohn's Trinity Church in New York and, apparently, spoken to the architect.[39] At least by the mid-1840s he was reading the works of that English zealot in the Gothic cause, A. W. N. Pugin. On 18 September 1846 he acquired from Ticknor's a copy of Pugin's *Contrasts*, probably in the second edition of 1841 (see appendix A). It was not very useful as a pattern book, but it was an impassioned and completely biased look at the differences between the "noble" Gothic buildings of the fifteenth century and the decadent classicism of the early nineteenth.

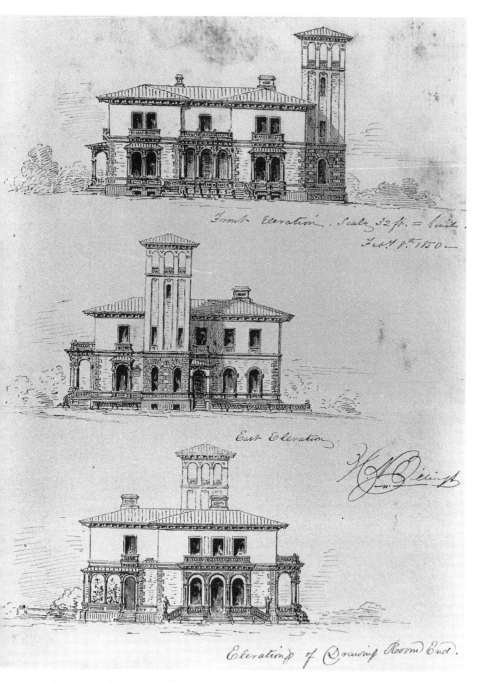

Fig. 51. Ink drawing by Hammatt Billings, elevations of a Perkins house, 1850 (Harriet Beecher Stowe Center, Hartford, Conn.)

Fig. 52. Hammatt Billings, Church of the Saviour, Bedford Street, Boston, 1846, exterior. To the right is the Massachusetts Charitable Mechanic Association building, 1857, by Hammatt Billings, G. J. F. Bryant, and N. J. Bradlee (photo by Southworth and Hawes; The Bostonian Society/Old State House).

Contemporary with work on the Boston Museum, Hammatt and Joseph designed the Church of the Saviour (later Second Unitarian) in Bedford Street for the congregation of the Reverend Robert C. Waterston (fig. 52). It was originally conceived in 1845, redesigned in 1846, and removed before 1881. The church was dedicated in November 1847, on the morning of the afternoon that saw the laying of the cornerstone of Joseph's own Gothic Church of the Messiah in Florence Street, a few blocks away.[40]

"The architect of . . . [the Saviour] has shown himself a master," according to the *Christian Examiner*, which does not name him. "In his hands the style is as plastic as it was four hundred years ago. There is harmony and symme-

try about the whole building,—a prevalence of leading lines all flowing upward.... The details are as beautiful ... and as a piece of architecture we must
call it a gem." But, our unnamed critic continues, as a Protestant, a Congregational, church, it failed, because in the Gothic "every thing was calculated to
stimulate emotion and repress thought." The long aisles, rows of impeding
columns and arches, and dark stained glass of the Roman Catholic style all
worked to make preaching difficult and hymn singing impossible.[41]

Billings was probably less worried about such criticism concerning the
Protestant use of Gothic than he was about his disastrous attempt to act as
contractor for the erection of the building. Our earliest notice is a document
dated 9 September 1845 in which the builder, Benjamin G. Russell, agrees for
four thousand dollars to erect in Bedford Street a church for the society
according to plans and specifications prepared by H. and J. E. Billings.[42]
Sometime between that contract and a second one, dated 1 April 1846, the
design must have been enlarged (and perhaps now called for stone rather
than wood or brick) and a new agreement made necessary. In the second
covenant Russell and Hammatt Billings jointly undertook "on or before the
first day of September [1847] ... in consideration of the sum of thirty-three
thousand dollars ... [to] erect build and completely finish a Stone church ...
in Bedford street ... [according to] plans and specifications ... made by the
said Billings.... And also ... provide all materials and ... all the labor and
works ... proper to said church."[43] Rough Newark freestone was to be used
on the exterior, and alternate chancel designs are mentioned (and now unlocated). Hammatt's lifelong financial problems apparently stemmed from this
ill-fated venture, for the cost of completing the building is given as seventy
thousand dollars in contemporary accounts, more than double the contract
price, and in the next decade it was reported that "he lost a great deal of
money" on the venture.[44] There is no evidence that he ever repeated his
mistake; there is much to suggest that this one error reverberated through his
subsequent career as he scurried to pay off his debtors.

The view of the exterior of the Bedford Street church preserved in a
photograph by Southworth and Hawes shows a fashionable early English
Gothic Revival building of broad planes set with pointed details enlivened
by planted moldings: it was certainly more faithful to contemporary (i.e.,
Puginesque) standards of Gothic design than to the medieval sources the
Christian Examiner's critic would have us recall. The single, asymmetrical
tower had a belfry but no spire; the body was articulated into nave, aisles
with clerestories above, and chancel. The design, then, lies somewhere be-

tween the granite Gothic of the 1830s and the advanced ecclesiastical style that Richard Upjohn (1802–78) was to bring two years later to St. Paul's, Brookline.

That the brothers kept abreast of current modes, and were especially aware of Upjohn's groundbreaking career, is demonstrated by the history of Grace Episcopal Church in Lawrence, Massachusetts. H. and J. E. donated plans for the board-and-batten Gothic edifice, which opened on 11 October 1846, the first building to be erected for religious worship in the city.[45] The small wooden structure was of a type just then being given broad usage by Upjohn. Five years later the brothers provided the congregation with the granite structure, which with some alterations, still stands in Jackson Street.[46] It was built according to their plans "but modified by the builders," perhaps in the absence of on-site supervision by one of the architects. The new church was consecrated on 5 May 1852, and thus must have been designed in 1851. It is a bell-cote type, which historian William Pierson has observed "during the 1850s . . . became common throughout the American Episcopal community" in the wake of Upjohn's popularization of a form introduced (by an unnamed English architect) at St. James-the-Less in Philadelphia (1846–48).[47] In fact, Upjohn had just erected such a church at St. Stephen's, Boston (1846). Both the original board-and-batten chapel in Lawrence and its stone replacement display proportions more broad than narrow, and the crispness of the granite forms of the existing building also distinguishes it from Upjohn's contemporary work.

That Hammatt is often alone credited with the designs for the Bedford Street church and the houses in Wollaston, Cambridge, and Newport demonstrates that the brothers acted separately as well as in partnership during the 1840s. In addition to the spireless Church of the Messiah, the details of which followed closely those of the Bedford Street design, Joseph produced two simple school buildings for Cambridge in 1847 and 1848, and he collaborated in 1847 with Joseph W. Ingraham, a member of the Boston School Committee, in the design of what with his untimely death in 1848 came to be called the Ingraham School.[48] What little architectural detail this austere building possessed was probably closer to Greek than Italian. J. E.'s early schools reflect the lead of Ammi Young at the Charlestown High School, erected in 1847, a fact reinforcing other evidence linking the two. The Ingraham School was characteristic of the simple, almost styleless works Joseph designed. His seems to have been an engineer's approach to architecture;

Hammatt's, an artist's. And when Joseph took his engineering skills elsewhere, as we shall see, Hammatt was left largely to design for other architects.

In the 1850s the brothers parted company. Joseph joined Charles F.
Sleeper in partnership from 1851 to 1853, and together they designed the first
building of the Auburndale Female Seminary (now Lasell Junior College) in
Newton (1851), the severe, Italianate National Theatre at Portland and Tra-
verse Streets in Boston (1852), and St. Stephen's Episcopal Church in Wilkes-
Barre, Pennsylvania (1853).[49] How they received the latter, a commission from
so far afield, remains a mystery. Joseph soon made other arrangements, however: in July 1853 he assumed the duties of civil engineer at the Charlestown
(later Boston) Navy Yard. Over the next dozen years he carried out a number
of major improvements there, some in the robust granite style of his pre-
decessor, Alexander Parris, his mentor, Ammi Young, or his contemporary
(and his brother's erstwhile collaborator), Gridley J. F. Bryant. His chief
monument there, and an area landmark for more than half a century, was the
239½-foot brick chimney (1857–58) of the Steam Engineering Building.[50]

With Joseph employed by the navy, we must picture Hammatt very busy
as a freelance illustrator and designer through the 1850s and into the 1860s.
He was one of the principal artists for *Gleason's* and later *Ballou's,* and for the
annual *Boston Almanac;* worked for Ticknor & Fields, John P. Jewett, and other
Boston publishers; projected a host of monuments; and turned out a pile of
miscellaneous graphic work. Among his independent architectural designs
during this period were a new entrance hall and staircase, no longer extant,
for the Athenaeum (1850), a corrective to the Cabots' unsatisfactory interior
which, according to Emerson, Billings said wanted greatness; a preliminary
design for the case of the Great Organ installed in George Snell's Music Hall
(1858; the definitive design was probably by Herter Brothers); and the canopy
over the Rock and the National Monument to the Forefathers at Plymouth
(1854–55).[51] There were also projects left on paper: a plan for a library
(1849), perhaps related to the Boston Public Library; a sketch for the extension of the federal Capitol, perhaps an intended entry in the competition of
1850 although it seems never to have been sent; and an undated elevation for
an Academy of Fine Arts, perhaps related to the short-lived Massachusetts
Academy of Fine Arts that succeeded the local Art Union in 1853.[52] In 1860
Billings produced a scheme in the competition for enlarging Boston City
Hall, but the commission ultimately went to Bryant, frequently a collaborator of Billings but here in association with Arthur Gilman.[53]

This elongated list of architectural chores does not represent all of Hammatt's work during the 1850s and 1860s, however. He also frequently collaborated with other architects, either overtly or covertly. His graphic talent cast him in the role of designer whether he joined his brother or others. He was what his older and better-known contemporary Alexander Jackson Davis called himself: an "architectural composer." He had a gift for picturesque composition that carried over from illustration to buildings and increasingly came into demand, and he was often called on to provide massing or skylines for the plans of others. It is probable that through such collaborations he had a greater impact on mid-nineteenth-century Boston architecture than can ever be properly assessed.

This aspect of his career stood out in the memories of others. James Jackson Jarves, who knew Hammatt's work well, wrote in *The Art-Idea* (1864) that in architecture "he has given evidence of a latent genius which in any other country would have been stimulated and developed to its fullest power. . . . The mere overflow of his mind would make a reputation for the common run of architects and artists. Indeed, we fancy, more is already due him in Boston than appears on the surface." Ednah Dow Cheney, who in the 1850s was briefly married to Hammatt's fellow artist Seth Cheney (who was also a brother of Billings's later clients at South Manchester, Connecticut), later remembered that "his pecuniary necessities forced him to work for other architects, who bought his designs and used them according to their own purposes." As late as 1920 Charles F. Read recalled that "many buildings were erected from his designs and he also assisted other architects in their work who did not possess his genius."[54] Much evidence sustains this testimony; there is ample documentation for Hammatt's roles as both credited design consultant and ghost.

Billings most frequently joined forces with Gridley J. F. Bryant (1816–99), the Northeast's busy architectural entrepreneur during most of the century, who over the decades had a number of design associates, partners, or both. He and Billings were in contact as early as 1848 when Billings drew a view of Bryant's new Suffolk County Prison (now called Charles Street Jail).[55] In 1855 they were associated with Luther Briggs in the planning and superintendence of "the buildings, streets, and improvements embraced by the operations of Mr. [Josiah] Quincy and the Mercantile Wharf Association" on Clinton Street.[56] In 1857 Billings designed "key-stones with emblematical heads" as well as "other statuary and alto-relievos" for the six-story Quincy granite commercial building, which once stood at 74–76 Franklin Street, that Bryant erected for the trustees of the estate of Joshua Sears.[57]

Also in 1857 a committee of members of the Massachusetts Charitable Mechanic Association, including architects Bryant and Nathaniel J. Bradlee (1829–88), produced a plan for their new building, then moved "to procure a design for the facades on Bedford and Chauncy streets. For this purpose they obtained the assistance of Mr. Hammatt Billings, who, in the course of a few days, handed in a sketch on a small piece of paper, about five inches by four."[58] (This description of Billings's graphic method is fully confirmed by the diminutive sketches in the Stowe-Day Library.) The committee requested him to develop his concept at a larger scale, and this "was with the plan drawn by the Committee" approved by the government of the association on 4 May 1857. The cornerstone was laid in September and the structure dedicated in March 1860.[59] The building, now gone, backed up to Billings's Church of the Saviour (see fig. 52); it consisted of two rental floors topped by the hall of the association on the third. The exterior was described at the time as Italian Renaissance modified by Lombardic or Romanesque details, which in nineteenth-century terms is accurate enough up to the French roof. The niches of the third story on the Chauncy Street elevation held figures of Charity, Labor, and Thought.[60] Were these, too, Billings's creations? There are drawings dated May 1857 in the Stowe-Day scrapbook for elaborately carved walnut fireplace-and-mirror frames that may have been intended for this same commission.

In 1859 Bryant and Billings submitted drawings for the Society of Natural History and the Horticultural Society in the Back Bay, but did not win the commission.[61] As we shall see, Billings and Bryant worked together in 1860 on the Phillips monument in Mount Auburn Cemetery and the unrealized Minute Man monument in Lexington, as well as on an unexecuted Soldiers and Sailors' monument on Boston Common in 1866.

Bryant was not Billings's only professional collaborator. The Tremont Street Methodist Episcopal Church in Boston was begun in 1860 and dedicated in 1862.[62] In various sources it is credited to Billings alone or to Billings designing for architects S. S. Woodcock and G. F. Meacham (fig. 53). According to one of Hammatt's obituaries, "when he was asked to draw a design for the exterior of that church, he walked to the spot to see the shape of the lot. Standing on the corner, he drew upon a piece of paper resting on his hat, the outline of the structure, to which he added a few slight embellish-

Fig. 53. Hammatt Billings for Woodcock and Meacham, architects, Tremont Street Methodist Episcopal Church, Boston, 1860–62 (Bufford lithograph; author's collection).

ments. It was the work of a few minutes."[63] Drawing or figuring on the top of a hat seems to have been relatively common in the nineteenth century. Daniel Maclise portrayed the English illustrator George Cruikshank in the August 1833 *Fraser's Magazine* sitting on a barrel sketching on his top hat, and the seated central figure in George Caleb Bingham's *Verdict of the People* (1854), in a practice that presages the "laptop" of current common usage, apparently tallies votes on his.[64] This is nonetheless a charming account of inspired picturesque composition and gives insight to this aspect of Billings's multi-directional career.

Billings's obituary in *Old and New* clearly states that the interior of the Tremont Street church was "not from his design." For Woodcock and Meacham, who supervised construction and probably provided the plan and interior design, Billings created an active silhouette, "with its spires of unequal height at [diagonally] opposite corners" for what was long regarded as "one of the finest church edifices in Boston . . . [and] one of the first . . .

constructed of Roxbury stone."[65] It is his most memorable ecclesiastical massing. Comparison to his Church of the Saviour of fifteen years earlier measures his leap from Gothic inspired by Pugin to richly colorful and active design inspired by Ruskin and his followers. We know that by 1851 he was buying and presumably perusing many of Ruskin's works (see appendix A).

The lithographic perspective view of the exterior of the church published in 1862 credits only Billings as architect.[66] His contribution to the massing of Woodcock and Meacham's church was recognized by his own effort. But as James Jarves and Ednah Cheney cautioned, this was not always the case. In the Stowe-Day scrapbook is a "Sketch of Church at New Britain, Conn./ Hammatt Billings, May 4th 1864." The drawing shows the church, three aisled without clerestory, and chapel set at right angles to one another, with a tower, three stories plus broach spire, placed at the reentrant angle (fig. 54). A lower tower and spire rises from the right side of the main facade. The style is English Gothic. It is, in short, a close adaptation of Hammatt's Tremont Street silhouette. Two other pieces of paper in the scrapbook show the complex in relation to the site, an irregular plot of land at the acute angle formed by converging, unnamed streets. The church faces down the single street created by their confluence.

The South Congregational Church located at the meeting of Arch and Main Streets in New Britain is an English Gothic design of red sandstone. It faces down Main with its chapel perpendicular to the chancel end of the nave. There are two towers and broach spires of unequal height, too, although the taller is to the right of the principal entrance, while the shorter nestles in the angle. This is the reverse of the relationship shown on Billings's sketch. Nothing in the South Congregational Church records mentions Billings, and there is no evidence of a competition for the design of the edifice. The building committee was appointed on 17 March 1864, the building begun in April 1865, the chapel finished and dedicated in March 1867, and the church itself dedicated on 16 January 1868.[67] The architect was George F. Meacham (1831–1917) of Boston. Since the church recognizably reflects Billings's sketch, dated just six weeks after the formation of the building committee, he was probably engaged as a silent design consultant by Meacham. We have here rather solid evidence of his ghosting for another architect. We know he worked with Bryant, with Woodcock and Meacham, and with his brother; for how many other architects did he work without receiving credit?[68]

Joseph Billings withdrew from the Navy Yard on 4 July 1866 and rejoined his brother in architectural practice following Hammatt's return from a brief trip to London in the summer of 1865. Hammatt had already submitted a losing (and now lost) design in the competition for Memorial Hall at Harvard and was to enter a "French Renaissance" design (also now unlocated) in the competition for the New York Post Office on City Hall Square early in 1867.[69] Although he lost again, in a field of over fifty entries in the post office competition he was one of five third-place winners and received a three-

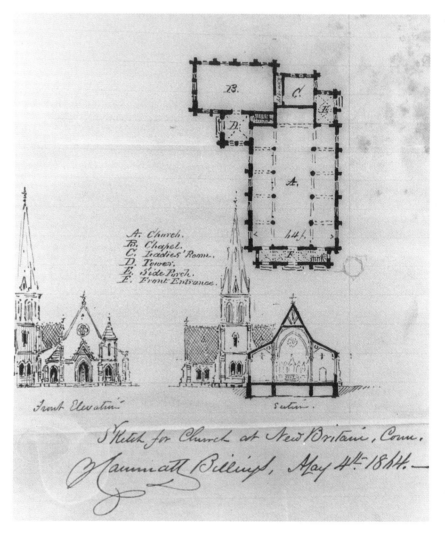

Fig. 54. Ink drawing by Hammatt Billings for a church at New Britain, Connecticut, 1864. This is probably a preliminary study for George F. Meacham's South Congregational Church (Harriet Beecher Stowe Center, Hartford, Conn.).

hundred-dollar premium.[70] With Joseph's engineering expertise again available to him, Hammatt's architectural career got a second wind. In the eight years until Hammatt's death the brothers created a large number of works in and out of Boston, several for important clients including Gov. William Claflin, Henry Fowle Durant, and the Cheney Brothers of South Manchester, Connecticut.

The "little village" of South Manchester was "the seat of the successful introduction of silk weaving in the United States."[71] The firm, founded in 1838, eventually included six of the eight Cheney brothers (George, Charles, Ralph, Ward, Rush, and Frank; Seth and John were artists who invested but had no active role in running the company). The business expanded from the mid-1850s, and by the 1860s it was booming.[72] Led by its president, Ward Cheney (1813–76), in the years immediately after the Civil War the company created a model industrial town that drew the attention of architects and reformers, as well as the popular press.[73] The village was scattered about a parklike area. The Cheneys built their houses within the village complex, landscaped the mills, and saw to it that all workmen's cottages were "designed with an artistic taste." The company supplied reservoirs for drinking water, the fire department, the light, power, and tramway companies, sewer and garbage services, a railroad and depot (1869), a school, and a "Hall for the social entertaining of the operatives." The Billingses were actively engaged in the architectural development of the village in the second half of the 1860s, although the complete extent of their contribution is not at all clear. Nor do we now know how they came to be the Cheney architects, although Hammatt had had contact with the family through the artistic brothers, Seth, who had died in 1856, and John, who by the second half of the sixties was in retirement in South Manchester.

All but one of the surviving drawings for Cheney Hall at South Manchester are signed by Hammatt alone, and the earliest is dated April 1866, so this may have been the commission that brought the brothers together again.[74] The building was opened in 1869 (fig. 55). According to an 1872 article in *Harper's*, the basement of the social hall was divided into rooms used by temperance lodges; a reading room and library occupied the lower floor, while the hall above was the site of multidenominational religious services as well as theatrical "representations" and temporary exhibitions; and the third floor housed the armory of the First Connecticut Militia. The building is on the exterior stylistically related to the Billingses' Frank Cheney House of the same time. The hall is a rectangular, two-story, red brick box with corner pavilions and a one-story arcaded entrance porch (with side pavilions added later). High mansards cap the pavilions and the main block. Details include pointed arches of polychromatic voussoirs surrounding round-arched openings at the main level, Gothic dormers, and Neo-Grec decorative accents inside and out. Hammatt here created an eclectic pile, part French, part English, in keeping with the emerging style of the post–Civil War era, but linked to his previous work by its classical balance. The restored building survives as part of the Cheney Brothers National Historic Landmark District.

Whether Billings provided drawings for the depot, the school house, or any other buildings, or the landscape planning at South Manchester remains an unanswered question, but he did design houses for at least two of the Cheney brothers, one of which remained on paper. Drawings now in a private collection for the existing house of Frank Cheney (1817–1904; later called "Miss Mary's" because his spinster daughter was long resident there; it is now New Hope Manor) are signed "H. Billings" and dated August 1866.[75] The plan is divided into halves by a ten-foot-wide hallway, which on the principal floor separated sitting room, main stair, parlor, and piazza from kitchen, service areas, and dining room. The arrangement is sensible, additive, and uncomplicated; the rooms plain but generously proportioned.

Fig. 55. H. and J. E. Billings, Cheney Building, South Manchester, Connecticut, 1866–69, exterior, from *Harper's New Monthly Magazine*, November 1872 (Boston Athenaeum).

Fig. 56. Hammatt Billings, Frank Cheney House, South Manchester, Connecticut, 1866, exterior (author's collection).

The interior woodwork is Renaissance Revival. On the three-story exterior the building is red brick with one-story porches and a piazza of Italianate details and a mansard roof punctuated with lucarnes (fig. 56).

In the Stowe-Day scrapbook are two sets of sketches dated June and September 1867 and July 1869 for a house for Ward Cheney plus a design for a desk for the same client.[76] The earlier scheme is based on the Frank Cheney plan but with a looser perimeter. The main rooms, presumably sitting room and parlor, are extended and enriched by rectangular and polygonal window bays; the main stair is moved across the ten-foot-wide central hall; and the kitchen is strung out along the axis perpendicular to it. The sketches of the exterior show Hammatt thinking of a pointed, polychromatic, and pictur-esque, presumably wooden, pile of a domestic establishment (fig. 57). The later scheme, signed by both H. and J. E., turns the central hall of the earlier plans into a beamed living hall with adjacent stairway in the center of the plan, eliminates the sitting room and parlor combination in favor of one drawing room at a right angle to the dining room, and includes a more extensive use of broad piazzas. The spaces now begin to spin around the stairway. With this scheme Hammatt joined the updated domestic planning ideals of his leading contemporaries.[77] Neither Ward Cheney project was ever built. Had Billings lived he would have presumably received the commis-

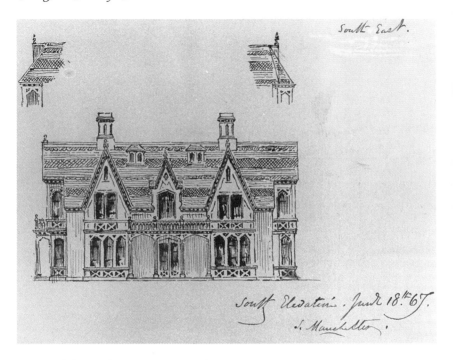

Fig. 57. Ink drawing by Hammatt Billings for the south elevation of the unbuilt Ward Cheney House, South Manchester, Connecticut, 1867 (Harriet Beecher Stowe Center, Hartford, Conn.).

sions for the Cheney Block at Hartford (1875) and for the unbuilt houses for Rush (1876) and James Cheney (1878) that went to H. H. Richardson; that is, if his architecture like his graphics had not begun to look old-fashioned.[78]

The early 1870s brought the brothers a great deal of work. There are a number of drafts in the Stowe-Day scrapbook for the Billings brothers' unsuccessful entry in the competition for the Connecticut State Capitol (1871–72).[79] The large number of recognized and supposed Connecticut projects, including a Second Empire competitive design for an insurance company building in Hartford, suggests that the Billingses' practice was expanding westward from the Hub toward the end of Hammatt's life, but most of the solid achievements of these years remained in and around Boston.[80] For the city the brothers projected a number of designs including important commercial work such as the Wesleyan Association Building in Bromfield Street (1869–71) and Joseph's demolished, colorful Odd Fellows' Hall at Tremont and Berkeley Streets (1871–72).[81] The president of the Wesleyan Association during 1868–72 was the prosperous shoe merchant William Claflin (1818–1905), twenty-third governor of the Commonwealth,

trustee of Mount Holyoke and Wellesley Colleges, and client of the Billingses for a domestic design in suburban Newton. The Wesleyan Association Building housed a Methodist family newspaper, *Zion's Herald*, the Theo-
logical School of Boston University, and other tenants.[82] In a letter of 3 April
1869 sent to the association to accompany preliminary sketches now unlocated, the Boston architectural firm of Hartwell and Swasey proposed
a number of variations for the "intended improvement of the Bromfield
House estate."[83] Their design, in a "style of architecture . . . largely and
successfully used in England for Civic buildings . . . [and] peculiarly adapted
to one . . . for religious and literary purposes," included an asymmetrical
tower and was probably Victorian Gothic. The association rejected this for
unknown reasons in favor of the Billingses' granite-fronted brick building of
French derivation, with Second Empire roofs and Neo-Grec rosettes and
other incised decoration. As historian Nancy Salzman points out, it is one
of the finest buildings to survive the Great Fire of 1872.

Also in the 1870s, the brothers designed the Cathedral Building at Franklin and Devonshire Streets, erected to replace a building of the same name
destroyed in the Great Fire. The first Cathedral Building was standing by
1864 on a site diagonally opposite 74–76 Franklin Street.[84] Although G. J. F.
Bryant is given sole credit for its design, here, too, there is evidence of Hammatt's ghostly hand. The Second Empire building was closer to the embellished facades of 74–76 Franklin (1857) than to other Bryant buildings in the
area. It was five stories of arcades and round-arched openings capped by a
mansard roof. At the second and fourth levels were keystones decorated with
human heads in the manner of Hammatt's work on the Phillips monument
at Mount Auburn of 1860, designed in association with Bryant, or the details
on 74–76, which this building was certainly intended to rival. In the center
of the fourth story of the Devonshire Street facade was an "R" set into the
axial window recess. This was the initial of the developer, Isaac Rich, who
was indeed rich: "probably the largest fish dealer in the U.S. . . . an extensive
wharf proprietor and ship owner," as well as real estate developer, who was as
early as 1852 worth a whopping $250,000.[85]

The first Cathedral Building vanished in the Great Fire of 1872 and was
replaced by 1874 with the second, a "handsome iron structure," as Edwin
Bacon described it (fig. 58). The new building was French-inspired and five
stories, but lacked the earlier building's mansard roof—that lumber pile in
the sky the proliferation of which through the center of the city had fed the
blaze and was legislated out of the rebuilt area.[86] The design is given to

H. and J. E. Billings, without Byrant, although Isaac Rich was again the developer. Hammatt's sketch for a fireplace frame for the building is in the Stowe-Day sketchbook.[87] The second Cathedral Building disappeared long ago; it was H. and J. E.'s definitive large contribution to downtown Boston, although for the same Isaac Rich they produced in 1873 a smaller and long-gone "New York iron front" at Summer and High Streets, a venue occupied by William Claflin and Co., wholesale boots and shoes.[88]

The architects worked the suburbs as well as the city. In the 1870s Hammatt turned out a set of ecclesiastical designs for greater Boston. The surviving Waverley (First) Congregational Church on Trapelo Road in Belmont of

Fig. 58. H. and J. E. Billings, Second Cathedral Building, Boston, 1873–74, exterior (Fine Arts Department, Boston Public Library, courtesy of the Trustees of the Boston Public Library).

Fig. 59. H. and J. E. Billings, Wellesley (Mass.) Congregational Church, 1871–72, exterior (after E. H. Chandler, *History of the Wellesley Congregational Church,* 1898).

1870 is a relatively low-budget, board-and-batten version of a Pugin-Upjohn Gothic design.[89] It features an asymmetrical entry tower with spire, a nave with transept, and an articulated chancel. In 1870 the Wellesley Congregational Church, under Rev. George Gardner Phipps, pastor from 1867 to 1878, appointed a building committee, which included Henry Durant, that selected the Billings brothers as architects for a new church.[90] Surviving drawings and specifications are dated March–May 1871; the dedication took place in July 1872. As at Waverley the building was wooden Gothic with corner tower and spire (fig. 59). It had a nave with side aisles, a pointed arcade across the front, an entrance porch at the base of the tower plus other pointed porches, and a chapel to the rear. According to the draft specifications, the building was to be "wood above the underpinning, with slated roofs and spire." The outside finish was clapboard; the inside finish was to be "narrow, matched and beaded ash vertical sheathing, capped" up to the side window sills, and plastered above. Pews were to be of black ash; the pulpit and railing to the platform, of black walnut. These specifications seem usual for Hammatt's buildings of the period. The church, which faced the railway

depot, burned to the ground on the last day of 1916, thus joining a year and a
half later H. and J. E.'s other local work, College Hall at Wellesley, as a
sacrifice to the flames.

For the suburbs during these last years, the Billingses turned out not only
churches, of course, but houses as well. For Governor Claflin they designed a
suburban villa in Newtonville. Claflin owned much property in the area,
including an Italianate home, the Old Elms, erected in the 1850s (designer as
yet unknown). The new house was for Claflin's daughter and businessman
son-in-law, Charles W. Ellis, but the preliminary sketches at the Stowe-Day
Library, and the contract drawings that are still in the house, all bear Claflin's
name; the drawings are dated July 1869. The preliminary plan shows a close
variation of the second Ward Cheney house project of the same year, and the
contract drawings show a close variation on that. As erected at 170 Otis
Street the structure was a stylistically updated version of the villas Hammatt
was designing in the 1850s, with tower, mansard roofs, and applied Neo-Grec
details.[91]

Although there survive many sketches for residential work, which seem to
date from the late 1860s or early 1870s, no others have yet been identified.
The one late suburban building that is known, other than College Hall and
the gatehouses at Wellesley, is the Thayer Library (it now houses the municipal waterworks) in Braintree, Massachusetts (fig. 60). It was commissioned
in 1871, contracted in March 1873, and dedicated in June 1874.[92] No competition is documented, but there is in a private collection an 1871 design for the
building by Luther Briggs and Company showing a towered Venetian Gothic
building.[93] The Stowe-Day scrapbook contains an unlabeled, undated drawing related to the Thayer, which shows alternate window treatments and
demonstrates that Billings originally thought of a towered silhouette as well,
although a lower one with classical details. The building erected in 1873–74
lacks the tower. It is a bichromatic, red brick and stone-trimmed, neoclassical
building with hip roof and triangular pediment. Here as at Billings's Mount
Holyoke library, as we shall see in chapter 7, we are reminded of Georgian
architecture.

The eclecticism of the brothers' post–Civil War work is demonstrated
by the contrast between this design and another contemporary project. Also
in the Stowe-Day collection is a Billings sketch dated December 1873 for a
public library at Haverhill, Massachusetts. The actual building was erected
during 1874–75 from the design of a local architect, Josiah Littlefield.[94] The
Billingses' project is Venetian Gothic, while Littlefield's descended from

Fig. 60. H. and J. E. Billings, Thayer Library, Braintree, Massachusetts, 1871–74, exterior; now the city water department (Society for the Preservation of New England Antiquities).

Kirby's round-arched Boston Public Library of the 1850s. No competition is mentioned in the library's records, so this sketch represents either an unproductive collaboration between the architects or Billings's fishing for a commission he did not catch. Hammatt's roots were in the classical tradition; that he could in the 1870s swing from Georgianesque to picturesque Gothic in contemporary buildings of the same function suggests the range of his architectural offerings at what should have been the crest of his career but was in fact the end of his life.

Hammatt Billings's architectural labors produced at least three very different works of more than passing importance in the history of nineteenth-century Boston building, one from early in his career, one from its middle, and one from near its end, and two of them now destroyed: the Boston Museum, the Tremont Street Methodist Episcopal Church, and the original building of Wellesley College. Three works in a career of nearly thirty years seem little enough, but for an architect of Billings's stature, and a jack-of-all-designs whose time was in constant demand for other work, it was an enviable achievement.

The majority of his buildings blend into the fabric of nineteenth-century Boston and its environs. Although it fits neatly between the careers of Bulfinch and Richardson, the body of Billings's oeuvre (excluding his early Boston Museum) does not, like theirs, represent the cutting edge of architectural innovation and achievement. Billings's was a more representative accomplishment. He was a form-giver not a structuralist. He kept abreast of the latest design ideas coming from England, France, and his colleagues in Boston and New York. Most of his buildings are composed of formal and decorative concepts that were the common visual coinage of the era. He was competent rather than brilliant; like his illustrations, his buildings quietly satisfied the functional and stylistic expectations of his patrons without rising very far above the general level of production of his time and place. Like his illustrations in *Ballou's* or books, Billings's buildings enhanced their surroundings without calling undue attention to themselves. And for just that reason the works of "his real profession" gain meaning, for in them rather than in those of a "signature" architect, we can see the norm, the standard by which the mediocrity or excellence of others might be judged.

7

"A Rare Achievement of Architectural Skill"

College Hall, Wellesley

THE CROWNING achievement of Hammatt Billings's career as an architect—one that occupied much of the labor of his last five years—came with his design of the original campus for Wellesley College. He "did indeed consider it his chiefest work," according to Edward Abbott, a journalist who served on the Board of Visitors to the college and was therefore in a position to know.[1] It was an accomplishment he shared with his brother Joseph, and that he owed to the continued patronage of Henry Fowle and Pauline Durant, for whom he had designed the library at Mount Holyoke in 1868, and who began the next year to plan their own institution "founded for the glory of God and the service of the Lord Jesus Christ, in and by the education and culture of women."[2] This was a work of the highest visibility because of the then rarity of institutions of higher learning that took women seriously. Wellesley College was the largest work of Hammatt's career, and it might have launched him onto other works of equal importance, and thus placed him more firmly within the history of American architecture, had he not died at the age of fifty-six, nearly a year before its opening. It might have done that anyway if it had not completely disappeared in a fire of March 1914. What Edward Abbott called in *Harper's* magazine a year after its opening "a rare achievement of architectural skill" thus all but vanished until recently from discussions of American architecture in general and educational architecture in particular.

The creation of the Wellesley College campus spanned from the spring of 1869, when the idea began to take shape, until September 1875, when the first students were admitted to the completed building. "Mr. Durant's Female College" was a "fine building," according to the poet Henry Wadsworth Longfellow, who drove out from Cambridge to visit the fledgling institution a month after its opening (and, ironically enough, in light of the earlier discussion, was treated to a row on Lake Waban in the college boat, the *Evangeline*).[3] The commission stood at an intersection marked by the productive last years of Hammatt Billings's career, the changing lives of the institution's founders, the evolving history of architecture for higher education in this country, and of institutions for the serious education of women that emerged in the years before and after the Civil War. Before we look closely at the culminating work of Billings's architectural career, then, we must look at the various historical factors that shaped the building program.

Henry Fowle Durant (nee Henry Welles Smith; 1822–81) was a Boston lawyer who changed his name to set himself off from other Henry Smiths, whose success at the bar led to grumbling about his methods, and who as a businessman profited perhaps unseemly much from the Civil War.[4] For these and other reasons (e.g., he was not a Unitarian; he did not attend Harvard), although otherwise of the type that constituted Billings's patronage, he stood outside the pale of conservative "proper Boston." He married his first cousin, Pauline Fowle (1832–1917), and established a country seat in what was then West Needham (the area became the town of Wellesley in 1881) near the celebrated horticultural domain of the Hollis H. Hunnewells, to whom he was distantly related through his mother.[5] Durant was an aesthete; his estate, like Hunnewell's, contained collections of art and nature. The deaths of the Durants' two small children dramatically altered the couple's lives, however. Henry sought solace in Evangelical religion, became an avid advocate for Christ, and led prayer meetings across New England. This brought him by July 1866 to South Hadley, Massachusetts, and to what was then called Mount Holyoke Seminary for Women, to whose students he preached and whose board of trustees he joined in 1867.[6]

It may be that the Billingses were recommended to Henry and Pauline Durant by William Claflin, for whom they also worked during these years (of course, the reverse could also be true). Their association with the Durants presumably began in 1868 when the brothers designed a library for Mount Holyoke College. It was during the presidency of Helen M. French (1867–72) that Pauline Durant offered the school ten thousand dollars for books if a suitable, fireproof library could be erected within three years. In May 1868 the Commonwealth of Massachusetts granted the school money to erect the library, and on 5 June the trustees appointed a building committee including, in fact apparently dominated by, Henry Durant. The Durants probably selected the architect. Hammatt's preliminary sketches for plans and an elevation dated 14 July of that year appear in the Stowe-Day sketch-book, while a portfolio of developed drawings (now unlocated) is mentioned in a letter of 28 May 1869. Foundations were laid in June, and the library was dedicated in 1870.[7] It was extended in 1886–87 by an addition to the north designed by Peabody and Stearns of Boston and demolished in 1904 to make way for a new library building.

Surviving letters from the brothers preserved in the Mount Holyoke Archives give us a glimpse of Henry Durant as a client preoccupied with details. They cover the period of construction from February 1869 to Christmas 1870. They contain references to Durant's "wishes," "desires," or decisions, specifically with regard to basics such as the color of the stone trim, the pattern of window lights, and the laying of the wooden floor. The letters leave no doubt that Henry Durant, during the period when the design of Wellesley's College Hall was under consideration, was a client who knew his own mind; that the architects and builders worked for him. And he not only closely watched the construction of the building, but in a letter of October 1870 dictated the administration of the library as well.

The Stowe-Day sketches (which are close to what was built) and old photographs depict a small brick structure to the north of and connected to Mount Holyoke's first seminary building (fig. 61). The connecting corridor shows up on the preliminary plans only as outline, but it too was designed by Hammatt, for in a letter of October 1869 a plan and section of it were said to have been sent out from Boston by the architects. The library proper stood on a broad rectangular plan extended by a polygonal bay to the west and a rectangular bay to the east. It rose into a boxy, high-ceilinged room that was meant to have galleries reached by spiral stairs, as we also learn from the correspondence. The intended effect was probably akin to what was finally realized in the larger library in College Hall at Wellesley (see fig. 68). Billings divided the floor space into corner alcoves by paneled, black walnut book-cases, while heavily molded trim outlined the doors and windows. He stenciled the ceiling and walls of the interior with delicate classicizing motifs.

The same vocabulary of decorative detail found on Cheney Hall at South Manchester, Connecticut—Ruskinian alternating brick and stone voussoirs in nonconcentric arches in the bays—was repeated on the gabled exterior here, as was the symmetrical massing. The end elevations of the Mount Holyoke library, however, appear in photographs to have been almost Georgian in effect. Habits of classical design learned in the 1830s clearly survived in Hammatt's works of the 1860s. The Durants were presumably delighted with the Billingses' services, for in the next year they commissioned the brothers to create the campus of their own educational endowment at Wellesley and presumably had a hand in picking them as the architects of the local Congregational meetinghouse as well.

Durant's religious conversion and his work at Mount Holyoke trans-

Fig. 61. H. and J. E. Billings, library at Mount Holyoke College, 1868–69 *(left)* with the original college building as enlarged *(right)* (Mount Holyoke College Archives).

formed him. As Helen Horowitz has pointed out, when he embraced religion Durant embraced a realm largely populated by women. When he and Pauline decided to memorialize their dead son, Harry, they turned their taste, enormous wealth, religious fervor, and architects to transforming their country estate into an institution for the higher education of women dedicated (as Durant wrote in his will of 1867) "to the service of the Lord Jesus Christ, by erecting a seminary on the plan (modified by circumstances) of [Mount Holyoke at] South Hadley."[8]

Higher education for women began in earnest in the United States in the second quarter of the nineteenth century with the establishment of "female seminaries." Mount Holyoke, founded by Mary Lyon (1797–1849) in 1837, was among the first of these institutions. It erected a building at South Hadley, Massachusetts, in 1838: a four-square, four-story, red brick, hip-roofed, late Federal block with central entry that was soon relieved by a two-story, light-painted wood piazza. It was, unlike the dormitories of traditional male colleges, an architectural form based upon the merger of house and asylum. The male colleges at Princeton, Harvard, or Amherst, all located in towns, were arranged in separate buildings with easy access to public life. Dormitories were planned as suites of rooms reached by individual entries and stairways, without long corridors, where a minimum of supervision meant a measure of independence (and legendary strife between "town and gown"). In the thinking of the era, in the "cult of domesticity," women ideally led private lives devoted to familial service. If higher education meant leaving home, then seminary women, like the inmates of an asylum, needed protection and supervision, and this meant establishing their colleges in remote locations and gathering all activities into one building.

At Mount Holyoke there was imposed upon the students a common existence based upon the hierarchial ordering of the "family" usual in asylums. The life of the female seminary student was a well-regulated one reinforced by architectural design. As in an asylum all aspects of student activity were housed under one roof, and rooms at each level were off a common corridor. At Mount Holyoke the central entry gave access to dining in the basement, the public rooms at ground level, recitation rooms at the upper level, and students' rooms on the floors above. The Durants knew Mount Holyoke and its architecture well. The detached library they added to its original building just after the Civil War was architecturally and programmatically the origin of their own donation at Wellesley. According to Henry Durant there was "no danger in having too many Mount Holyokes."[9]

The Durants were not inclined to copy the austere block that first housed Mount Holyoke, however; they saw no conflict between architectural beauty and the pursuit of Christian learning. For more specifically architectural inspiration they started with Matthew Vassar's recently created college at Poughkeepsie, New York. In building Vassar College the beer baron (1792– 1868) sought to create a lasting monument to himself and a permanent memorial to his riches; he therefore engaged a fashionable New York architect, James Renwick Jr. (1818–95), to design a suitably impressive pile. Vassar may have shunned Mary Lyon's preference for simplicity, but he and his advisers followed her lead in choosing the model for the architecture and the organization of his college. Renwick had, among his many other credits, designed any number of asylums and like institutions, most recently the mansarded Charity Hospital on Roosevelt Island in New York City (1858– 61). He adapted the form and the organization for Vassar in 1860–61; it opened in 1865.

Renwick gave Vassar a huge, symmetrical, Second Empire pile: a tripartite, five-story, mansarded pavilion formed the center of the vast horizontal composition stretching five hundred feet in length (fig. 62). The pavilion was connected to five-storied, clustered end pavilions by three-story wings. External materials were red brick set in black mortar with blue freestone trim. The central pavilion was the epicenter of the institution. The male college president spent his working and his private hours there; it housed his office and his residence as well as those of the lady principal, the recitation rooms, parlors, a small library, dining room, and chapel, music rooms, art gallery, and science laboratories. Male professors and their families lived in the slightly less ornate end pavilions, and the students' and unmarried women teachers' rooms stretched along the wide, single-loaded corridors within the even plainer connecting wings. Provisions for safety included iron doors that could divide the huge structure into five sections in case of fire.[10]

Vassar's architecture was sharply focused. It clearly expressed institutional control, the hierarchical and paternal familial social structure that unfolded beneath its vast and continuous series of mansards. With all the members and facilities for all the activities of the college huddled under one roof far removed from the distractions of urban life, Vassar College in 1865 formed the perfect model of the ideal mid-nineteenth-century establishment for the higher education of women in the United States.[11]

Wellesley College grew from these earlier examples. Henry Fowle Durant, as Helen Horowitz has so happily put it, filled the shell of Vassar with

Fig. 62. James Renwick, Jr., College Hall, Vassar, Poughkeepsie, New York, 1860–65 (Special Collections, Vassar College Library).

the soul of Mount Holyoke. On 10 October 1869 he wrote to Gov. William Claflin to say he was going to apply for incorporation of "a Female Seminary (something after the general plan of Mt Holyoke) . . . to give education of the highest standard to young ladies of the middle classes at very modest prices," and asked him to join the board of trustees of his "eminently Christian College." Claflin did join the board when it was incorporated in 1870, although its majority was composed of men of the cloth.[12]

Durant also wrote that he did "not expect to build the Seminary for two years at least," but he had in fact already engaged the architectural services of the Billings brothers for work at the site. There exists a preliminary study for the campus's East Lodge, a close variant of what was actually built, that is signed by "H. & J. E." and dated 31 March 1869.[13] Design work on the principal building occupied the next two years, with nearly definitive elevations drawn after the laying of two cornerstones in August and September 1871. The second stone held a box containing a Bible and an inscription reading in part: "Except the Lord build the house, they labour in vain that build it" (Ps. 127:1). The first brick was put in place on 2 May 1872, and the building opened its doors three and a half years later (fig. 63).[14]

For the Durants' picturesquely landscaped, three-hundred-acre estate across Lake Waban from the Hollis Hunnewells, Billings designed two gate lodges and the commandingly sited main building reached by a serpentine road between them. The scheme—a huge building housing all aspects of the institution and guarded by gatehouses at the public roads—found its inspiration not only in the spirit of Mount Holyoke, as Durant had stated as his intention, but in the overall form of Vassar College, and in the process transformed both sources.

The visitor entered the campus (but never on the Sabbath) past either West or East Lodge (although these were in fact northwest and southeast of the great building), both of which are extant but internally altered. Such gates and gatehouses were a standard feature of gentlemen's estates in mid-nineteenth-century England and America, appearing for example in several plates in Richard Brown's *Domestic Architecture* of 1852.[15] Durant had, before his son's death, planned to establish him in just such a gentleman's estate on these grounds. West Lodge, which appears on the definitive 1875 map of the campus but is otherwise undocumented, is a picturesque cottage in the English manner. It originally sported high-pitched gable roofs of imbricated slate and still displays walls of small particolored granite stones interrupted

Fig. 63. H. and J. E. Billings, College Hall, Wellesley College, 1871–75 (photo by A. H. Folsom; Wellesley College Archives).

Fig. 64. H. and J. E. Billings, East Lodge, Wellesley College, 1869–70 (Wellesley College Archives).

by a polygonal and a rectangular bay, details found also on East Lodge. The preliminary sketch for East Lodge shows it reversed and slightly different from what was reduced and erected. Its T-plan and ornamental Flemish gables might descend from plate 51 in Brown's book, but the imbricated slate pattern of the roofs and the polychromatic random granite walling enhance the picturesque effect (fig. 64). This little structure seems to have set the keynote for the more imposing Wellesley Town Hall of 1882 by Shaw and Hunnewell, as well as other local buildings.

In keeping with the principles of siting within a picturesque park that descend from eighteenth-century England, College Hall was located so as to rise dramatically above the lake to the south, or to emerge gradually as a lofty and activated pile as the visitor crossed the rolling and wooded terrain beyond the gatehouses. This was markedly different from the initial view the visitor still receives of Renwick's building at Vassar, which spreads out frontally, laterally, and symmetrically at the end of the straight road from the single gatehouse. As we shall see, that difference in siting called forth some differences in the building at Wellesley.

The evolution of Billings's design for College Hall is preserved in a series of drawings now in the college archives. What appears to be the earliest of these contains an undated (but probably from August–October 1871) and unsigned schematic plan of the principal floor and an unfinished north

elevation (fig. 65). This is the sole preserved document attesting to intercourse between the architects and their clients at Wellesley. Here the designer first attempted to arrange into a geometrical pattern the verbal building program given him by the founders. They had surely referred him to
Renwick's Vassar; he took it as a starting point only. In this preliminary
scheme, the 361-foot-long horizontal Second Empire edifice is composed of
a four-story-plus-mansard central pavilion connected by three-story-plus-
mansard wings to three-story-plus-mansard cross-axial wings (which remain
mere outlines on the sheet). The symmetrical elevation is close to Renwick's,
perhaps because the ultimate picturesque siting above Lake Waban has not
yet been considered, but the internal arrangement differs significantly from
that at Vassar.

This is clearly a sketch produced as the basis for discussion, with many
features unresolved, including the treatment of the ends of the east and west

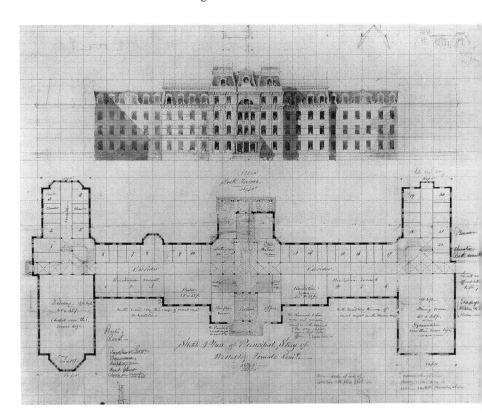

Fig. 65. Ink and wash drawing by Hammatt Billings of the preliminary plan and elevation of
College Hall, Wellesley, 1871 (?) (Wellesley College Archives).

transepts and the overall length of the building. At this stage there is much in doubt, much that draws forth comments, presumably from the Durants as well as the architects, that are recorded on the sheet, but the final distribution of parts is here in embryo. Office, reception room, bathroom, and matron's room occupy the corners of the central pavilion, while twin stairs occupy the center. Parlor and recitation rooms line the north side of the continuous, double-loaded, east-west corridor, thus preserving as much as possible the sunny, southern view over Lake Waban for students' rooms, while the library and chapel above occupy the eastern transept and the dining room with gymnasium above is located in the western transept. Students are housed in suites composed of a bedroom and a parlor. As student life at Wellesley was to be somewhat more relaxed than at Mount Holyoke or Vassar, Billings's schematic plan lacked the rigidly hierarchical architectural ordering of Renwick's building.

The flux of thinking about these arrangements is recorded in the spontaneous comments inked or penciled on the sheet. These range from single-word queries about "Reading Room," "?Sunshine," or "Tower" to longer notes about the possible placement of the "Principal's rooms" above reception, chemistry lecture room and laboratory in the basement, the location of music rooms at the ends of the corridor separated by glass partitions, and the means of connecting the dining room to the kitchen. Although College Hall is here *in nuce*, there were to be further changes in subsequent plans, especially in the final ordering of rooms, the addition of the tall, slender tower to the west, the placement of the kitchen in a detached building to the northwest, and the interior of the central pavilion. And the building continued to grow. By July 1871 it had reached an overall length of 454 feet on the cellar diagram, while the final arrangement appears on a set of plans that seems contemporary with the opening of the college in 1875, where it stretches out to 475 feet with the main corridor continuing well beyond the east and west transepts.

As at Vassar, Wellesley's main building provided spaces for the development of the entire student: for her mind, her body, and her soul; but the Durants went beyond Vassar in providing for the aesthetic experience as well. The visiter entered Renwick's building at the second level, up a grand flight of steps into an entrance hall divided by Corinthian columns with a double staircase located across the broad corridor and receding upwards. In the final arrangement at Wellesley, as shown on the definitive plan dated 1875, Billings swept away the clutter of his original schematic. The central pavilion now

Fig. 66. H. and J. E. Billings, the Centre, College Hall, Wellesley, 1871–75 (photo by Seaver; Wellesley College Archives).

contained the spatial, social, and emotional core of the institution. This was
a skylighted five-story "Centre" reached at ground level from the one-story
porte cochere on the north (fig. 66). This was a revisiting and updating of
the Corinthian Hall of Billings's Boston Museum of a quarter of a century
earlier. The space was defined at ground level by an arcade resting on polished Hallowell granite columns and surmounted by tiers of balustrades and
fluted iron Corinthian colonnades open at each floor and rising to the fifth
level. Standing on the ground floor of red slate and black and white marble,
the visitor looked "up through the great opening to the very glass-capped
roof, story rising above story, column ranging upon column, balustrade
crowning balustrade," according to Edward Abbott.[16] The ornamental free-
classical details of the balustrades, executed in Western ash, were different at
each level and not unlike similar details at Cheney Hall in South Manchester,
Connecticut, just recently completed by the brothers. A huge marble jar-
diniere planted with palms filled the bottom of this light-shot well and
marked the intersection of the axis from the entry and the long east-west
corridor reaching from the kitchen facilities on the west to an entrance on
the east. From its unveiling in 1886, Anne Whitney's statue of a seated Harriet Martineau presided over the space, one of a large number of objets d'art,
statues, paintings, photographs, prints, and drawings (some by Billings himself) that graced the building almost from its opening. In 1876, for example,
Elihu Vedder supervised the hanging of his just-finished *Cumean Sibyl* in the
ground-floor corridor just off the Centre.[17] At first glance the student knew
she had entered a world of art and architecture undreamed of by Mary Lyon
at South Hadley or, indeed, by Matthew Vassar at Poughkeepsie.

To make room for his Centre, the communal gathering place and colle-
giate focus, Billings moved the stairs (from their location in his original
schematic) to the southeast and southwest corners of the center square;
secondary stairs occupied the angles between the east-west corridor and the
lateral transepts (fig. 67). The northern corners housed a reception room
and a recitation room. The dining room remained on the ground floor in the
western pavilion, while the kitchen and steward's apartment were housed on
this level in a detached building. The library occupied the north range of
the east transept. The female "President"—not, as on earlier drawings, the
"Principal"—had a suite of rooms adjacent to the reading room and guard-
ing the eastern entrance. (The first to occupy the position, Ada Howard, was
a graduate of Mount Holyoke.) Female faculty lodgings were distributed
throughout the building. Student suites and recitation rooms filled out the

plan. In what one hopes was an oversight in the drawing and not in the building, just one bathroom, with four water closets and two baths, was located at the far eastern end of the building, convenient to the president but not to the student whose room was placed in the southern wing of the western transept more than four hundred feet away!

The upper floors were better served: there were bathrooms to either side of the center. The chapel over the library occupied the second and third levels of the northern wing of the eastern transept. Music shared the upper level of the detached kitchen building with the gymnasium. A hospital, "carefully sheltered from the bustle of the building proper and occupying its sunniest and brightest corner" at the west end of the corridor, was "one of the most pleasing precincts of all" in Abbot's opinion. On the fourth level mineralogy and chemistry occupied the north side of the center. On the fifth level the natural history cabinet was in the center, while physics occupied the eastern transept and the natural history laboratory and the art gallery occupied the north wing of the western transept. Trunk rooms filled out the attic spaces. Sixteen recitation rooms were more or less convenient to the more

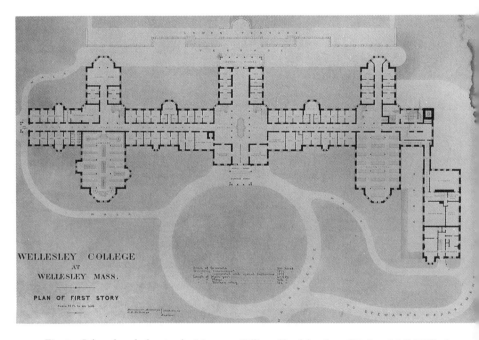

Fig. 67. Ink and wash drawing by Hammatt Billings (?) of the plan of College Hall, Wellesley, 1871–75 (Wellesley College Archives).

Fig. 68. H. and J. E. Billings, the library, College Hall, Wellesley, 1871–75 (Wellesley College Archives).

than three hundred students housed in pairs in comfortable two-room suites on the first four levels. The majority of these suites, with southern windows, offered sunshine and eye-catching views over the lake. Such was the flexible architectural distribution of Durant's academical village under one roof.

The main gathering places within this "village"—other than the focal Centre and the circulatory corridors and stairways, all eventually enlivened by paintings and statues—were the library, chapel, dining room, gymnasium, natural history collection, and art gallery. The library (fig. 68), on the ground floor of the northern arm of the western transept opposite a reading room in the southern arm, provided shelf space for a very generous allowance of books. The room was the fulfillment of Billings's library design for Mount Holyoke. It was, characteristic of the era, divided into alcoves of solid black walnut on two levels, and, in time-honored fashion, decorated with the busts of famous authors. According to the *Boston Journal* the Pompeian red walls were inspired by Wilhelm Zahn's study of antique ornament.[18] This room formed in Abbott's opinion the "gem of the building," and it was indeed the most handsomely appointed room.

The chapel located on the floor above the library was a cavernous space despite the Gothic details and stained glass windows, one the gift of William

Claflin. Perhaps Durant's Evangelicalism accounts for the fact that this was more lecture hall than inspirational venue. The illustrator of Abbott's *Harper's* article struggled to give it some character by his dramatic lighting. The art gallery on the top floor of the western transept was divided into alcoves, spotted with reproductions after the antique, and lighted through a monitor in the roof. The other large rooms were more useful in appearance than ornate. Many of them, including the dining room, contained black walnut seating furniture made for the building, and presumably designed by Billings. Some of these chairs survive.

Durant and Billings were as concerned with the physical comfort and health of the students as with the visual amenities. The immense building was originally lighted with gas. It was heated by steam generated in boilers located like the gasworks in the detached kitchen wing and distributed through a main tunnel in the basement into brick chases serving every room above. Sunshine and fresh air were fundamental requirements. Abbott especially remarks on the efficiency of the ventilation, with pure air constantly supplanting impure.[19] Freshwater came from an artesian well. The drainage, both natural and artificial, was described as "faultless." The college's early publications stressed the building's "pure air and water, sunshine, good ventilation, and drainage." Unfortunately, as the devastation of the fire in 1914 proved, the provisions for fire security, such as fire doors capable of isolating the library and a detached kitchen wing, were inadequate. Certainly the Centre, an open flue at the core of the building, was a perfect conduit through which to spread the conflagration.

In the course of studying the arrangement of Durant's building program Billings continued the even distribution of important rooms across the entire layout that first appeared in his schematic. However, the external architectural form of the first elevation eventually lost the emphatic centrality of Renwick's Vassar in favor of what Montgomery Schuyler was to call a building that "scatters."[20] It lost, too, some of its Vassar-inspired Frenchness after the initial elevation. Despite the axial balance in plan and dominant mansard, the building—with its commanding position on top of the lakeside hill now established—took on the animated asymmetrical look of contemporary English design. It was "set off at various points with towers, bays, porches, pavilions, and spires," as Abbott wrote. It was a "massive accumulation of wings and porches, towers and gables" according to another contemporary account.[21] Advanced elevation drawings, that of the northern flank dated October 1871, that of the southern or lake side clearly later (since it envisions

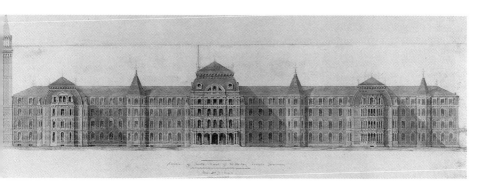

Fig. 69. Ink and wash drawing by Hammatt Billings of the south elevation of College Hall, Wellesley, after 1871 (Wellesley College Archives).

a tower closer to what was realized), show the slender Italianate campanile that was built at the western end of the building—perhaps the fruit of Billings's reading of Ruskin's *Stones of Venice*—but he is undecided about how to animate the skyline above the chapel (fig. 69).[22] In the later drawing he seems to think of a monitor there, but he finally chose a high flèche to punctuate the eastern transept, and delicate finials at salient points across the skyline. Sheets of studies for an imaginative variety of cross-shaped, presumably iron roof ornaments for the chapel wing and elsewhere can be found in the scrapbook at the Stowe-Day Library.

The elevations were, like Vassar's, built of red brick set in black mortar with brown freestone trim, but they were visually more active. Although Billings did take his departure from Renwick's mixture of segmental and half-round arched openings, Wellesley's walls were organized into three or four stories of half-round and segmentally arched openings composed of alternating brick and stone voussoirs beneath pointed roof dormers. Vertically stacked oriels gave further relief to the finished exterior. A reporter for one Boston newspaper found that the structure's "great surface is broken by bay windows and picturesque projections, which, with the arms of the cross, prevent all monotony, and help make masses of shadow, which on summer days add so much to the attractiveness of the building."[23] Classical granite colonnades formed the one-story north and south porches; a screen of fragments from these demolished colonnades has now been reassembled above the lake.

For the Durants, Billings created a vast, picturesque pile situated in a vast picturesque park, a one-building college following the institutional precedents and developing the architectural leads of Mount Holyoke and Vassar. When it was finished it represented the ideal architectural embodiment for the higher education for women just after the Civil War. Or so it seemed. In fact, as is so often the case, the building was obsolete as soon as it opened its doors. Exactly contemporary with the creation of Durant's Wellesley was the development of Smith College at Northampton, Massachusetts. When Smith opened, also in 1875, it was based upon a very different premise about the ideal arrangement for women's higher education. Smith was integrated into a town, not hidden behind closable gates in a rural setting, and it placed administration and classrooms in one building but quartered its students in houses moved from other local sites. That is, it sought to preserve the domesticity of women by placing them in domestically scaled dormitories, not in one huge seminary building. The layout at Smith was, then, decentralized, and this pattern was to have an impact on institutions of higher education for women in the years to come.[24] Bryn Mawr followed Smith in this pattern, and coincident with the death of Henry Fowle Durant in 1881 and the increasing enlargement of its student body, Wellesley also began to splinter into smaller units with the construction of Simpson Cottage, designed by Ware and Van Brunt of Boston in the same year. Simpson was the first of several residential cottages (and, to be sure, other, larger dormitories) erected over the next decade and the only one to survive.

In the period between its completion and its destruction thirty-nine years later, Billings's College Hall had gradually become the largest but just one of many buildings on the evolving campus of Wellesley College. Immediately after its destruction in 1914, Martha Shackford and Edith Moore published a commemorative booklet in which they wrote that Hammatt Billings's College Hall, this "landmark in the history of the education of women," "with its light and sunshine, its wide outlook over lake and campus, its artistic Centre and its countless associations[,] . . . [became] only a memory."[25] Shackford and Moore did not leave the only monument to the building, however. Its existence is recalled in a memorial erected at the centennial of the college near the original site, a memorial composed of surviving, fire-scarred fragments of its once-proud colonnades. These remnants visually recall not only an educational landmark but a major work of Hammatt Billings's career. These remnants and this study fill the void in educational and architectural history created by the building's destruction.

8

"Some Lasting Memento of Their Worth"

Monuments

"MAN HAS KNOWN few greater stimuli to architectural and artistic creativity than the attempt to transcend his own mortality" wrote the architectural historian Howard Colvin.[1] Hammatt Billings designed transcending monuments of two kinds: private or funereal memorials, and public or patriotic markers. His career began in the decade that saw the introduction of the rural cemetery movement in the United States, with its emphasis on the uplifting delights of landscape design, horticultural display, and funerary art, and he frequently answered the call to provide visible recollections of the dead "by some lasting memento of their worth."[2] His career also began in an era of growing nationalism followed by sectional strife, an era that awakened to the memories of the founding legends and Revolutionary battles as important lessons in citizenship, and it carried into the post–Civil War era when fresh patriotic sacrifices demanded fresh and permanent commemoration. Answering these different consecrated and hortatory demands formed a significant part of his multifarious career. As architect and designer of public and private memorials Billings anticipated the diverse accomplishments of Richard Morris Hunt (1827–95) in the 1880s.[3]

Billings labored long and lovingly over the commemorative arts. Funereal and patriotic memorials appear first and last among his designs. The best evidence of this comes from a scrapbook now in the Boston Public Library that includes drawings for a rich assortment of monuments dated as early as mid-August 1845, near the beginning of his activities as a designer, and as late as mid-September 1874, two months before his death.[4] The grave markers were intended for a number of cemeteries in and around Boston, including Forest Hills in Jamaica Plain, Woodlawn in Everett, Mount Hope in Dor-

chester, and especially Mount Auburn in Cambridge, and range from inscribed tablets to classical and Gothic tabernacles, vaults, obelisks, sarcophagi, and figural designs. The list of patrons here as elsewhere in Billings's
career reads largely as if it were drawn from a who's who of elite Bostonians.
It should come as no surprise that he created memorials for some of the
oldest and some of the richest families of Massachusetts.

Billings's work as private memorial maker began as grim Calvinist beliefs
gave way among fashionable Bostonians to a more optimistic Christianity.
As Washington Irving wrote early in the nineteenth century, "[The grave] is
a place, not of disgust or dismay, but of sorrow and meditation."[5] The
concept of an attractive, elegiac cemetery represented a change of attitude
toward death in the 1830s and 1840s that was reflected in the design of grave
markers as well as burial grounds.[6] The blunt "Here lyes ye body of" beneath
a crude death's head carved into a simple gray slate slab, the common stone
of seventeenth- and eighteenth-century urban churchyards, gave way in the
early nineteenth century to suburban landscapes dotted with white marble or
polished and colored granite. These materials were piled into complex architectural compositions often embellished by lovely images and inscribed with
hope-filled messages reflecting the kinder belief in death as the portal to a
promised reward.[7] John C. Loudon, whose English books on landscape design were influential in the United States, wrote that cemeteries should improve "moral feeling" and taste. They should be educational and contain
ornamental tombs, landscaping, and plantings. They should be, in short,
"schools of the arts," with the man-made landscape and markers creating a
balance between nature and culture.[8] The American John Jay Smith elabo-
rated on this when he wrote that a cemetery "properly designed, laid out,
ornamented with tombs, planted with trees, shrubs, and herbaceous plants,
all named, and the whole properly kept, might become a school of instruction in architecture, sculpture, landscape-gardening, arboriculture, botany,
and in those important parts of general gardening, neatness, order, and
high keeping."[9] Such artistic cemeteries quickly became the aim of tourists,
who were led from point to point, like visitors to a museum, by illustrated
guidebooks.[10]

The landscaped cemetery demanded new kinds of commemorative art,
and that was an architectural challenge met by a number of designers and
publicists.[11] American authors followed the lead of Englishmen such as
George Maliphant, whose *Designs for Sepulchral Monuments* of 1835 could be
found in the library of the Boston architect Richard Bond (1798–1861).[12]

This is a folio of thirty-one engraved plates depicting neoclassical and Gothic "mural tablets" and free-standing memorials, many in the form of sarcophagi. Among the Americans concerned with improving cemeteries was John Jay Smith (1798–1881), author, promoter, and one of the founders of Laurel Hill Cemetery in Philadelphia, who in 1846 published a folio of essays on rural cemeteries illustrated with designs for monuments drawn from Loudon and others. The uses, laying out, and management of cemeteries are discussed in the first half of Smith's text, then a brief essay on monuments introduces a portfolio of lithographed designs from Italy, France, England, and America. "As the design of cemeteries is to provide family burial, not merely for the present, but for all succeeding generations, too much importance cannot be attached to the form and manner of the improvements made in them," he wrote, adding that the services of an architect should be sought. Monuments built to last, he added, ought to be composed of few pieces and never veneered. His plates depict pedestals, obelisks, columns (some whole, some broken, some topped with urns), and sarcophagi. There is an eclectic mix: some are Gothic, most classical (Greek and Roman), one Egyptian. He reproduces American designs by the stone mason John Struthers and the architect John Notman, both of Philadelphia, the architect Russell Warren of Rhode Island, and others. "A great change is perceptible in the style and elegance of the monuments put up in America since the founding of rural cemeteries," he wrote. "This taste has been improved by employing the best architects to make designs, very few persons having had any guide in the shape of engravings to direct their views."[13]

In his *Original Designs in Monumental Art*, a series of lithographs that began to appear in 1851, the Boston (later New York) architect Paul Schulze (1827–97) provided a rather more sophisticated visual guide to the design of funereal monuments. In his brief text (Schulze was an architect not an author) he remarked on the neglected opportunity the new attitude presented, and in his plates offered a large collection of headstones, railings, and monuments in the form of Gothic, classical, and Baroque obelisks, columns (some broken), sarcophagi, crosses, *aediculae,* and canopies, some with and some without sculptural embellishment.[14] Schulze's plates tower in sophistication above those of Smith (fig. 70). How many of his designs were actually realized remains to be seen, but they did have an impact. The Boston Public Library scrapbook of Billings's projects, some of which were erected, strongly resembles Schulze's gatherings.

Mount Auburn in Cambridge was dedicated in 1831 as the earliest of the

ELEVATION.

HALF GROUND PLAN.

Fig. 70. B. W. Thayer
lithograph from Paul
Schulze, *Original Designs
in Monumental Art,* 1851
(Fine Arts Department,
Boston Public Library,
courtesy of the Trustees
of the Boston Public
Library).

rural cemeteries in America.[15] With its founding the deceased "would lie in his own grave, with a monument to mark it, and cared for by the [Massachusetts] Horticultural Society."[16] Billings knew the grounds well. In an illustrated article in the *Boston Almanac* for 1857, he not only touted Mount Auburn's touristic potential but criticized many of the prominent features of the Cambridge site, finding Jacob Bigelow's Gate and Chapel, as well as the Tower, far below his aesthetic standards. "A visit to Mount Auburn," he wrote, "is one of the indispensables to a stranger sojourning in or near Boston, and few places present . . . a more varied combination of elements to attract attention and awaken thought." But, he continued, it "is not the sole illustration of the fact that something beside[s] good intention is necessary to do honor to the dead in imperishable forms; but there is here, perhaps, a greater variety of inconsistencies, a more unlimited display of fancy, caprice, or whatever . . . than in most other great cemeteries." Great art requires unity of thought, he wrote, a harmony of the parts to the whole, but at Mount Auburn "this is entirely lost. The visitor passes from one [monument] to another, struck with equal astonishment at the bizarre fancies which meet his eye at every turn." He found something to praise in two architectural and two sculptural monuments, those for the Sharp and Knight families, and those for the Magoun household and Nathaniel Bowditch. The former was a Gothic pinnacle of a type he had already used elsewhere (and did he indeed design it?), while the latter two were primarily sculptural. Although he wished for a "decent pedestal" for the Bowditch memorial, he called Robert Ball Hughes's 1847 figure "the best statue of its kind in America," perhaps because the seated figure holding a book reminded him of, and indeed perhaps inspired, a similar figure he created in 1854 on his National Monument to the Forefathers at Plymouth.[17]

There are among Billings's designs for funereal monuments in the Boston Public Library scrapbook projects for markers that are sculptural, such as the figure of Faith dated 1870, but despite his admiration for the Sharp and Bowditch memorials at Mount Auburn, the majority of Billings's cemetery monuments were primarily architectural rather than sculptural, even when they contained figural embellishment. His Tuckerman monument at Mount Auburn contains a portrait; his Shaw monument in the same cemetery holds an ancient relief; his Phillips memorial sports decorative heads; and his Damon column is topped by a capital carved with the symbols of the four Evangelists, but all are primarily architectural in design, and while he did create religious figures, he seems never to have incorporated those secular and overtly

Fig. 71. Ink and graphite drawing by Hammatt Billings of the Robert Gould Shaw monument, Mount Auburn Cemetery, 1848 (Fine Arts Department, Boston Public Library, courtesy of the Trustees of the Boston Public Library).

sentimental or narrative sculptural elements so common to nineteenth-century grave markers.[18] His work in this field, as in his architecture in general, progresses from the classical to the eclectic. He must have thought of this body of work as a corrective to the "unlimited display of fancy" he abhorred in other markers in Mount Auburn Cemetery. Considering the wide variety of his own funereal designs, we might not completely agree that he succeeded.

His early apprenticeship with the classicists Asher Benjamin and Ammi B. Young is reflected in one of his earliest dated monuments, that dedicated to

Robert Gould Shaw at Mount Auburn, a drawing for which appears in the library scrapbook (fig. 71). Shaw (1776–1853) had an estimated worth of $1.5 million in 1852, a staggering sum that placed him among the eighteenth richest men in the commonwealth at a time when $100,000 was a large fortune.[19] He was a merchant and philanthropist, and grandfather of the Civil War hero of the same name who is remembered in Augustus Saint Gaudens's masterful relief facing the Massachusetts State House in Boston.[20] Billings gave this fifteen-foot grave marker the form of an Ionic marble and brownstone *aedicula* enclosing a Greco-Roman relief of the first century B.C. imported by Shaw from Athens.[21] It stands on a prominent site facing Bigelow Chapel and Martin Milmore's later sphinx, and bears the date 1848, a full five years before Shaw's death.[22]

Billings designed a huge classical memorial for Jonathan Phillips (1778–1860) in association with Gridley J. F. Bryant, as we know from a photograph of a wooden model of it in the library scrapbook (fig. 72).[23] Phillips was a Harvard-educated businessman and state politician, estimated to be worth $1 million in 1852.[24] His impressive monument took the form of a sarcophagus resting on a high rectangular pedestal (fig. 73). As we see in the model it was to have been embellished with wreaths, stars, swags, leaves, and heads. The executed version, a dense gray granite pile more than twenty feet in height, omits the decorations on the pedestal, but the sarcophagus itself is surrounded by neoclassical and neo-Egyptian heads of a type similar to those Billings was using on Bryant buildings downtown.[25] The Phillips monument has a commanding presence near the main entrance to the cemetery, above the circular garden to the north of Jacob Bigelow's chapel. A more ornamental version of this type of memorial is shown in a sketch of a draped and beflowered coffin atop an inscribed pedestal within a symbolic enclosure of corner blocks and low iron fence. It too is among the designs in the Public Library scrapbook.

Billings provided a classical *tempietto* for Robert Shaw as a fitting setting for his antique relief and a classical sarcophagus for Jonathan Phillips, but he

Fig. 73. Hammatt Billings for G. J. F. Bryant, Jonathan Phillips monument, ca. 1860 (photo by Cervin Robinson, © 1996).

also designed memorials for Mount Auburn in medieval and Gothic styles. His monument to Joseph Tuckerman (1778–1840) is signed on the base by both the designer and the sculptor, Joseph Carew of Cambridge and Boston. Although Carew's low-relief profile of the deceased was inspired by classical work, the monument itself is in color, silhouette, and details more medieval than antique (fig. 74). Tuckerman, that "pioneer in American social work," was a sickly Unitarian clergyman who devoted the last decade and a half of his life to ministering to the unchurched poor of Boston. His monument is a rectangular block of brownstone inscribed on three sides, with the profile portrait signed "J Carew" on the front beneath a gently curving hip "roof" carved into faux slates.[26]

Billings's 1857 *Almanac* sketches of Mount Auburn may have been in preparation for a major addition to the embellishment of Cambridge's garden of graves in the form of the tomb of J. B. Whall he designed for Gridley Bryant in 1858 (fig. 75). It stood on the garden circle beneath the Bigelow chapel near the Phillips sarcophagus. It was more architecture than mere monument: in plan a Latin cross twenty-three by twenty-eight feet, in mass a vaulted structure in the "early pointed Gothic" according to a contemporary description, with transepts "arranged in tiers as receptacles for the dead." It could accommodate eighteen bodies. Despite Billings's criticism of the disharmony among the various markers at Mount Auburn, his neighboring Phillips and Whall monuments only added to the cacophony. As the writer of an item in the *Mt. Auburn Memorial* noted, "the contrast between the older tombs and this modern one is most striking."[27]

Also designed for Gridley Bryant was Hammatt's 1858 monument to the Brewer family prominently placed near the chapel in Mount Auburn (fig. 76). The occasion for the memorial was the death at age fifteen of Gardner Brewer (1842–57), son of Gardner (1806–74) and Mary Weld Brewer (1804–88).[28] The elder Gardner was a member of the firm of Sayles, Merriam, and Brewer, "one of the oldest and most extensive commission houses in Boston," a man estimated to be worth four hundred thousand dollars in 1852.[29] The *Boston Evening Transcript* for 31 August 1859 rhapsodized over this work. Its ecstatic account notices "with pride and pleasure in each succeeding visit to this beautiful city of the dead, that there at least the noblest feelings of gratitude and respect for departed friends, beautify the resting place of loved ones, and there it is that true Art finds employment." The editors call the Brewer monument "the most beautiful temple [*sic*] yet erected in the cemetery," and it alone "is worth a visit to Mount Auburn." Billings's

Fig. 74. Hammatt Billings and Joseph Carew, Joseph Tuckerman monument, Mount Auburn Cemetery, 1840s (photo by Cervin Robinson, © 1996).

design was "in the Italian gothic style of the Cathedral of Milan, so admirable for its airy and lovely composition."[30]

The Brewer monument is of a type that Billings had first studied as early as 1845, as we know from a sketch so dated in the Boston Public Library scrapbook. At young Brewer's death the designer must have dusted off this

Fig. 75. Hammatt Billings for G. J. F. Bryant, J. B. Whall tomb, Mount Auburn Cemetery, 1858 (Mount Auburn Cemetery).

pen-and-ink drawing of a Gothic tabernacle, slightly altered it, and offered it to the family. As erected, it is about twenty feet high and, again according to the *Transcript*, "wrought in white Italian marble, by Richard Barry," whose name is inscribed in the base. Barry executed many other monuments in Mount Auburn, and he was to work elsewhere for Billings. The stone monument was richly worked. The paper gives a minutely detailed description, noting the "highly ornate" carved floral design of the crown molding of the base, the "*feulletted* pannels [*sic*]," containing on the front simply the word "Brewer," the capitals with "vines and scrolls," the "four gothic pointed arches highly decorated," the pinnacles and crockets, and the whole "crowned with an octagon[al] spire and finial of an Eternal Cross." The cruciform terminal is now missing, and the stone weatherworn after nearly a century and a half, but the work still impresses as a relic of a past attitude toward interment.

The Italian Gothic element Billings introduced for the sketch adopted for the Brewer monument continued in his work for Mount Auburn after the Civil War, when it combined with the richness of contemporary eclecticism.

Fig. 76. Hammatt Billings, Gardner Brewer monument, Mount Auburn Cemetery, 1858 (photo by Cervin Robinson, © 1996).

Other projects began to assume rustic shapes. Two unidentified drawings (one apparently for the Hanson family) of 1871 in the Public Library scrapbook exhibit the latter characteristics, for example, while the monument erected to the memory of John Wade Damon (1792–1863), designed in August 1869, displays a rich assortment of motifs (fig. 77). The original setting and immediate vicinity of the monument have been altered over time, but the Damon shaft itself is preserved. It rises some thirty feet into the air. A rectangular base embellished at the corners with colonnettes supports a column surmounted by a pinnacle in the form of a miniature church spire. The column is belted a third of the way up its height with vertical grooves below. Its capital is enriched by carved corner symbols of the Evangelists.[31]

Billings also memorialized deceased members of families and organizations not interred at Mount Auburn. For the estate of the Yale-educated merchant Edmund Dwight (1780–1849), a founder of Chicopee and Holyoke, Massachusetts, as well as of the American Antiquarian Society in Worcester and president of the Western Railroad, a man who reportedly left nine hundred thousand dollars at his death, Billings created in 1851 a Gothic monument and landscape setting in Forest Hills, Jamaica Plain.[32] Its location is on Walnut Avenue in an originally "sheltered nook with a pleasant sunny aspect, and back of it rises the steep, high rock, its summit crowned with shrubs." The rock is Roxbury puddingstone; the summit now supports a water tower. The plot was defined on the sides by "thickly-growing pines" and in the front by a "heavy and beautiful balustrade of [brown]stone and bronze." The monument itself is a brownstone pinnacle some fifteen feet tall composed of an octagonal pointed arcade resting on a base and surmounted by a crocketed spire.[33] The Public Library scrapbook contains plans, elevations, and a perspective of this design.

The Cushman monument on Burying Hill in Plymouth, a twenty-seven-and-one-half-foot obelisk of Quincy granite erected in 1858 is probably from a design by Billings. He memorialized less affluent clients as well. The *Boston Evening Transcript* for 16 July 1860 contains notice of the dedication, on the twenty-first, of the "Printers' Burial Lot" in Mount Hope Cemetery, Dorchester, a cemetery that, according to an 1852 account, "is calculated to be a blessing to the city generally, and afford a rural resting place as desirable as Mount Auburn, at a fifth of its cost."[34] The monument was designed by Billings and executed by the marble works of Richard Barry, who also executed the Brewer monument and many others in Mount Auburn. Officially the memorial of the Franklin Typographical Society and Boston Printers'

Fig. 77. Wash drawing by Hammatt Billings of the John Wade Damon monument, Mount Auburn Cemetery, 1869 (Fine Arts Department, Boston Public Library, courtesy of the Trustees of the Boston Public Library).

Union on Mt. Hope Avenue, this is a modest monument: a slender stone obelisk above a socle and stylobate, the whole some eighteen feet tall, surrounded by flat oval gravestones. Ornament is held to a minimum of classical motifs. The Boston Public Library scrapbook also contains a beautifully rendered late design for an obelisk embellished with incised Neo-Grec floral motifs. Notes indicate that the shaft was to be of polished red granite; the base, polished Quincy granite. It is dated April 1870 and was intended for Woodlawn Cemetery, presumably in Everett, but has not otherwise been identified.

This account of Billings's work on private memorials would not be complete without mention of the "Bowditch" or "Whittier" sundial. It was a minor task, one that demonstrates that little jobs were part of the life of a jack-of-all-designs who was always ready and willing to accommodate his patrons. Henry Ingersoll Bowditch (1808–92), physician and abolitionist, acquired in 1852 an English silver sundial face, which he had set into a copper disk engraved with the signs of the zodiac. Sometime between then and 1855 when he put it in place in his garden in Weston, a Boston suburb, he asked his friend, the poet John G. Whittier, for some verses, and Hammatt Billings, "whose taste I deem better than that of any other artist in our country for such a purpose . . . to engrave the motto and Whittier's initials" on the copper.[35] Here is another endorsement by one of Billings's Brahmin admirers.

There are in the Boston Public Library scrapbook three variant sketches for a wall-mounted memorial tablet dated 1870 and dedicated to the educator Thomas Sherwin (1799–1869) who had once been Billings's headmaster at English High.[36] This is a Ruskinian or Venetian gable on columns with inset trefoil tablet. Another sketch of 1873, and a flap over one of the earlier designs, changes this into a Civil War memorial crowned by the figure of Victory flanked by a soldier and a sailor (fig. 78). This switch from personal to patriotic memorial characterizes the scrapbook drawings as a whole. Among the designs are not only funereal projects from every decade of Billings's professional career, but a number of sketches from the late 1860s and early 1870s for individual and collective commemorations for those who fought for the Union. Some are identifiable and some are not, and not all his work in this category appears in this gathering. Billings as designer of public monuments appears in the early 1850s, the years in which the Union came increasingly under attack. As early as 1854 he proposed a colossal figure of Faith for Plymouth to commemorate the forefathers as figures of national focus. This was just one of other colossal monuments he proposed during

Fig. 78. Wash over
graphite drawing by
Hammatt Billings of a
Civil War monument,
1873 (Fine Arts
Department, Boston
Public Library, courtesy
of the Trustees of the
Boston Public Library).

this period, including an earlier one to Daniel Webster in Boston and a later
project to commemorate the Battle of Lexington. Only the Plymouth monument was erected, although it was altered, reduced, and delayed until after the
Civil War. Its long gestation and national importance require separate discussion (see chap. 9).

The earliest of the postwar memorials would have been the most prominent both in size and in location. In 1866 Hammatt, here as so often in
partnership with Bryant, won a competition among some thirty entrants for
the design of a memorial to be erected on Flagstaff Hill in Boston Common.[37] For this Soldiers and Sailors' Monument, Billings eschewed the co-

Fig. 79. Wash drawing
by Hammatt Billings for
an unrealized project for
a Soldiers and Sailors'
Monument, Boston
Common, 1866.
Hammatt Billings and
G. J. F. Bryant, architects
(Fine Arts Department,
Boston Public Library,
courtesy of the Trustees
of the Boston Public
Library).

lossal vision he had espoused for public memorials in the 1850s in favor of a
type that went back in this country at least to Robert Mills's Washington
Monument in Baltimore (1813–38); that is, a figure perched atop a column or
shaft. In this case Billings drew a cruciform base embellished with four
historiated reliefs elevated on a stylobate cornered by what look like sarcophagi and supporting an inscribed *aedicula*, which itself upholds a Doric
column enriched with fascies (fig. 79). This is in turn surmounted by a
twenty-foot standing figure of Liberty leaning on her sheathed sword with a
palm branch in her right hand and in her left holding a laurel wreath above
her head. The overall height was to be 120 feet. A rather large drawing exists

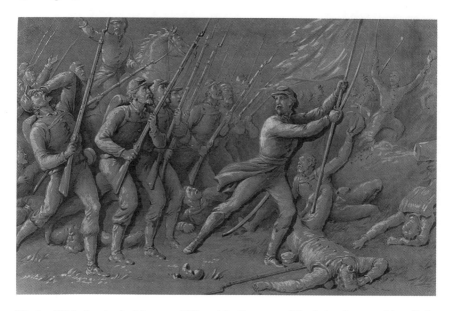

Fig. 80. Wash drawing by Hammatt Billings, *The Charge*, 1866. The design for one of the reliefs on the Soldiers and Sailors' Monument, Boston (Corcoran Gallery of Art, Washington, D.C., Museum Purchase, Membership Association Fund, 1951).

for one of the base reliefs. *The Charge* is a spirited scene of Union troops sweeping left to right following their standard bearer over the bodies of fallen enemy (fig. 80).[38] It is a reworking of motifs Billings had first drawn in the 1840s as illustrations of the Mexican War.

Although the foundations for the Soldiers and Sailors' project were actually begun, the estimate of the cost at one hundred thousand dollars began to look unrealistic, and work was quickly halted.[39] Early in 1870 Billings apparently tried to offer a reduced monument, an alternate design that is preserved in the Boston Public Library scrapbook in a number of versions (fig. 81). All show a Union soldier upon a simpler column rising from a base; one is twenty-three feet high and two are dated 1870. *The Charge* reappears on one version. But this design apparently failed to impress the commissioners, for at the end of 1870 Martin Milmore won a second competition (Billings's second project may have been submitted to this competition), and the existing monument, erected from Milmore's design, was dedicated in 1877. Billings's presence on Flagstaff Hill was not entirely erased, however, as Milmore's monument clearly embodied many of his ideas as well as those of any number of other precedents, including monuments to Henry Clay in Lexington, Kentucky, and Stephen A. Douglas in Chicago.[40]

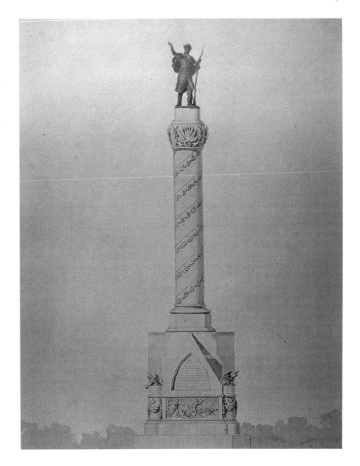

Billings had better results with his less-elaborate design for a war memorial in Concord, Massachusetts, also begun in 1866. His forty-nine-and-
one-half-foot Soldiers' Monument standing opposite the Town House is a
rough-faced Concord granite obelisk rising above an inscribed cubical base
(fig. 82).[41] The shaft is a stack of paired blocks, each tier oriented at ninety
degrees to those above and below; the pinnacle is of dressed stone. There are
many variations on this obelisk form in the Public Library scrapbook. Ralph
Waldo Emerson, a member of the building committee which "sought the assistance of an architect eminent for taste and skill," spoke at the dedication
on 19 April 1867.[42] He gave a rich, contemporary reading of such a work. "It is
a simple pile enough,—a few slabs of granite, dug just below the surface of
the soil, and laid upon the top of it, but as we have learned that the up-heaved
mountain, from which these discs or flakes were broken, was once a glowing

mass of white heat, . . . so the roots of the events it appropriately marks are in the heart of the universe." And he continued: "The art of the architect and the sense of the town have made these dumb stones speak. . . . 'T is certain that a plain stone like this, standing on such memories, . . . mixes with surrounding nature,—by day, with the changing seasons,—by night, the stars

Fig. 82. Hammatt Billings, Soldiers' Monument, Concord, Massachusetts, 1866 (Society for the Preservation of New England Antiquities).

roll over it gladly,—becomes a sentiment, a poet, a prophet, an orator, to every townsman and passenger, an altar where the noble youth shall in all time come to make his secret vows." It was a characteristic nineteenth-century analogy in which geological forces are harnessed to human meaning.[43]

The library scrapbook also contains four sketches dated between July 1873 and October 1874 that are variations on the design of a soldiers' memorial for Braintree, Massachusetts. The concept—the ubiquitous Union soldier standing at rest on a pedestal—existed by 27 June, when the town decided to erect a granite figure after a model submitted by Messrs. Batterson and Confield of Hartford on a pedestal designed by H. and J. E. Billings, "whose skill and judgement as architects stand in the foremost rank."[44] It was dedicated in June 1874 and is still there, one of the innumerable stone or metal Union soldiers on granite bases that grace town centers across New England.

When Billings was not hired to design the whole monument he might be chosen to embellish or to create just the base, as at Braintree and Boston. He was asked, for example, to provide a relief or reliefs for the base of Richard Greenough's 1855 statue of Franklin in front of (now Old) City Hall, Boston, a memorial sponsored by the Massachusetts Charitable Mechanic Association. This was a request he turned down, it seems, because the money was not right. In letters of 1854 Emerson mentions Billings as providing "the relief" for Greenough's statue.[45] A month later the designer received a letter from Robert C. Winthrop of the association, which reads in part:

> We were all sincerely desirous that the very best Boston talent should be employed in illustrating the career of our great Patriot-Philosopher & Mechanic, & we had earnestly hoped that you might have found it acceptable to furnish the designs for the Bas Reliefs. We were compelled, however, to propose it to you as a matter of business, as . . . the funds . . . did not afford us any too wide a margin for the work in hand. The Committee . . . have been extremely reluctant to abandon . . . the benefit of your pencil, but they are unwilling to press you further into a service for which you have conceived so decided a repugnance.[46]

The existing reliefs are signed by Greenough and Thomas Ball. Although he did not contribute to the creation of the statue, Billings did produce for *Ballou's* a view of its dedication as well as a view of the completed work.[47]

In 1867 Billings provided his old friend Thomas Ball with the design for the Quincy granite pedestal for his statue of Washington erected in the

Public Garden.[48] As early as April 1859 a committee of artists chaired by Benjamin Champney and including Hammatt Billings had resolved to raise funds for the erection of an equestrian statue of the Revolutionary War hero modeled by Thomas Ball.[49] Billings's decorations in the Boston Music Hall for a fair held in November to raise funds for the enterprise are discussed in chapter 10. In the wake of the Civil War, Billings was commissioned to provide a pedestal for the statue, a pedestal he seems to have created with one eye on Michelangelo's pedestal for the Marcus Aurelius on the Capitoline Hill in Rome. The ensemble dedicated in 1869 placed Ball's bronze equestrian general atop Billings's eighteen-foot-high Quincy granite base. At its unveiling Frank Leslie's newspaper called the base "beautiful in outline and majestic in general effect," but by 1881 Arthur Dexter was complaining that it was "too high; and the consequent foreshortening mars the effect of one of the finest works in our city."[50] Comments such as this show the early fading of Billings's historical presence.

The public and private memorials created by Billings demonstrate the range of his commemorative designs. Nothing seemed to have been beyond his attention; no period in his career seems to have been without works of memorial art; no commission seems to have been too opulent or too small for his talents. He saved the major part of his energy in this department of art, however, for his "great design," his vision of a colossal figure of Faith to commemorate the landing of the Pilgrims at Plymouth. It was to occupy his time from early in the 1850s until his death in 1874.

9

"Well Calculated to Promote Fraternal Feeling"

The National Monument to the Forefathers

THE NATIONAL Monument to the Forefathers at Plymouth, Massachusetts, is Hammatt Billings's largest and most complex commemorative design. He conceived it in the early 1850s, and much reduced, it was finished and dedicated in the late 1880s, well after his death. One of a number of colossal monuments designed by Billings at midcentury, it was the only one to come to any sort of fruition. Although not fully realized as he conceived it, this is the best documented of Billings's many works, and it reflects in essential ways his role as interpreter of public sentiment at the height of his career. The study of the history of the Forefathers Monument can tell us much about the design, meaning, and fate of what was intended in the mid-nineteenth century to be among the most significant of national memorials. It can thus tell us much about nineteenth-century American culture.[1]

The Forefathers Monument is an 81-foot apparition of solid Hallowell granite composed of a 36-foot figure of Faith bestride an octagonal, 45-foot pedestal surrounded by seated 15-foot figures of Liberty, Education, Law, and Morality. *Faith* is a large-featured, 180-ton, classically draped female who stands with one foot on a representation of Plymouth Rock (fig. 83). She holds a Bible in her left hand and points heavenward with her right.[2] Her only other significant attribute is a single star above her forehead. The heroic ancillary figures, each weighing 20 to 25 tons, are seated on diagonal buttresses. *Liberty* (fig. 84) is a carapaced male wearing a helmet, draped with a lion's skin, cradling a sword in his right arm, and holding a broken chain in his left hand. Small figures on the sides of his chair represent Peace (woman holding a cornucopia) and Tyranny (king laid low). On his pedestal is a relief depicting the landing of the Pilgrims. *Education* is a draped woman

Fig. 83. Hammatt Billings and others, National Monument to the Forefathers, Plymouth, Massachusetts, 1854–89 (photo by Cervin Robinson, © 1994).

Fig. 84. J. H. Mahoney after Hammatt Billings, *Liberty* (detail of the National Monument to the Forefathers), 1888. The relief is of the *Landing of the Pilgrims* (photo by Cervin Robinson, © 1994).

pointing to a book in her lap. The small figures on her chair represent Wisdom (bearded man with book and globe) and Youth (woman and child). The relief on her pedestal depicts the signing of the Mayflower compact. *Law* is a draped male also holding a book. His chair is supported by *Mercy* (draped orante) and *Justice* (woman with scales and sword). *The Treaty with the*

Fig. 85. J. H. Mahoney after Hammatt Billings, *Treaty with the Indians* (relief on the National Monument to the Forefathers), 1888 (photo by Cervin Robinson, © 1994).

Indians is shown in relief (fig. 85). *Morality,* finally, is a woman holding a book inscribed "God" who sits above a relief showing the embarkation from Delft-Haven. Her chair contains small figures representing an Evangelist (writing in a book) and a prophet (Moses holding the tablets of the Law and looking to heaven). There is no mistaking the meaning of any of this, for the name of each figure is clearly inscribed in the stone.

There are also inscribed panels, two of which list the names of the passengers on the *Mayflower.* The principal text bears this dedication: National / Monument / to the / Forefathers / Erected / by a / Grateful People / in Remembrance of / Their / Labors, Sacrifices / and Sufferings / for the / Cause of Civil / and / Religious Liberty.

In Plymouth today it is the "1620" Rock beneath its 1920 McKim, Mead, and White—designed setting that is the aim of the modern pilgrim as it has long been popularly assumed to have been the point of landing of the original Pilgrims. Before the early nineteenth century no such honored site was in evidence. In the eighteenth century the Rock was embedded in a wharf. It gained some attention in the Revolutionary era, for in 1774 an attempt was made to free it that resulted in its splitting in two (this was seen as an omen of separation from England). The lower part was left in place, the upper moved to Town Square where it stood in casual display until 1834 when it was again moved, this time to a fenced place of honor in front of the new uptown hall of the Pilgrim Society. In 1880 it was rejoined to its lower half at the present site.[3]

Colonial indifference to the landing was replaced in the early nineteenth century by a veneration of the past born of growing national self-consciousness. The placement of part of the Rock in front of Pilgrim Hall was no accident. The Pilgrim Society was founded during the bicentennial anniversary of the landing for the express purpose of providing "a plot for the erection of a monument to perpetuate the virtues, the enterprise, and the unparalleled suffering of the ancestors."[4] But realization took time. Thirty years later, in May 1850, with few funds on hand, the society was still talking, still resolving "to erect a monument on or near the Rock."[5] With the advent of midcentury, the plan began to take on a more definite shape.

Word of the Pilgrim Society's 1850 resolution to erect a monument seems to have reached Portsmouth, New Hampshire, by early the next year, for in a note to the *Boston Weekly Museum* in January 1851 the Reverend Rufus Wheelwright Clark (1813–66) of that city wrote that "if the monument should bear any proportion to the singularity of the event which it would . . . commemorate, it would tower above all similar works . . . in our country. Let us erect . . . a monument of New-England granite, which, like the hopes of the Pilgrims, shall ascend to the skies, pointing heavenward." Apparently before a designer had begun to work, then, three essential characteristics of the monument as erected had been proposed: its colossal size, its native material, and its upward point. Since the Reverend Clark mentions no figure, however, he probably had in mind a column or obelisk to rival those previously dedicated to Washington and the Revolution in Boston and Baltimore or Washington, D.C. In any event, a note a year later in the *Boston Transcript* explicitly made such a connection: "It is proposed," it said, "to erect upon that portion of the . . . Rock which still remains at the water's side . . . a towering column of granite which shall only be exceeded in its dimensions by that now erecting at Washington."[6] Where the unidentified writer found this (mis)information is unknown.

These references make it certain that there were minds at work on the proper form for a memorial at Plymouth from very early in the decade, but in fact it was not until June 1853 that the trustees of the society appointed a committee "to advertise for the plan of a monument on or over Plymouth Rock & offer $100 premium for approved design," and that proposal having met with some difficulty in committee, it was not until the meeting in July 1854 that the society's president was authorized "to obtain plans for a monument, and submit same with estimates to the Board."[7] The premium was now set at three hundred dollars. In what we shall see was a significant provision, the trustees reserved the right to refuse all proposals. A call for submissions appeared in the *Boston Transcript* (and probably other papers, including those in New York) in August, and by November the trustees had in hand proposals from "Schultz," "A. Noury," and "Bond" of Boston, as well as "Asboth & Zucker" and another, unnamed entrant from New York.

These projects stemmed from architects about whom we know all too little. Richard Bond had designed Gore Hall in the Gothic style and the Italianate Lawrence Scientific School for Harvard College in the 1830s and 1840s. "Schultz" was probably Paul Schulze who was soon to win the competition to build Harvard's new Appleton Chapel.[8] More important, he was in the 1850s publishing a series of designs for funereal and other monuments. They are largely architectural with some secondary sculptural embellishment. Noury appears in Boston directories for 1853 in association with one E. A. Launay. He was probably the André Noury described as the "unknown French architect" who provided the preliminary plans for the Boston Theater of 1854.[9] Alexander Sandor Asboth (1811–68), a Hungarian patriot, had studied engineering and fought with Louis Kossuth. Asboth fought again for the Union during the Civil War and died (as the result of battle wounds) as U.S. Minister to the Argentine Republic.[10] Gerhard Zucker remains a shadowy figure.[11]

With the exception of Asboth and Zucker's, we know nothing about the submitted proposals. We know little enough about Asboth's. When the projects were received the trustees voted to ask the partners for "more accurate information concerning the nature of the material suggested ['zinc &c for images']," and at a later meeting, on 20 December, when "Col. Asboth" was said to be "entitled to the premium," some members still wanted more information and alternative designs with and without "allegorical & other decorative figures." If the proposed monument could stand without these figures, it too must have been largely architectural with secondary sculptural accents, rather than anthropomorphous. Judging from the designs in Schulze's portfolios this was perhaps also true of the other proposals.

Despite the fact that it does not appear in the trustees' minutes at this point, there was one more proposal in the works. Since early 1854 Hammatt Billings had been thinking about a Forefathers Monument that was very different from those predominately architectural designs. In a letter to Billings of 26 March 1854 Catharine Beecher, whose sister's *Uncle Tom's Cabin* Billings had illustrated just two years earlier, wrote that she had "heard your . . . time was to be given to *your great design*" after completing other work in hand.[12] By the end of May, a full three months before the Pilgrim Society's call for proposals appeared in the Boston papers, that "great design" had advanced far enough for its creator to describe it to Winslow Warren of the Pilgrim Society. In a letter to Billings of the first of June, Warren acknowledged receipt of the proposal (this communication apparently does not survive) but noted that the trustees "are not at present authorized to act . . . upon . . . any particular design," although they would soon call for ideas. He went on to caution Billings, however, that the trustees had been charged to erect the monument on or near the Rock, and that the magnitude and cost of his project would mean its rejection as evidence suggested that the public would not contribute money for "structures of this sort." Warren was clearly referring to the problems and delays experienced by the Bunker Hill and Washington Monuments. And he was also clearly referring to a proposal for a monument that was great in size and removed from the Rock, and this suggests that Billings's concept was generally formed between March and May 1854, for it conforms in these particulars to what was finally accepted.

In his resistance to Billings's showy project Warren may have been reflecting, among more generally suspicious Protestant attitudes toward figural plastic art, a specifically local prejudice. At least according to the sculptor Horatio Greenough (1805–52) New England balked at grandeur. "I have just finished a colossal bust of Franklin," he wrote on 25 February 1839, "which I think of sending to Philadelphia or New York, as I find you Bostonians are not fond of the colossal."[13] Answering Winslow Warren two days after hearing from him, Billings began a yearlong campaign to overcome such resistance, to win the commission for a colossal figure by explicitly linking the monument along a continuum between a heroic past, an indebted present, and a thankful future. He insisted that the descendants of the Pilgrims think "no monument can be on a scale of too great grandeur, nor can it be made too imperishable, to express to the full the sense of obligation which is felt

towards them, and the grateful affection with which their memory is cherished." As to cost, he continued, "certainly it is within the means of a nation
of twenty three million of freemen to erect such a memorial as shall convey to
a . . . remote posterity the memory of this event, characterized by Mr. [Dan-
iel] Webster as 'the greatest in our history.'" Having evoked the memory of
the region's late, great, orator and statesman, he asked for permission to
present his ideas to the full committee, to counter the impression that his
scheme was "little less than Quixotic."

Nothing of Billings's argument was original; it was, rather, common
enough in the period among those who favored erecting memorials (there
were, of course, others who did not). In his letter to Warren, Billings seems
to draw upon ideas expressed at least as early as 1819 in an article on a
proposed Scottish national monument in *Blackwood's Edinburgh Magazine*. It
remains to be seen whether he read the original paper or encountered its
ideas as reechoed and amplified by others. Nationalism, filiopietism, and the
continuity of past events with future hopes are all expressed by the author,
who was the younger Archibald Alison (1792–1867). The monument, Alison
asserts, is "best suited to animate the exertions of her [Scotland's] remotest
descendants . . . it will stand at once the monument of former greatness, and
the pledge of future glory."[14]

Five days after his note to Warren, in a letter of 8 June 1854 to an unnamed recipient (probably the Plymouth antiquarian William Russell), Billings began to apply what must have been formidable powers of persuasion
in defense of his design and its projected price against Warren's objections.
"As the grandeur of the proposed mon[umen]t would be the great part upon
which I should rely in addressing the public mind, & costliness is a mere
matter of circumstance to be taken into consideration, not by itself, but in
connection with many others," he needed to show the design to the trustees.
And to this end he was having made a model, which, on the twelfth in a letter
to Richard Warren of the society, he said will probably be ready about the
first of July. "Much depends upon the energy and system with which the
public is addressed," he wrote. "The success of any design, is predicated upon
the effect which its magnitude and grandeur will have in awakening the
feeling of the Public and in the method by which I propose to collect the
funds." By the late spring of 1854, then, Billings had a design in hand and a
scheme in mind for raising the funds necessary to erect it, and he wanted to
meet the trustees to show off his model and explain his proposal. Meanwhile, he began to enlist powerful political support outside of Plymouth by

proposing to show the model to Gov. John H. Clifford. Clifford was then honorary president of the Massachusetts Academy of Fine Arts, a short-lived Boston artists' club of which Billings was a director.[15] All of this, it should be remembered, occurred before the trustees voted definitively to advertise for proposals! Billings had clearly heard tell of the project from contacts close to the Pilgrim Society.

By the end of 1854 Asboth's design had been premiated and early in February 1855 he asked the committee to appoint him architect of the monument. But at this point the names of Asboth and Billings, which had not previously appeared in the trustees' minutes, crossed paths. At their February meeting the trustees authorized a letter to Asboth informing him they were not ready to appoint an architect, and that, although he was entitled to the premium, they did not feel bound to erect his design. They then appointed a committee to confer with Billings about his proposal. Two weeks later, on 27 February, Billings appeared before the trustees (although no model is mentioned in the minutes, it can be assumed that it was presented at this time). Billings's lobbying had paid off.

The trustees' minutes for 28 May 1855 describe Asboth and Zucker as "two Hungarian gentlemen of New York." In an undated, unsigned, and un-addressed letter in Billings's handwriting preserved at the Pilgrim Society that must stem from this time, Billings wrote that he felt "that the honor of the country is somewhat concerned in the affair, and that as it is to be a National Mon[umen]t it should be the work of a native artist." Billings might claim John Howland of the *Mayflower* as his ancestor, and he here seems to use the xenophobic prejudices of the contemporary Know-Nothings to promote his cause.[16] Billings's politics are not completely understood, but evidence suggests his sympathy, at least, with the Whigs.[17] And as we shall see, Billings's monument seems to reflect political ideals that were Whiggishly inclined, at least as those ideals were dedicated to Union-saving as championed by Daniel Webster and Edward Everett, among others. In any event, this nativist appeal also worked. In March Asboth and Zucker were voted the three-hundred-dollar premium, paid, and, in effect, dismissed. In early April the trustees named a committee to negotiate with Billings, and on 23 May 1855 the two parties signed a contract for not one but two monuments, a document that also gave Billings the authority to solicit the funds necessary for their erection. His triumph was complete.

Billings, it seems, thought the site for the monument on or near the Rock stipulated by the society, while it had historical validity, offered little as an appropriate venue for his grand vision. He therefore split the society's proposal in two. The contract called, on the one hand, for a "mon[umen]t of granite decorated with four bronze statues" to be erected "over or upon" the Rock and to be completed within three years of 1 August 1856. This was to comply with the society's wishes to commemorate the landing at its putative site. But the contract also called for a second, more imposing monument, Billing's "great design." He was to erect on land he would select in Plymouth within one-half mile of the Rock, and which he would donate to the Pilgrim Society, the National Monument to the Forefathers, "a plan and complete description and specifications of which accompany this document" (but now seem to be lost). It was to be completed within twelve years. Billings was appointed architect and superintendent, with the authority to solicit and receive subscriptions for these works in the name of the Pilgrim Society.

The designer hired the Reverend Willard M. Harding (d. 1880) as the general and financial agent for fund-raising for the Forefathers Monument. Expenses were estimated at $300,000. Money would be solicited in a nationwide, grassroots effort through a system of state or regional representatives. Premiums were offered for donations. In the original proposal of 1855 every contributor would receive a certificate printed from a steel plate. Donations of $5.00 would earn a steel engraving of the monument and a life membership in the Pilgrim Society (fig. 86). A donation of $50.00 added a bronze medal to the engraving.[18] A 20-inch bronze statuette (fig. 87) was offered for $100.00, a 30-inch statuette of bronze and silver for $500.00, and a 36-inch statuette for $1,000.00.[19]

As we shall see, funds came in slowly and were significantly disrupted by the Civil War. Nonetheless, these cast and engraved premiums insured a broad distribution of knowledge about the appearance of Billings's colossal monument. And we know Billings's first design for the National Monument to the Forefathers from such sources. In his letter of 8 June 1854 he wrote that he had a small, sketchy model of the project that was unsatisfactory and that he had made arrangements to have made "one much larger & finish it perfectly before exhibiting it to the Public." He thought it would be ready by the first of July. This may well be the "miniature model . . . by J. A. Jackson" that was exhibited two years later at the Fair of the Massachusetts Mechanic Charitable Association, and that may well be the approximately 7-foot-high plaster model of the monument that once stood in Pilgrim Hall and is now housed in the Plymouth Public Library.[20] John Adams Jackson (1825–79) was a Boston sculptor who returned from a European sojourn in 1854. We know from documents at the Pilgrim Society that he modeled the smaller metal statuettes of the monument that went for premiums to donors to the cause, but these documents stem from 1857–58, so the model exhibited in 1856 cannot have been one of them.[21] The second source of our knowledge of

Fig. 86. Steel engraving by Rawdon, Wight, Hatch, and Edson after Hammatt Billings, Pilgrim Society Certificate, copyright 1856 (author's collection).

the original design is the series of engraved views of the monument that began to be published soon after the signing of the contract. These disagree with one another in details—suggesting that in some particulars the design was still in flux—but, with the accompanying description, they provide us with a generally accurate conception of Billings's original proposal. The

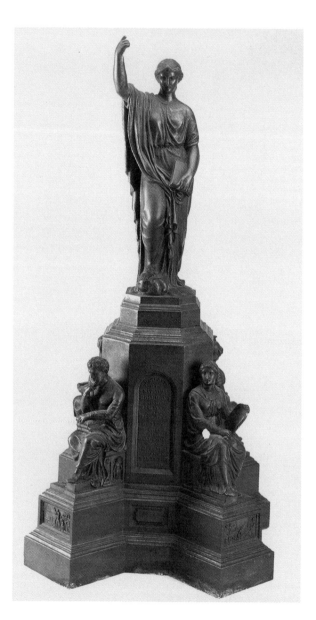

Fig. 87. John Adams Jackson after Hammatt Billings, premium statuette of the National Monument to the Forefathers, 1857–67 (The Frances Lehman Loeb Art Center, Vassar College, gift of Henry-Russell Hitchcock, in honor of Agnes Rindge Claflin).

statues and the engraved premiums make it certain that Billings's design was to produce a more graceful and lithe figural composition than that finally achieved nearly a quarter of a century later.

The primary figure in Billings's proposal represented Faith (or the "Spirit of Religion" in some early descriptions). As depicted in an engraving published in 1856 in the *Illustrated Magazine,* she conforms in most details, excepting those of her drapery, with the statue modeled by Jackson and the view on engraved certificates copyrighted 1 September 1855. The magazine describes an immense monument: a 70-foot granite figure rising above an 83-foot base. She stands "upon a rock, holding in her left hand an open Bible, while the other hand is uplifted towards heaven." That was intended as an oratorical gesture: "Looking downward, as to those she is addressing, she seems to call them to trust in a higher power."[22] The 40-foot ancillary figures, "emblematic of the principles upon which the Pilgrim Fathers proposed to found their Commonwealth," were *Morality, Law, Education,* and *Freedom.* The inscribed panels were to be of "porphyry, serpentine, or other hard stone" and the inscriptions inlaid with white marble. The project called for reliefs depicting the departure from Delft-Haven, the signing of the social compact in the cabin of the *Mayflower,* the landing at Plymouth, and the first treaty with the Indians, all of white marble. (We might expect to find the first Thanksgiving depicted on such a monument, but while it was an important feast day in Massachusetts at the time, it did not gain its current national prestige until the presidency of Abraham Lincoln.)[23] The base would contain a chamber, twenty-four feet in diameter, with stone staircase leading to a platform at the feet of *Faith* from which local landmarks might be viewed.[24] This description of Billings's proposal contains characteristics not found in the monument as erected. In the event, Liberty replaced Freedom among the principles of the Pilgrims; *Law* lost his beard, some of his books, and his thoughtful posture; the design of the chairs upon which the allegorical figures are seated changed; and the entrance, interior room, and viewing platform were eliminated. In addition, the rock upon which *Faith* stands became (early on in the evolution of the work) Plymouth Rock, an emphasized feature that required a change in her stance and other changes in her drapery.[25] But more significantly, the existing 81-foot memorial, as overbearing as it is, scarcely measures up to the colossal 153-foot overall height of Billings's proposal. The monument as erected is big, but the original conception had the dimensions to stir the blood.

Which was, of course, the point. Billings wrote as much in his letter to the trustees. He had carefully measured his monument against the colossi of history. The first published descriptions said it was intended to be "the grandest work of the kind in the world." "In magnitude . . . [it was to] far exceed any monumental structure of modern times, and . . . equal those stupendous works of the Egyptians."[26] According to the *Illustrated Magazine* of 1856, *Faith* was to be "larger than any known statue, excepting that of the great Ramses . . . and the Colossus of Rhodes; and the sitting figures . . . nearly equal in size to the two statues of Ramses in the plain of Luxor." In 1860 appeared the *Illustrated Pilgrim Almanac,* sold "in Aid of the Monument Fund," with a series of engravings after drawings by Billings of ancient and modern colossi including the Colossus of Rhodes, a marvel of the third century B.C., and Giovanni Battista Crespi's early seventeenth-century San Carlo Borromeo on the Lago Maggiore, some 70-feet high on a 37-foot pedestal (fig. 88). Billings tied his monument to this colossal tradition. He must have thought a huge figure better embodied his ideas than a huge column or obelisk, although he was certainly aware that both existed as precedent. Billings conceived the first colossal figure to be eventually erected (however reduced) in the United States, although Bartholdi's Statue of Liberty has precedence of dedication.

When Billings began to think about a monument to the forefathers there were two outstanding national memorials for him to study: the Bunker Hill obelisk in Boston and the Washington Monument in the District of Columbia. Begun in the 1820s but not finished because of difficulties with fundraising until 1843, Solomon Willard's 220-foot granite shaft celebrated a memorable Boston battle of the Revolutionary War.[27] Billings knew it well for he had provided a drawing for an engraving of it for the *Boston Miscellany* in 1842, and he must have known of the long struggle to raise monies for its erection, for Richard Frothingham, to another of whose books Billings had contributed an illustration, told its history just before Billings began work on the Forefathers project.[28] As historian John Seelye has pointed out, Plymouth's Forefathers Monument was intended to rival that on Boston's Bunker Hill.[29]

The Washington Monument took even longer to erect. Thinking about it began in the mid-1830s, but Robert Mills's project for a 600-foot obelisk rising through a Greek Doric circular colonnade was not accepted until 1845. The cornerstone was placed in 1848, but work ceased from lack of funds in 1856, and the monument was not finished (without the intended colonnade) until well after the Civil War.[30] It was a controversial design from the mo-

JULY.

Fig. 88. Wood engraving after Hammatt Billings, *San Carlo Borromeo* by G. B. Crespi, from *The Illustrated Pilgrim Almanac*, 1860 (Special Collections, Clapp Library, Wellesley College).

ment of its publication, and like the Bunker Hill obelisk, was of a type Billings consciously sought to avoid for his Plymouth memorial. The *Boston Transcript* of 26 February 1850 published a letter opposing a federal grant-in-aid for the Washington Monument, which it called a national disgrace for the usual reason that it mixed incompatible styles (the eclecticism of the post–Civil War era was rarely condoned in the first half of the century). Hammatt Billings was among the many Boston architects, painters, and sculptors who signed the statement, so he must have been gratified when in December 1855 he received a letter from the architect Charles A. Alexander (1827–88), another signatory who was then resident in Portland, Maine, praising his proposed monument for Plymouth. Alexander urged that it be widely published so the public might "see the contrast between it and the huge pile which is so likely to disgrace the country in the shape of the 'Washington National Monument.' " Alexander went on to praise Billings's project for a unity of architecture and sculpture that was "too often lacking today."

The fashion for erecting monuments had its detractors at midcentury (not of course among the trustees of the Pilgrim Society), and the fashion for complicated allegorical monuments that had marked the late eighteenth century had waned by the middle of the nineteenth. Although there was no lack of precedent for colossal sculpture dedicated to national significance, all of the other proposals for the Plymouth memorial, from that of the Reverend Rufus Clark to those of the other competitors, were apparently mainly architectural, and the trustees, we remember, had questions about Asboth and Zucker's use of allegorical embellishments on their design. There was in general some resistance in U.S. monumental art of the mid-nineteenth century to what the sculptor Thomas Crawford (1813–57) called, a year before Billings's proposal, "the darkness of allegory," an allegory that Horatio Greenough disparaged as a "puerile adhesion to an antiquated . . . conception."[31] We can now understand another reason for Winslow Warren's initial objection to Billings's proposal. It flew in the face of those contemporary prejudices. It was to be both architectural and sculptural, but it was largely allegorical, and it was huge. For the Forefathers Monument Billings chose to create a colossal figure rather than a purely architectural composition.

In this he was not alone either in the United States or in the western world. Colossal figures have thrilled people from antiquity to the present.[32] A rash of projected and executed examples, many dedicated to rising nationalism and reflecting the late eighteenth-century quest for the sublime, broke out in the early nineteenth century: John Flaxman's 1799 proposal for a 230-foot *Britannia* for Greenwich and Ludwig von Schwanthaler's considerably smaller bronze *Bavaria* (a 60-foot figure on a 15-foot pedestal) are examples.[33] Billings published a view of *Bavaria* in his *Illustrated Pilgrim Almanac*. "Le grandiose, le sublime, tel est son partage," wrote Lesbazeilles of such works in the 1870s.[34]

Nor were all precedents European. In the United States several colossal statues had been proposed, although in the majority these had not been allegorical designs but "portraits" of Washington or others. Among the alternate designs Robert Mills submitted for the Washington Monument in the District of Columbia in 1836–40, for example, was one contemplating a 110-foot robed Washington atop a 100-foot cubical base. And in 1845 the team of Thomas Crawford, sculptor, and Frederick Catherwood, architect, proposed for the City of New York a cast-iron, 75-foot Washington atop a 55-foot pedestal bearing Revolutionary scenes in relief.[35]

Although Washington was the subject of most of these colossal projects, he was not the focus of them all. For example Henry A. S. Dearborn (1783–1851), a Whig lawyer, congressman, author, and promoter of the Bunker Hill Monument as well as designer of Mount Auburn Cemetery in Cambridge and Forest Hills Cemetery in Jamaica Plain—and thus very probably known to Billings—suggested in 1838 the erection at Buffalo on a massive granite pedestal of a 100-foot bronze figure of New York governor De Witt Clinton (1769–1828). The governor would be "holding aloft in one hand, a flambeau, as a beacon light, to designate . . . the entrance, and pointing with the other, the direction of the route of the Erie Canal."[36] No more came of this notion than came of Dearborn's later proposal for a 42-foot Corinthian column surmounted by a flaming urn to honor the memory of John Eliot, the seventeenth-century "Apostle to the Indians."[37] Billings probably knew some of these or other prototypes; perhaps they quickened his desire to provide a colossal figure for the Forefathers Monument. But he emphasized the allegorical in his design, and he also created his own sources.

In addition to other of his far-ranging activities, as we know, during the 1850s Billings was designing patriotic, multifigured, historical and allegorical illustrations for the periodical press. His one identified wood-engraved title page for P. T. Barnum's *Illustrated News*, dated January-July 1853, represents Liberty bestowing the laurel on the Arts and Sciences (fig. 89). She holds a raised wreath in one hand and a pike with liberty cap in the other, is "Americanized" by a feathered headdress (Cesare Ripa in his *Iconologia*, first published in 1593, depicted America with such a headdress), and stands on an arc within which is shown the U.S. Capitol with T. U. Walter's new wings but not his dome. The wreath and the headdress were used again by Thomas Crawford for his statue *Freedom* of 1855–58 (eventually placed atop Walter's new dome), although he added an eagle's head to the headdress and rejected the liberty cap at the insistence of Jefferson Davis, then secretary of state.[38] Resting on the haunches of the arc enclosing the Capitol in Billings's engraved allegory are seated females representative of Arts and Sciences, figures that reappear somewhat transformed on Billings's Pilgrim Society certificate of 1856 (see fig. 86). Between them in the *Illustrated News,* a putto sculpts a portrait bust of Michelangelo. In this composition, then, the dominate figure is a draped, upright female at the top of a triangle of figures, and this is the two-dimensional equivalent of Billings's coeval free-standing colossal design.

Billings's architectural projects of the late 1840s and early 1850s were largely Italianate in style. The portrait of Michelangelo in the *Illustrated News,* a reference that reminds us that Billings was to be called during his lifetime the Michelangelo of his day, may also point to a distant source (in time, place, and form) for the designer's composition here as in the Forefathers Monument: the tombs of Giuliano and Lorenzo de' Medici (1519–34) in the

Fig. 89. Wood engraving by Frank Leslie after Hammatt Billings, *Liberty Crowning the Arts and Sciences*, title page of the *Illustrated News*, New York, 1853 (author's collection).

New Sacristy at San Lorenzo in Florence.[39] There, figures representing the times of the day lounge on the convex top of the sarcophagus, and seated figures of Lorenzo and Giuliano clad in military dress surmount the composition. Billings borrowed the triangular arrangement, the Giuliano for his representation of Freedom (later, Liberty; see fig. 84), and the head-in-hand thinking posture of the Lorenzo for his original statue of Law. (The comparison of such works, of course, points out that Billings was likened to Michelangelo for the range of his work not the quality of his design.) In his dependence upon Michelangelo, Billings seems to have led the way, but it should also be noted he had sources of inspiration closer to home. His representation of Law, for example, could also have been suggested to him by Robert Ball Hughes's seated figure of Nathaniel Bowditch in Mount Auburn Cemetery. The original model for it stood (and still stands) in the entrance hall of the Boston Athenaeum, which Billings had remodeled in 1850. In 1857 he wrote that it was "the best statue of its kind in America."[40] Billings's design differed from all such sources, however, in its colossal dimensions.

We first heard of Billings's "grand design" in Catharine Beecher's letter of March 1854, but he had in fact been thinking big in the realm of monumental art for the preceding year and more. Daniel Webster died at Marshfield, near Plymouth, Massachusetts, in October 1852. By the end of the year the City of Boston had published *A Memorial of Daniel Webster* containing a view of his home in Marshfield after Hammatt Billings, a resolution that "a permanent memorial of our illustrious and lamented fellow-citizen be provided," and a tribute to "the colossal grandeur of his intellect."[41] The idea of a memorial quickly merged with the plan to lay out a park opposite the Common on land acquired by the city in December 1852. Throughout the next month the *Boston Transcript* discussed the idea of a public garden as the site for a Webster statue. On 13 January 1853, for example, the newspaper proposed a colossal figure on an island in a pond in a place to be named Webster Park. And the next month, *Gleason's*, Boston's illustrated monthly, submitted its "plan of the Public Garden," having had "Mr. Billings sketch for us . . . an artistic design of what . . . [it] *should be*". At its center Billings proposed "to place a colossal statue of Daniel Webster, elevated upon a high pedestal, decorated at the angles with appropriate figures, and the faces ornamented with scenes in relief" (see fig. 96). Although the *Transcript* for 24 March 1853 reported that there was thought of turning the sketch into a working plan, nothing came of either this colossal statue or Billings's Public Garden scheme in general.[42]

Nonetheless, Billings's projected *Webster* contained the Forefathers Monument in embryo. It looks to have been conceived as some forty-five feet high. Although that was far short of his reach at Plymouth the next year, already present are the standing oratorical figure, its octagonal base, the reliefs, and the supporting figures seated on the diagonal (one is in the posture of a thinker, but none is, alas, identified). When he heard, long before the public announcement, and probably through the Boston "old boy network," the financial and intellectual elite whom he served as designer, that the Pilgrim Society contemplated erecting a monument to the forefathers, Billings had merely to enlarge this concept and substitute the appropriate allegorical figures.

Fig. 90. Steel engraving by A. C. Warren after Hammatt Billings, certificate of the Lexington [Mass.] Monument Association showing the proposed Minute Man Memorial by Billings, Thomas Ball, and G. J. F. Bryant and a view of the Battle of Lexington, copyright 1861 (author's collection).

The Webster and *Faith* were not Billings's only designs in colossal statuary. At the end of the 1850s he joined as designer the sculptor Thomas Ball and the architect Gridley J. F. Bryant, with both of whom he had collaborated and would again on other memorials, on the project for a monument to the battle of Lexington.[43] In the words of Edward Everett, who spoke in 1859 on behalf of the design, it was to be the work of "Hammatt Billings, a distinguished native artist"; in a notice in the *Boston Evening Transcript* it was said to have been "commended on both sides of the Atlantic."[44] The main image, Everett said, was "the figure of a Minute-Man, who, leaving his accustomed labors, and seizing his musket . . . has hastened to confront the disciplined battalions of arbitrary power. . . . It is to be of bronze and of colossal size; elevated upon a lofty pedestal of granite . . . with niches for the insertion of appropriate *relievos,* emblematic of the events of the day; the whole to be of a magnitude and in a style of execution worthy of the great event, creditable to American art, and in harmony with the national feeling" (fig. 90).[45] This too became an unexecuted memorial, its realization thwarted by the rupture of national life that marked the next years. It was superseded by Daniel Chester French's popular, life-size *Minute Man,* designed and put in place not in Lexington but in Concord in 1871–75.[46]

The Webster, Forefathers, and Minute Man colossi, all conceived during the tremulous 1850s, show Hammatt Billings and his patrons attempting to focus not only upon past heroic events but also current political aspirations by designing monuments dedicated to the founding, creating, and sustaining of the national union. In this they paralleled his illustrations for *Ballou's* of the same period. Of the three projects, the Webster and the Minute Man remained on paper, but however shrunken and inelegantly executed, Billings's design for the National Monument to the Forefathers now stands in Plymouth. What ideas did he think the monument should embody, and once they were chosen, how did he decide to represent them?

The most likely place to find the answer to these questions is in the patriotic speeches delivered at the annual celebrations of the landing and other commemorative occasions, especially those of the famed New England orators of the day such as Daniel Webster (1782–1852) and Edward Everett (1794–1865), as well as somewhat lesser but nonetheless influential figures such as the Reverend Lyman Beecher (1775–1863) or the Boston lawyer Rufus Choate (1799–1859), who served with Billings on the board of directors of the Massachusetts Academy of Fine Arts in 1853.[47] A modern historian has pointed out that such oratory "stocked and restocked the common mind with a store of selected memories." It sought to create a "communal experience of affirmation . . . to create a state of consciousness: . . . to make the abstract real."[48] The Forefathers Monument was to do this in another art, in effect to be a visualization of such oratory, a patriotic speech in historiated stone. *Faith*'s gesture, we remember, was originally oratorical.

In the first half of the nineteenth century a growing national consciousness developed into a form of ancestor worship that played off legends of the founding. Since the 1760s there had been irregularly spaced celebrations commemorating the day of the landing at which prominent men delivered speeches with appropriate sentiments. If in our own day we find the intentions of the Pilgrims complex and not entirely benign or self-sacrificing, the mid-nineteenth century harbored no such doubts.[49] In 1820, the year of the founding of the Pilgrim Society, Daniel Webster in a celebrated address instructed his audience that it stood "on the spot where the first scene of our history was laid; where the hearths and altars of New England were first placed; where Christianity, and civilization, and letters made their first lodgement, in a vast extent of country, covered with a wilderness and peopled by roving barbarians." And later, he exhorted his listeners not to forget "the religious character of our origin. Our fathers were brought hither by their high veneration for the Christian religion. . . . They sought to incorporate its principles with the elements of their society, and to diffuse its influence through all their institutions, civil, political, or literary." Faith, filiopietism, and a free social system: these were constituent elements in the midcentury use of the newly enhanced founding legend. And these would find visible expression appropriate to the era in the Forefathers Monument.[50]

The celebration held thirty-three years later, in August 1853, in accordance with the resolution of the May meeting of the Pilgrim Society as "a highly appropriate and fitting tribute to the memory of the Fathers of New England, and also a proper season for taking measures to erect a monument in the town, on or near Forefathers' Rock," featured a speech by Edward Everett, then a U.S. senator. "There are two Master Ideas," he said, "by whose influence the settlement of New England may be rationally explained. . . . [and] these Great Ideas are GOD and LIBERTY. . . . I mean profound religious faith . . . [and] civil liberty." The political code of the Pilgrims, he went on, "united religion and liberty, morals and law."[51] If we add education to this list we have the iconographical program of the National Monument to the Forefathers, designed in the year after this speech and dedicated three and a half decades later.[52]

Billings must have been aware of the currently popular view of the primacy of religion among the reasons for the forefathers' departure from the Old World. "What sought they thus afar?" poetized Felicia Hemans in 1826: "They sought a faith's pure shrine!"[53] To give shape to this cause the designer could have drawn upon a variety of sources. There was, of course, the Renaissance-Baroque iconographical tradition—more accessible to the nineteenth century than to us—in which Faith ("Fede Cattolica") is presented (by Cesare Ripa for example) as a draped female wearing a helmet and carrying, in her lowered left hand, the tablets of the Old and the book of the New Testament, and in her raised right hand, a heart from which projects a lighted candle.[54] Despite its Catholic origins this icon, somewhat transformed to be sure, gained following in the nineteenth century even among Protestants. In another type, that represented by Antonio Canova's *Religion* of 1814 or Santo Varni's colossal *Faith* in Genoa of about 1850, the draped female exhibits a radiating aura around her head, and she supports the upright Latin cross (Varni's figure carries a book, the Bible certainly, in her left hand). Billings learned of this tradition at some time in his career, for in 1870 he drew a related figure of Faith, probably as a design for a cemetery marker.[55] The candle or other symbol of illumination used in the iconographical tradition, however, gave way in Billings's Plymouth work to the oratorical gesture, the beckoning finger pointing heavenward. He rejected the helmet, as well as the aura of the second type, in favor of a single star, succinctly emblematic of the heavens (or is it the star of empire?), and he gathered the Old and New Testaments into one Bible. Billings eliminated some overt signs of religion, the cross and the aura, while retaining the book, perhaps because he thought the former too Roman Catholic for a monument to Protestant forebears. It is possible that Winslow Warren's dislike for the initial proposal stemmed from a Protestant mistrust of such popish representations of religion.

Billings's representations of Education, Law, and Morality are unexceptional. They are seated draped male or female figures holding a book or a tablet which, without his labels, could represent almost anything. His embodiment of Freedom (later, Liberty) as a seated male warrior, however, deserves comment. In contemporary illustrations, even in those by Billings himself, as in 1853 in the *Illustrated News* for example (see fig. 89), or in *Ballou's* for December 1855, Liberty is a classically draped female whose posture closely resembles that of the Faith of his monument (although the reasons for the posture vary). Billings here adopted the common type.[56] As this figure represents Faith on his monument, however, perhaps to avoid misreading or visual confusion he picked a dramatically different representation of Freedom. For formal prototype he found inspiration in Michelangelo's armored figure of Giuliano de' Medici from San Lorenzo; this he adapted to an iconographical tradition representing Fortitude, or Courage, to serve his purpose. His original figure held no sword, as we know from the model now in the Plymouth Public Library, unlike what was finally put in place on the finished monument, but the attributes of his *Freedom* and many representations of Courage otherwise agree: helmet, armor, and lion skin. In the iconographical tradition one representation of Courage is a warrior in the guise of Hercules draped in lion skin or subduing a lion.[57] By adding the broken chain of slavery, Billings, with characteristically nineteenth-century insouciance, adapted this unrelated tradition to his programmatic needs.[58] No relationship has yet been (or is ever likely to be) established between Billings's figure and the similar, *neo-Florentine* representation of Courage used by Paul Dubois in the mid-1870s for the tomb of General Juchault de Lamoricière in the Cathedral of Nantes, unless they reflect a common source, but they would certainly appear to be first cousins (Dubois's figure, of course, lacks the chain).[59] Billings's turning to Michelangelo, it should be noted, precedes by two decades Dubois's, although the latter is said to have had precedence in France.

Each of *Faith*'s ancillary figures in Billings's proposal was accompanied in turn by two supporting figures on the sides of the chair who amplify his or her message, and a relief depicting one of four remembered events in the story of the Pilgrims. History also occupied Billings's ceaseless pencil throughout the 1850s, and these narrative reliefs were extensions of his work for the engravers at *Ballou's* and elsewhere. They were also part of that nineteenth-century artistic "series of dramatic departures, landings, arrivals, and discoveries, [that were] symbolic touchstones of the nation's destiny, [and] implied that America itself was an apocalyptic revelation," as recently discussed by Wendy Greenhouse.[60]

The departure from Delft-Haven and the signing of the compact aboard the *Mayflower* were scenes specific to the Pilgrim story, while the landing and treaty with the Indians were events shared with other immigrant groups. Billings's iconography combines tradition with some innovation. Early versions of his *Compact* and *Landing* are known from the engraved Pilgrim Society certificate of 1856. For these compositions, as in his work for *Ballou's*, Billings relied upon the neoclassical rules for narrative art, with figures arranged in a shallow space and balanced left, right, and center. In his *Signing of the Compact*, associated on the existing monument with the figure of Education, the setting aboard the *Mayflower* is barely suggested. Male Pilgrims stand or sit around a carpeted table as one of them signs the document in what looks like a work descended from the portrait groups of Frans Hals or, perhaps more likely, a composition dependent upon John Smibert's 1729 *Bermuda Group* (it too depicting an assembly of new arrivals) or one of its progeny in the work of Robert Feke or Charles Willson Peale (see fig. 86).

Landings of the Pilgrims and other groups had been treated more often in American art, so Billings could here draw upon a tradition both more varied and more specific. John Vanderlyn's large *Landing of Columbus* was in the U.S. Capitol rotunda by 1847. The event at Plymouth Rock appeared in Samuel Hill's engraving of about 1800 that formed the source for any number of painted versions, including that of Michele Felice Cornè, and the same depiction is found, sometimes augmented, sometimes not, among the illustrations in such popular publications as the *History of the Pilgrims* of 1831 or the *United States Book* of 1833.[61] By the time Billings turned his attention to the episode, the Pilgrim Society had in its own collection Henry Sargent's mammoth canvas of about 1813. Finally, Peter Rothermel's dramatic *Landing* of 1854 culminates the series.[62] Historian Vivien Fryd has written that these are scenes of passage, of the transformation of the Englishman into the American, as well as in some depictions of the newcomers' "potential dominance over indigenous peoples."[63] The transformation of the actors from sea-borne Europeans to landed colonists is clearly depicted by Billings, whose *Landing* is linked to his figure of Freedom, but Fryd's latent victim is nowhere to be seen as the men and women of the *Mayflower* gather to light the first fire of freedom. It was usual in depictions of the landing to give prominence to the Rock of legend, but Billings follows Sargent in down-playing it within his multifigured composition. (Somewhere along the line this relief was significantly changed to emphasize, in the more common version now on the monument, the passage from boat to Rock; see fig. 84).

The *Departure*, which Billings placed beneath *Morality*, and the *Treaty with the Indians*, associated with the figure of Law, round out the historical reliefs. The *Departure* was probably best known in the 1850s from the huge canvas of 1836–43 by Robert W. Weir in the U.S. Capitol rotunda, depicting the departing Pilgrims praying at Delft-Haven aboard the ill-fated *Speedwell*. Ashbel Steele used it as the frontispiece for his 1857 biography of William Brewster.[64] Billings's design is independent of this tradition. Assuming that what is on the monument now generally reflects his original composition, he concentrated on the translation from land to ship, with some figures waving farewell, some grieving at departure, and others busy preparing the ship for sailing. Treating with the Indians was a more universal subject by the 1850s. Benjamin West's 1771 depiction of William Penn and the Delawares at Shackamaxon was probably the best-known version, reappearing over and over again in copies, in framing prints, in popular publications, and in the abundant versions of the peaceable kingdom by the Quaker Edward Hicks.[65] In 1827 another version carved in sandstone by Nicholas Gevelot appeared in the U.S. Capitol.[66] Billings's composition here too stands apart from this tradition, if, again, we can assume that the present relief represents his design. The scene is usually set out-of-doors, while he correctly represents the negotiations of a Leonardesque grouping indoors, with onlookers, both Pilgrims and natives, standing around a table at which one of each of their number negotiates, probably Massasoit for the Indians and John Carver for the Pilgrims. And is that much-traveled Squanto who seems to translate for the negotiants and assumes a pose reminiscent of Christ at the center of Leonardo's *Last Supper* (see fig. 85)?

In showing the *Compact* and the *Treaty* as similar indoor scenes, Billings seems to link them, in the conception of his day, to suggest visually that the agreement among Europeans was akin to harmony between races. (We, of course, are no longer so certain.) He also composed both *Departure* and *Landing* as, appropriately, outdoor events memorializing the "sea change" that would make free Americans of persecuted Englishmen. The meanings of the historical reliefs on his monument were enhanced by these interactive commentaries.

Hammatt Billings's National Monument to the Forefathers was thus intended at one level as historical "text" to be read according to mid-nineteenth-century interpretations of the past. Its meaning spreads out from top to bottom, from the heaven-sent Faith which was then believed to have fueled the Pilgrims' journey, to the social principles and civil institutions that were seen to have been established under her guidance, to the qualities these were either sustained by or fostered themselves, to the scenes of human history that accounted for the transference of those ideals to the New World. But at a second level the monument was intended to focus the United States of the 1850s upon common national origins for current political ends. A complete reading of Billings's text must also take into account its historical present as well as the distant past.

If the fervent filiopietism of the second quarter of the nineteenth century provided a patriotic context for the National Monument to the Forefathers, this context must be extended to include the onrush of events in the decade of the 1850s tending toward the dissolution of the nation, for that gives it even deeper meaning. As the historian Neil Harris has observed, "a society turns to an extended reliance on symbolism to prop up sentiments which require support." And he also notes that symbols "proclaim an allegiance to a cause . . . or a creed in danger of being forgotten."[67] The decade that saw the rising tide of secessionism, that witnessed, among many other well-known, sectionally divisive events, the Mexican-American War of 1846–48, the Fugitive Slave Law of 1850, Bleeding Kansas of the summer of 1856, and John Brown's raid at Harper's Ferry in October 1859, also saw a cresting of interest in the arrival of the Pilgrims, an interest of which the proposed Forefathers Monument was to be the most visible sign. Literary works devoted to the Pilgrims had appeared earlier, of course, ranging from Felicia Hemans's ten-stanza "Landing of the Pilgrims in New England" of 1826 to the children's *History of the Pilgrim's* of 1831, but the number of serious works that appeared in the 1850s is astonishing. It includes the publication of documents and guidebooks, the writing of histories, of biographies, and of fictional works. It includes (to name just one of each type from a long list) William S. Russell's *Pilgrim Memorials* of 1846 (second edition, 1855), E. H. Bartlett's *Pilgrim Fathers* of 1853, Ashbel Steele's *Chief of the Pilgrims . . . the Life . . . of William Brewster* of 1857, Nathaniel B. Shurtleff's edition of *Records of the Colony of New Plymouth*, 1857–61, and Henry Wadsworth Longfellow's "Courtship of Miles Standish," begun in 1857 and first published in 1858. And it should also be noted that William Bradford's *Of Plymouth Plantation* first appeared in its entirety in 1856. Although these were regionally focused, their reach was wide. Most students of the period agree that, in the succinct statement of the art historian Angela Miller, "in the 1850s the Northeast laid claim to being the privileged carrier of national identity."[68]

Modern historians such as Wesley Frank Craven and Lawrence Buell have discussed the uses of history in the middle of the nineteenth century. Craven points out for example, in *The Legend of the Founding Fathers*, that New England writers had a "special influence on the development of our national historical tradition" and that histories of New England depicted it to be the story "of a God-fearing community dedicated to the fulfillment of a religious ideal" that was also a political ideal: the right of self-government. It was a reading of history that created a common tradition, and Craven goes on to remind us that "one function of tradition is to provide a focus for the sentiment that binds men together in hours of trial. . . . The past and future are cherished together in a way that reminds us of our national inclinations to make of the past a guarantor of the future."[69] This was exactly Billings's choice of arguments in defense of his proposal to Winslow Warren.

Legends of the founding, in particular of the landing at Plymouth, provided the stuff of national tradition, of common memory. And it was to that national tradition that Billings and his patrons looked in creating a monument to remind all citizens, North and South, of their collective heritage during the trying 1850s. His aim, it seems, was not only to give shape to the words of the great orators of his day, but to the historians as well, in the cause of preserving the national unity for the progeny of his time through the celebration of a shared heroic origin. In a time in which national principles were forgotten "art was a means of coping with the problem," again according to Neil Harris. He quotes William Hoppin, who in 1846 wrote that monuments render the "idea of country in a visible shape. . . . We need something tangible. . . . We need the outward types."[70] This appears to have been Billings's intention: to enlist the colossal tradition to celebrate a collective memory in the service of current events.

"Americans of Emerson's generation worked assiduously to create a past usable for their purposes, and Whiggish Bostonians led the crusade," according to a recent observer.[71] Billings's mentors for the meaning of the monument, men such as Webster, Everett, and Choate, were all stout Whigs and Unionists, men who believed disunion would be worse than slavery, who—much to the disgust of more dedicated abolitionists—compromised in the hope of saving the integrity of the civilization of the founders. Among the letters apparently solicited by Billings after his proposal had been accepted by the Pilgrim Society was one from Josiah Quincy (1772–1864) endorsing the design as embracing "everything, piety, patriotism & veneration could desire."[72] A second letter, from Edward Everett himself, who was about to launch his nationwide series of lectures on George Washington as a salve to sooth sectional wounds, tied the inspiration of the past to the fears of the present in a succinct statement of the monument's meaning.[73] "Its colossal dimensions symbolize the magnitude of the event & the moral grandeur of the characters commemorated," he wrote. "The erection of such a work on the scale proposed, implying as it does the co-operation of the descendants of the pilgrims in every part of the Country and of all who are now in the enjoyment of the goodly heritage for which . . . we are so largely indebted to the Pilgrim Fathers, is well calculated to promote fraternal feeling throughout the Union, and deserves the encouragement of every patriot."[74] And Everett's interpretations echoed from across the Mason-Dixon Line in a letter from Henry A. Wise (1806–76), the governor of Virginia (who was a prewar Unionist but eventually joined the secession and fought for the South).[75] He wrote from Richmond on 2 January 1856 that "Well may we all unite, the sons of the Cavaliers with their [the Pilgrims'] true sons [i.e., New Englanders], in building a monument founded upon these four corners of perpetuity [Morality, Education, Law, and Liberty] & pointing to Heaven for immortality."

The gathering gale of disunification was stronger than these verbal and visual sermons of unity, however, and would soon fan the nation into a firestorm of belligerent divisiveness. And that would of necessity delay and transform the realization, as it swept away some of the meaning, of Hammatt Billings's "great design." The diminished result was anticlimactic.

Cornerstones for the canopy over the Rock and for the Forefathers Monument were laid on 2 August 1859 with Pres. James Buchanan and the designer in attendance.[76] The canopy was finished in 1867 (fig. 91). It was destroyed in 1919 to make way for the present pavilion sponsored by the Colonial Dames of America. Despite the provision given in the contract, where four figures of bronze are particularly mentioned (a design for which no drawings or other descriptions seem to survive), Billings's canopy was without anthropomorphous embellishment. It took the form of an arcuated granite baldachino of Baroque design but Tuscan simplicity with four scallop shells, the medieval symbols of pilgrimage adopted at Plymouth for her Pilgrims, dotting the skyline.[77] The use of the baldachino form and the shell motifs may have contributed to the downfall of this structure. It quickly evoked criticism. As early as 1882 Herbert Adams called it "pretentious," and a "mausoleum," lamented that it "overshadows the Rock itself," and noted—in an allusion demonstrating shaky art history but firm conviction—that it "reminds the beholder of the canopy over the altar of St. Peter's" in the Vatican. And that was certainly the wrong signal to send out from the stepping stone of historically Protestant New England. He hoped for its removal, a sentiment that grew into the Colonial Dames' "improvement" at the time of the tercentenary.[78]

Billings's canopy was, then, realized just after the war, but the collection of funds for the monument, with premium statuettes cast in 1867, continued to lag behind expectations. Just before his death in November 1874 Billings, perhaps on the theory that half a monument is better than none and more likely to be realized so long after the fervor of its original proposal, significantly cut it in size, and a contract was signed for the construction of the pedestal with the Bodwell Granite Company of Vinalhaven, Maine. It was finished in 1875 when Hammatt's surviving brother and partner, Joseph, assumed the duties of supervisor.

Oliver Ames of North Easton, Massachusetts, donated the figure of *Faith;* it was carved at the Hallowell Granite Company in Maine. But the figure was no longer, as originally intended, the product of small gifts from across the nation, nor was it completely Hammatt's creation. Early in 1875 Joseph asked the sculptor William Rimmer (1816–79), with whom Hammatt had studied anatomy in 1864, to make a nine-foot model after his brother's design to be used as a guide to the full-scale figure. (There is no explanation why Jackson's earlier model was no longer adequate, unless that

Fig. 91. Hammatt Billings, canopy over the Rock, Plymouth, Massachusetts, 1854–67; destroyed 1919 (author's collection).

is somehow explained by the change in size.) Differences of opinion arose between the two because Rimmer altered the figure, changing her raised arm to the present crooked one, for example, thus losing the oratorical reference, and freeing her upraised thumb in an awkward gesture, despite keeping one eye on the Venus de Milo while he worked.[79] Nor was Rimmer the only sculptor to intervene. One Edward Perry reworked Rimmer's model at Joseph's request, and at the Hallowell yard the figure was carved by an employee, Joseph Archie, who, although he kept one of Hammatt's early engraved views hanging from the scaffold, apparently made further changes.[80] The result, put on the pedestal in August 1877, was a composite work representing six different minds and hands: Hammatt Billings, Jackson, Rimmer, Joseph Billings, Perry, and Archie. The result was severely criticized when it was new, and it has not improved with age.[81]

Morality was set up the next year. She was the gift of the Commonwealth of Massachusetts and modeled by German-born Carl H. Conrads (b. 1839), who also signed the embarkation relief beneath it. In 1873 Hammatt had made definitive drawings for the reliefs and apparently asked the young Daniel Chester French to model them.[82] Although French appears to have made some small sketches (which do not seem to have survived), apparently nothing came of that initiative. *Education* was next, the work of Alexander Doyle (1857–1922) of New York following Billings's design, with its relief of the compact (somewhat altered from Billings's original) modeled by English-born John M. Moffitt (1837–87). Roland Mather of Hartford paid for them; they were put in place in October 1881. Joseph had died in 1880, as had Willard Harding, who had been Hammatt's financial agent from the beginning, and another long hiatus ensued. *Freedom* (changed from Hammatt's *Liberty*), the gift of Congress, and *Law*, paid for by subscription, with their reliefs were modeled by Welsh-born J. H. Mahoney (1855–1919), an employee at Hallowell, and put in place in the autumn of 1888. Although Billings had won this commission in the 1850s by speaking against foreign intervention in the creation of a national monument, by the end of its execution, immigrants were indeed giving it shape. The finished conglomerate was dedicated on 1 August 1889, long after the original design had lost much of its meaning. In the period between then and now it has slowly become a largely forgotten relic of an imperfectly remembered past.

Hammatt Billings's colossal 1850s vision of national unity based upon a shared reverence for the founding legend, as delayed, reduced, and transformed, is only partly realized in the existing monument above Plymouth

Fig. 92. Steel engraving by the American Bank Note Company, certificate of the American Committee on the Statue of Liberty, 1883 (New-York Historical Society).

harbor. It was dedicated three years after the unveiling of Auguste Bartholdi's Statue of Liberty on a pedestal by Richard Morris Hunt in New York harbor.[83] Its plodding presence and its provincial location have relegated it to obscurity, while *Liberty*, a lively figure of contemporary "high-tech" engineering situated by the Golden Door, the principal late nineteenth- early twentieth-century gateway into the United States, has become globally symbolic of the nation. Billings's *Faith* represents the dated beliefs of one religious group; Bartholdi's *Liberty* still embodies the hopes of many displaced peoples. The granite of the Forefathers Monument is emblematic of its traditional regionalism; the ironwork of *Liberty*, emblematic of her modern internationalism. The undoubted relative importance of the two colossi as realized has, however, like the relationship between their dedicatory dates, clouded the relationship between their inceptions. Billings's colossal vision of 1854 was well known across the country after 1855 through engravings and small replicas, and it ought now to be understood as a meaningful antecedent to Bartholdi's statue, which was conceived in 1865. Billings's struggle to solicit monies for its erection from the entire country, while it proved only partly successful because of the turmoil of the 1850s and the disruption of the Civil War, clearly anticipated similar fund-raising efforts on behalf of *Liberty* (cf. figs. 86 and 92). As lugubrious as the executed monument now seems, as neglected as it has now become, Billings's original design should assume its place as the first proposed and eventually partially realized colossal allegorical representation of the abstract principles upon which, in the reading of the mid-nineteenth century, the nation was founded and hoped to survive.

IO
"From the Pencil of Billings"
Festivals, Fireworks, and Furniture

AMMATT BILLINGS made himself available to supply the various design needs of a broad spectrum of clients both public and private. As one accomplished in all departments of art he frequently found himself called upon to provide suitable forms for a variety of public displays during the 1850s and 1860s, some more ephemeral than others. These ranged from street-spanning arches and parade-enhancing floats to pyrotechnical exhibitions, the decorating of fairs, and the draping of bunting on buildings. He also produced drawings for a variety of more tangible public and private decorative works ranging from clock frames to organ cases, light standards, and commercial and domestic furniture. The sources are filled with references to three-dimensional designs "from the pencil of Billings." An account of his far-ranging career must include some discussion of these miscellaneous, sometimes unfruitful but often highly visible chores. In his role as creator of a bewildering diversity of Boston public works, transient or permanent, Billings anticipated the multi-faceted later careers of Richard Morris Hunt and Stanford White in New York City.

Freshwater was introduced to the center of Boston by aqueduct from outlying Cochituate in 1848. For the celebration of the arrival of the public supply held on 25 October, Moses Kimball of the Boston Museum contributed a Water Arch spanning Tremont Street opposite his flag-bedecked theater. On the way to ceremonies focused on the gusher at the Frog Pond on the Common, a water jet illustrated by Billings in his title page to *The Boston Book* of 1850, a great procession of citizens animated with banners and floats passed up Tremont Street beneath the arch (fig. 93). Its vaguely Moorish design, with a central horseshoe opening spanning the street flanked by ornate sidewalk openings, was a rare exotic creation of Billings's architectural career and probably sprang from the nineteenth-century association of this nonwestern, therefore "non-historical," and therefore frivolous style with celebratory or light-hearted festival. Its theatricality, appropriately funded by the impresario Kimball and erected by the "master machinist of the Museum," was achieved by a more than fifty-foot-high frame, presumably of wood, covered with white cotton cloth. Ornament of trefoils designed by S. P. Hines edged the openings; a brilliant color scheme of white, crimson, and gold, and appropriate quotations from Shakespeare, enlivened the set piece.[1]

Fig. 93. J. H. Bufford lithograph after Hammatt Billings, Water Arch on Tremont Street, October 1848. Billings's Boston Museum is to the left. (Boston Athenaeum).

Hammatt's Water Arch was one of a long line of transient festival arches erected in the nineteenth century to honor famous men and significant events, although these were usually based upon classical precedent. It was a line that included Charles Willson Peale's Arch of Triumph in Philadelphia of 1783–84, and Stanford White's Washington Arch in New York of 1889. As historian Paul Baker has remarked, White "became a central figure in New York's expanding civic life and celebrations" in the 1890s. The Water Arch and other temporary public works put Hammatt Billings in the same position in Boston during midcentury. He anticipated White's honorary role as "municipal commissioner of public beauty," or, perhaps more accurately in Billing's case, of public sentiment.[2]

Less than two years later the public again called upon Billings to give visible expression to a common sentiment, but this time it was one of grief not joy, as the occasion was prompted by an untimely death rather then a life-sustaining fluid. Moses Kimball was again the moving force. Pres. Zachary Taylor died in office on 9 July 1850. The following day Kimball rose in Common Council to propose a committee "to make suitable arrangements for celebrating the obsequies" of the president.[3] The hero of the battles of Palo Alto and Buena Vista in the Mexican War, a war that was unpopular with many a New Englander, and a president caught up in the crises of the compromise over the extension of slavery, an arrangement lamented by many in the North, Taylor nevertheless enjoyed a personal popularity on both sides of the Mason-Dixon Line that outweighed his mild beliefs and his lukewarm Whiggishness.[4] The president was buried elsewhere on 13 July, but Boston held its own commemoration of his passing with a solemn parade on 15 August. On that day Henry Wadsworth Longfellow recorded in his diary that "everybody is rushing upon the town to see the funeral procession of President Taylor, and the 'catafalque drawn by Mr. Billings,' as the papers announce it."[5]

Billings—who was just about this time working on scenes of the battles of the Mexican War—created an impressive and unprecedented catafalque, or funeral car as the papers were eventually correctly to call it, that drove the journalists to heights of descriptive wonder (fig. 94). Edward Hennessey of the upholstery firm of Russell, Hennessey, and Phelps built the wheeled float. Its base was 8 feet by 15 feet; the structure was 13½ feet high; and the frame was covered with 100 yards of black velvet drapery. "The top rests upon eight arches," according to the *Transcript*, and "is surmounted with eight

Fig. 94. Hammatt Billings, funeral car for Zachary Taylor, 1850 *(Boston Evening Transcript)*.

black plumes. . . . The sides of the upper portions . . . [are] ornamented with the arms of the various states, emblazoned with silver. . . . The sides of the body . . . [bear] appropriate wreaths . . . indicating the battles won by the lamented Hero, interspersed with other wreaths of silver lace, ornamented with his cipher." "The interior of the canopy was heavily lined with rich white satin and silk. The plinth or base . . . upon which the bier rested represented a sarcophagus, gorgeously draped with the somber festooning of black velvet fringed with heavy trimmings of silver lace. On the top of the car was [sic] placed eight black urns, containing over two hundred ostrich plumes." The car was drawn by twelve black horses decorated with black plumes.

The whole presented a spectacle "of unprecedented magnificence." Still according to the *Transcript:* "In beauty of design, richness of material, and elaborate taste" the funeral car "probably stands unsurpassed by any thing of the kind ever executed in this city. The style . . . was strictly Roman." Boston stood indebted to Billings for setting the tone of the occasion: "to his excellent skill and good taste may be ascribed his success in producing what has been concluded to be both chaste and magnificent." Billings had the editors of the *Transcript* in his hip pocket.

Billings not only designed the Zachary Taylor funeral car but draped Faneuil Hall top to bottom in black relieved occasionally with strips of white, designed badges of mourning, and otherwise made the meaning of the proceedings tangible and memorable to the citizens of Boston. Such decorative commissions seem to have formed part of Billings's many public services, although we know too little about these highly fugitive designs. For a visit of the Prince to Wales to Boston in 1860, Billings, as so often during these years in association with Gridley Bryant, was again called upon to provide the decorations, although exactly what was produced remains uncertain.[6]

Descriptions of such evanescent works, when they do occur, are usually frustratingly brief, but we know one of these decorative commissions in some verbal detail. In 1859 Billings was a member of a committee organized to raise funds for the erection of Thomas Ball's statue of Washington, a monument eventually set up on Billings's pedestal in the Public Garden. For the Washington Statue Fair held in November 1859 in the Boston Music Hall, an interior for which he was just then designing the case for the Great Organ, Billings provided the "original and unique" designs for "the more complete adoption of the Oriental style of embellishment than has been customary in this country"; that is, in accordance with the current theory of associationism or the use of appropriate style for certain kinds of usages, he again employed "non-historical" and therefore nonserious forms to create a festive atmosphere.[7] He had for another festive occasion, in his Water Arch of 1848, also resorted to eastern sources; we are not told here, however, whether he turned to Islam, India, or China for his inspiration. Whatever their source, Hammatt's designs were carried out by the little-known builder-architect Charles Roath.

As usual the *Transcript* pulled out the stops in describing the decorations "which will give a gorgeous scenic effect to the entire premises." Billings placed a "spacious arch" outside the Winter Street entrance. In the center of the hall rose "a beautiful fountain and fairy-like summer house, in Oriental style, while the sale tents [filled with objects of *virtu* and presided over by the wives of the city's patriciate] ... form[ed] a square ... beneath ... the balcony, from which ... project[ed] a series of splendid parti-colored canopies covering ... the tables." The second balcony was hung "with Oriental pendants, suspended from gilded poles, and with such variety of emblazonment as to shed a particularly brilliant lustre upon the scene below." In another issue of the paper we hear of a "charming rural grotto" filled with the rarest flowers and an art gallery erected on the Music Hall stage. All in all, the paper concluded, "a labyrinth of beauty . . . surrounds the spectator." All in all, we can agree, this must have been one of Hammatt's more fully realized effects.

The Water Arch, the funeral car, and the Music Hall decorations were transitory designs; even more ephemeral were the pyrotechnical displays created by Billings to celebrate Independence Day on Boston Common. These were spectacles attended by great crowds and reported in great detail by the popular press. They were not always the "bombs bursting in air" of present-day displays of fireworks, but often series of elaborate patriotic devices hung upon two-dimensional frames. George Phillips, who was one of the (probably inflated estimate of) 150,000 spectators at a display in 1845, described the framework as standing "against the sky, like a fantastic temple."[8] Four years earlier Billings had described the Fourth as "this high holy day, the Jubilee of Freedom."[9] It is unlikely that he had a hand in this earlier event, as he was just at the beginning of his career, but he did provide like designs in the early 1850s, two of which are minutely recorded. These in fact anticipated by a few years his patriotic illustrations for *Ballou's*, so once again we see a consistency in his wide-ranging career.

In 1851 rain on the Fourth of July delayed the celebration until the eighth. The "crowning glory" of the evening was the "entirely new and original" pyrotechnical display designed by Billings and operated by James G. Hovey (fig. 95).[10] It stretched 125 feet from side to side and rose 75 feet into the air, "the largest and most gorgeous pyrotechnical structure ever produced in this country, . . . and when fully on fire [it] lit the entire sky." The theme was Our Union's Basis, an apt if hope-fraught sentiment at the beginning of the decade that saw federation unravel. At the base of the display the motto Peace and Prosperity underscored the fiery depiction of Liberty flanked by Washington and Lafayette. The words "Law, Union, Liberty" arched above the central female with Phrygian cap, shield, and eagle, surrounded by the seals of the original states in 10-foot circles. "The whole [was] surmounted by thirty-one stars [symbolic of the coeval count of states] . . . scrollwork, and . . . '1776.' " When the "mottos, inscriptions, and various colored decorations" burst into flame, there were "universal shouts of approbation" from an estimated 100,000 spectators. Clearly Billings had achieved another public success.

Two years later he topped himself. The "closing piece of [the] series of fireworks" displayed in 1853 far surpassed all earlier creations. It was "drafted expressly for the occasion" by Billings and again fired by James Hovey. The evening concluded with "the bursting of mines, bombs, rockets and heavy batteries of Roman candles," but the centerpiece was again a framework of colorful emblems designed with an eye on current politics supported by economic improvements. The spectacle was a Whiggish "Grand National Emblem . . . representing our inland intercourse and oceanic navigation,

Fig. 95. Wood engraving after John H. Manning from a design of Hammatt Billings, fireworks display, Boston Common, July 1851 (*Gleason's Pictorial Drawing-Room Companion*, 1851; author's collection).

prospering beneath the fostering folds of our national flag."[11] An "enormous structure," 300 feet long and 75 feet high, it was "by far the largest ever fired in America."

Gleason's provided its readers with a full description of the patriotic drama in two parts:

Part first consisted of a Gothic [sic] temple, formed of three arches, and supported by four columns surmounted by emblems of plenty. In the centre arch was the genius of Liberty surrounded by a halo of light, standing upon the implements of warfare, and upholding the liberty cap and olive branch. From the centre of the arches, upon either side, was seen, in graceful festoons, the flag of the United States overhanging the motto, "We unite all in brotherhood,"—and gathered in folds to the foot of the columns. Under the arch upon the right, at the base of the piece, was represented a Locomotive with a train of cars resting upon a bridge, and beneath the arch upon the left a Steamship riding upon the water. In part second, the locomotive and train moved at the ringing of the bell, to the right, one hundred feet, stopping at a station house; while at the same moment the steamship, rocking upon the billows moved to the left one hundred feet towards a lighthouse.

Billings's Fourth of July emblem for 1853, then, appears to the twentieth-century reader as a forerunner of animated neon display. To his contemporaries, however, it was further proof they had in their midst a person capable of visibly, publicly, and dramatically expressing their common hopes for national survival. During the 1850s fireworks joined periodical illustration and designs for colossal monuments as various aspects of Billings's visual support for the Union-saving ideals of his Whiggish friends.

Earlier in the same year (1853) Billings had been asked by the editors of Gleason's to sketch a proposal for a Public Garden at the foot of the Common, one which was to contain a colossal statue of Daniel Webster (fig. 96; see chap. 9). According to Gleason's editors, in Hammatt's sketch "a wide avenue . . . communicates on three sides with Boylston, Charles and Beacon streets. In the centre of the ground is a large square area surrounded by an ornamented wall, crowned with vases, and in the middle of each of the four sides of this enclosure, is a large opening for the great avenues which run from the sides to the centre area." The figure of the celebrated orator was to occupy the center. "Around the statue the enclosure is laid out in parterres, with vases, etc., interspersed. . . . The four great avenues . . . it is proposed to line with forest trees of all kinds indigenous to New England, and the spaces between are to be laid out in picturesque lawns, groves, etc., with fountains."

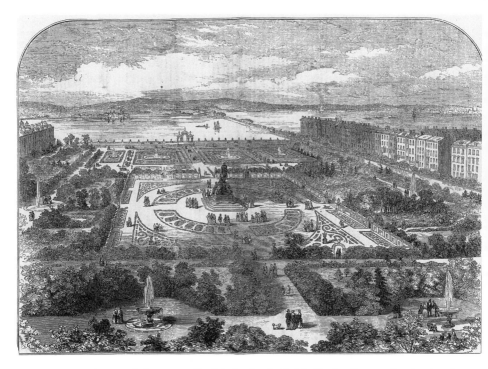

Fig. 96. Hammatt Billings, unrealized design for the Public Garden, Boston, 1853. A colossal statue of Daniel Webster was to stand in the center of this formal public space (*Gleason's Pictorial Drawing-Room Companion*, 1853; author's collection).

The description goes on to say that "West of the centre enclosure the ground is laid out as a flower garden, with hedges, clumps, etc. of the smaller trees and shrubs. Fountains, vases, etc., etc., would appropriately embellish this portion of the ground which continues to the esplanade or terrace, a long walk, forming the western border of the garden, and ornamented on the water side with a balustrade with alcoves and seats," as well as a central archway framing the view of the vanishing waters of the Back Bay. Hammatt here proposed a major public space, a characteristic mid-nineteenth-century garden design using a combination of formal and informal motifs and a catalogue of classical ornamental devices. This is a fleeting glimpse of what he might have achieved as a designer of large spaces, had he been commissioned to lay out other grounds, thus adding landscape architecture to his many other major credits.[12]

Apparently nothing tangible came of Billings's project for the Public Garden. The present layout was planned in 1860 by Boston architect

George F. Meacham (but we might recall here that Billings occasionally ghosted projects for him). Billings also designed public "furniture" that might have embellished such a place. A numbered series of six variant drawings shows what appears to be a fourteen-and-one-half-foot cast-bronze outdoor light standard with glass globes that dates from late August and early September 1870. Although nothing more has yet surfaced about this lamp stand, including whether it was ever manufactured, these are definitely not idle jottings, for one drawing bears an inscription, not in Billings's hand, that reads "Approved, generally," is dated 1 September 1870, and is signed with the initials "H. P." Another sheet seems to contain the definitive design, for it bears the date 3 September although it displays only the penultimate base, for that is contained on a paper flap that covers the inscribed date (fig. 97). All this results in a lamppost that is a collection of motifs including female figures emerging from foliage upholding faceted glass globes, a base bedecked with dolphins, and a shaft belted with cast eagle, cornucopias, and the letter "P." The scale is public rather than private, but the identity of "H. P." remains to be discovered. The series as a whole demonstrates an intense study of the design. A note on one drawing reads "This [globe] would be placed obliquely on the post so that the central face would be of glass." The resulting standard is ornately classical, elaborate, lavish, and accomplished in decorative design.[13]

Not all Billings's public works were so ephemeral. He also created more lasting decorative designs to enhance existing public spaces shaped by others. One of these was a relatively minor work that, however, as executed can still be seen in an important place by important people: it graces the parapet of the balcony facing the rostrum in the auditorium of Bulfinch's venerable Faneuil Hall. This is his design for a wooden frame for the so-called Children's Clock, a gift to Boston from its youngsters.[14] The composition, carved in 1849 by "Mr. Hobbs from a design by Billings" and gilded by S. Curtis, incorporates emblems of the arms of the Commonwealth of Massachusetts flanking the clock face.[15] So, for a century and a half, eminent speakers both charismatic and boring have (certainly unknowingly) contemplated Billings's work as they timed their lectures. The dedication in January 1850 included a reading of Henry Wadsworth Longfellow's "Building of the Ship," a piece described at the time as an "Ode to the Union."[16]

A second decorative commission was for a much larger work which, in the end, was only Hammatt's in a minor way. The Music Hall on Winter Street in Boston was designed in 1852 by the architectural firm of Snell and

Fig. 97. Wash drawing by Hammatt Billings, design for a light standard, 1870 (Harriet Beecher Stowe Center, Hartford, Conn.).

Gregerson.[17] By the end of the decade a drawing for the case for the Great Organ (built by E. F. Wackler of Ludwigsburg) had been accepted. "A most chaste and beautiful design by Hammatt Billings . . . [that] provides a noble central position" for a statue of Beethoven, "it will be constructed here [in Boston] under . . . [his] eye," according to a notice of 1859.[18] In June 1862 the annual meeting of the Music Hall Association heard that the "case (a superb design by Hammatt Billings) lies finished in New York," and by May of the next year Wackler was installing the organ in the hall, with the architectural casework still mentioned as a "superb . . . design by Billings."[19] But by April

1860 Billings had in fact turned over control of the project to the New York firm of the craftsman Gustave Herter (1839–83). In October 1863 *Dwight's Journal of Music* reported to its readership that "it was decided that the work should be committed to the brothers Herter," but that "the general outline of the *facade* followed a design . . . by . . . Billings, to whom also are due the drawings from which the Saint Cecilia and the two groups of cherubs upon the round towers were modelled. These figures were executed at Stuttgart; the other carvings were all done in New York, under Mr. Herter's direction."[20] The Great Organ was inaugurated in November 1863, and in December *Dwight's* summed up the contributions of Billings and Herter by reporting that "the beautiful case was constructed by the Brothers Herter of New York, the germ of the plan being a design by Hammatt Billings of Boston, who was the first to recognize the improvements suggested by the artist builders, and to urge the adoption of their modifications of his plan."[21] Everything we know of Billings's personality lends credence to this account of his unselfish reaction to the change in control. It left him credited with the original overall concept and three pieces of sculpture, and it left at least one of his obituarists believing that the "deviations made by others from his original design were not improvements."[22]

The Great Organ survives but not in its original location (fig. 98). It was moved from the Boston Music Hall in 1897, and in 1904 installed in the Methuen (Massachusetts) Memorial Music Hall, a work of the architect Henry Vaughan, where the public can enjoy its booming sound and marvel at its imposing presence to this day.[23] It is a wooden Baroque pile of American black walnut, "almost exactly the size of a first-class, five-storied city house" according to one nineteenth-century reporter, or a seventeenth-century Roman neighborhood church facade.[24] It contains six thousand pipes and stretches forty-eight feet across and sixty feet high. Billings's St. Cecilia crowns the central axis of this mammoth case piece, between the towers capped by his groups of putti. These exemplify his work as a designer though not a carver of sculpture.

Published reaction to the Great Organ was not as favorable as Billings was accustomed to hear from the critics. In *The Art-Idea* of 1864, James Jackson Jarves, who elsewhere in the same book finds much that is favorable to say of Hammatt's drawing and his architecture, describes the design as "an incongruous, grotesque whole, made up of details partly taken from the Christian art-idea and partly from the pagan, gigantic caryatids and classical masks intermixed with puny cupid-angels, a feeble St. Cecilia, and inane and commonplace ornamentations, . . . and the entire mass made the more emphatic in its offensiveness by its want of adaptation to the size and aesthetic character of the [Boston Music] hall over which it domineers so unpleasantly." In *The Bostonians* Henry James also took a swipe at the huge piece,

Fig. 98. Hammatt Billings and Herter Brothers, organ case, 1859–63. Originally installed in the Boston Music Hall; now in the Methuen (Mass.) Memorial Music Hall (author's collection).

calling it "the great florid, sombre organ, overhanging the bronze statue of Beethoven."[25] Bostonians of the mid-nineteenth century were critical of the overwrought, the overbearing, the oversized.

The Great Organ was indeed oversized furniture, a vast eclectic case piece dominating the interior of the Music Hall. Billings also sketched domestic and commercial woodwork, furniture, and decorative arts for some of the public and private buildings he designed. Most of these drawings are preserved in the scrapbook at the Stowe-Day Library in Hartford.[26] The majority seem to date from after the Civil War.

Billings often designed the decorative features of the buildings he erected as architect. The Stowe-Day scrapbook contains drawings for interior and exterior details connected to known buildings and some that are unassigned. There are sketches of corbels, cornices, screens, gas fixtures, ornamental grills, fences with gates, balustrades, fretwork, columns, pilasters, capitals, finials, dormers and weather vanes, patterns for incised ornament, and newels. The variety and much of the design were clearly inspired by the latest English ideas, especially those expressed by Charles Locke Eastlake's *Hints on Household Taste* of 1868 (American edition, 1872). There are also watercolors of geometric designs for panels that descend from the published works of Owen Jones, especially his *Grammar of Ornament* of 1856 (reprinted in 1868), as well as designs for interior decorative treatments and for free-standing furniture. Throughout there are drawings of conventionalized floral patterns so characteristic of the last half of the nineteenth century.

One sketch, dated 24 September 1873, shows a Neo-Grec bank tellers' screen intended to be built of carved wood and frosted glass surmounted by large acroteria. A number of drawings show paneled interiors with or without fireplace and mirror frames. This series stretches from 1857 to 1874; the designs range in style from Renaissance Revival to Neo-Grec to Eastlake. The earliest, dated 14 May 1857, is a Renaissance Revival fireplace frame surmounted by a mirror.[27] Below the mirror the frame was to be "carved in oak or walnut," above, "stucco colored and gilt." Another Renaissance Revival design, dated 31 January 1868, is for a drawing room, paneled above a wainscot, with fireplace and mirrored overmantel (the mirror is shown alternately round and rectangular). This was a commissioned design, for a Mr. Burnett or Barnett, who is otherwise unknown. There is a sketch dated 7 March 1874 for a fireplace frame for the "private counting room[,] 2nd. story[, in the second] Cathedral building." The facing around the opening as well as the shelf and its backing were to be of marble, according to the notes, the "Woodwork made by McNutt & filled for $95.00." (Could this be the J. J. McNutt of the Novelty Woodworks, a "creature" H. H. Richardson said in a letter of 24 September 1876 who should be "debarred from estimating on any of the church furniture" at Trinity, Boston?) It would appear that the marble facing was itself to be lined with tiles, while the woodwork sported a Neo-Grec decorative vocabulary. In the design of another, unassigned and undated fireplace frame, the ornamental touch and coloristic pattern are greatly energized, with a frame continuing around the overmantel mirror above "Panels in deep colors and [illegible word] gold." The fireplace surround was to be of "Dark grey marble facing with [incised sunburst patterns of] black lines," while the incised woodwork was to be "Oak, gold and marone [sic]." Nowhere is the enriched eclecticism of the Neo-Grec more in evidence than in this thumbnail sketch.[28]

In the Stowe-Day scrapbook are also a number of designs for free-standing furniture, including desks, sideboards, a table, and a secretary, furniture that anticipates the work of the Aesthetic Movement that reached its apogee in the decade after Billings's death. Whether any detached pieces were actually made and now survive is unknown. There is a drawing for fronts and sides of undated variant designs for desks for a Mr. Jewett and a Mr. Rogers. One has horizontal and diagonally grooved panels; the other is surmounted with a spindle gallery; both have chamfered structural members. These are constructional pieces characteristic of the English reform movement of the 1870s as publicized by Eastlake.[29] The "Eastlake School of Art," according to Ambrose Bierce, "scorns concealment of methods and as frankly discloses its means as an end."[30] There is also a related design for a desk for Ward Cheney of South Manchester, Connecticut. Designs for what appear to be two sideboards appear in the scrapbook, neither dated but both probably from the 1870s. One is a lightly sketched elevation of a three-bay piece with more detailed studies of incised ornamental patterns, finials, and pulls. The other is a more monumental piece, also three bays wide but broader and bulkier, with incised diagonal paneled doors beneath the counter, and a standard assortment of Neo-Grec decorative motifs, also incised, above.

There are, finally, two late sketches that best demonstrate Billings's range and stature as a skilled decorative designer influenced by contemporary English thinking. His most richly ornamented furniture design shows up in a drawing of the front and side of a secretary, dated 4 August 1874, just months before his death. This was conceived as an effervescent piece of constructional Gothic, roughly eight feet from floor to the tops of the pin-

Panel
11¼ × 19¾.

Aug. 4th 1874

Fig. 99. Ink and graphite drawing by Hammatt Billings, design for a secretary, 1874 (Harriet Beecher Stowe Center, Hartford, Conn.).

nacles, enlivened by carved and incised "free classical" ornament and four perhaps inlaid, more likely painted, historiated panels (fig. 99). According to notes on the drawing, these panels were to depict "Girl spinning with distaff, Cupid behind her takes hold of the shaft," "Girl reading is distracted by Cupid," "Cupid's eyes bandaged playing on a lyre," and "Cupid [illegible word] putting on a helmet." All this suggests a piece conceived for a young woman, otherwise unidentified. This secretary shows Billings as an accomplished designer in the latest English furniture fashion. Here he updates the Eastlakian mode with figural panels inspired by the work of William Morris, Philip Webb, and others.

The second design is for a table. It is more subdued than the secretary but equally important (fig. 100). Although lacking the decorative fireworks of the secretary, it is nonetheless both au courant and prophetic. Exhibiting the principles of "simplicity, functionalism, and honesty of construction" expounded by Eastlake's *Hints*, this undecorated trestle table, some eight feet

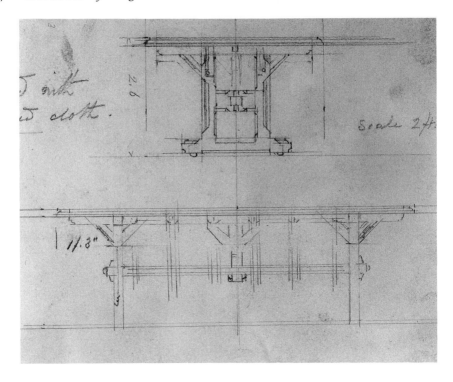

Fig. 100. Graphite drawing by Hammatt Billings, design for a table, ca. 1870s (Harriet Beecher Stowe Center, Hartford, Conn.).

long, with braced top, molded edges, and pronounced mortise and tenon joints, bridges the gap between the Gothic Revival of Billings's youth, and the Morris-inspired Arts and Crafts Movement that was to have such an impact upon furniture and other decorative design in the quarter of a century after his death.[31] These late pieces, the secretary and especially the table, suggest that, like A. W. N. Pugin in England, Hammatt Billings in the United States at the end of his life was poised to become a forerunner of the Arts and Crafts Movement.

Afterword

HISTORY IS LONG and memory short. History is not the same as memory; what we remember happened is only part of what did happen. It is arrogant to think that only what we remember or what appeals to us now should form the basis for the writing of history. If we care to recapture the past, we must include in that past that which the past thought was important, whether that assessment seems "correct" according to current standards. One function of history is to correct our selective recall. The past must be searched for significant people and events that have escaped our memories. The writing of history is cyclic, of course, like any other fashion, but we owe it to the past and to ourselves to at least begin our interpretation with what the past thought about itself.

The career of Hammatt Billings illustrates the problem. "Hammatt who?" was the question that usually greeted the announcement of occasional research over the past decades. Why bother with someone who has not floated on the surface of contemporary memory? With all the "important" work to be done on "important" figures, easily recognized names like Eakins or Homer, Upjohn or Richardson, Darley or Nast, why light very small candles in very dark corners? If Hammatt Billings had been of any consequence his name would still be alive. He cannot have been of any importance or he would be remembered.

The present-day observer pokes himself in the eye with attitudes of that kind, blinds herself to the rich possibilities of recovered history. And stands not on the shoulders of giants but on a haughty height from which to look down upon the judgments of another era. This study of the career of Hammatt Billings has cited his contemporaries over and over again as valuing his work—his public service—at the level of creative genius. Emerson placed him on a par with, among other luminaries, Margaret Fuller, Horatio Greenough, Daniel Webster, and Wendell Phillips, on a par, that is, with individuals we do remember and continue to respect, at least for their historical importance. These assessments of Billings's achievements come from myriad sources over a long period. They reflect the standards of the place and time in which he worked. By discounting Billings because he is so slightly remembered, the present has discounted the judgment of his peers and set its own standards above theirs. The result has been a cultural Alzheimer's. This study has undertaken its scholarly cure.

Taken as a whole, Billings's career ought to have an important place in the study of American popular culture. That place he earned by his work, and by the role of that work as witness to the public life of the past century. Billings's works in many media illuminate for us the trauma of the 1850s. Histories of American illustration, of American memorials, of American architecture are incomplete without recognition of Billings's achievements. Histories of nineteenth-century Boston, especially of its public, ceremonial life, are lacking without his presence. Even if we adhere to current standards of artistic quality, thereby finding much of his work not to our taste (which from the perspective of this Afterword would smack of faulty method), we must still recognize the bewildering variety of his contributions to the cultural life of his day.

Billings saturated the field of design in mid-nineteenth-century Boston. No one else comes to mind who was so highly praised in so many departments of art, whose presence so thoroughly permeated the popular culture of the period, who served such a broad constituency, whose talent showed itself in so many different lights. His career rivals that of England's A. W. N. Pugin in breadth, but where Pugin's varied art graced the lives mainly of the English aristocracy, Billings spread his diverse gifts more democratically across the spectrum of American society. A sizable portion of the population of nineteenth-century Boston that read books or periodicals, attended church, school, or the theater, buried its dead, celebrated civic festivals, envisioned the past or current events, attended concerts or art exhibitions, sang songs, or lived the commercial life of the city could not do so without encountering something of Billings's presence.

Like better-remembered nineteenth-century fine artists, Billings was acquainted with, worked for, and influenced many of the commercial, financial, political, intellectual, and cultural leaders of his time, but his work cut across class lines. Through his ever-present labors in the public life of the people he reached the middle and lower classes as well. His career has *historical* importance, whether or not we have until now remembered it, however we might judge the quality of its products.

This study has tried to recover what is now recoverable of the life and work of Hammatt Billings because it is worthy of being remembered as part

of the cultural and popular history of nineteenth-century Boston in particular and the United States in general. The work of remembering should not
end here. For all the many facts and things listed or discussed in this book,
more data requiring more interpretation seem to emerge at regular intervals.
To the future belongs a more complete remembering of Hammatt Billings's
role in our collective past.

Appendix A
Billings's Books

Beginning in 1845 Hammatt Billings (HB) bought books from the bookstore of William D. Ticknor (later Ticknor and Fields) at the corner of Washington and School Streets in Boston. These purchases were recorded in a ledger now preserved at the Houghton Library, Harvard University (fMS AM 1185.14[1], f. 129; [2], f. 492; [3] f.169; and [4], f. 516). After 1858 entries are not specific enough to identify titles. From 1845 to 1858 (with some missing years) the notations are brief, often cryptic, and at times illegible, but so far as they can be identified, HB acquired the publications listed below. Where possible, I have translated the notations into full bibliographical information. Where I am uncertain I have given the original notation in parentheses.

1845

1. 16 August: John Henry Parker, *A Glossary of Terms Used in Grecian, Roman, Italian, and Gothic Architecture* (Oxford, 4th ed., 1845), 2 vols. ($10.00).
2. 4 September: Charles Knight, ed., *The Pictorial Edition of the Works of Shakspere [sic]* (London, 2d ed., [1845]). HB purchased one fascicle on this date ($0.63), another (no. 44) on 16 September ($0.62), and others (nos. 47 through 55) on 4 November ($6.75).
3. 22 September: William H. Wright, *A Brief Practical Treatise on Mortars, with an Account of the Process Employed at the Public Works in Boston Harbor* (Boston, 1845). ($1.25).
4. 24 September: *Elements of Geometry and Trigonometry*, translated from the French of A. M. Legendre, by David Brewster, revised and adapted to the Course of Mathematical Instruction in the United States by Charles Davies (Philadelphia, 1844). ($1.25). HB could have purchased the abridgement.
5. 24 October: (Durer Passion Christ). ($5.75).
6. 18 November: (Moores Melodies). Perhaps the first volume of John W. Moore, *The Musician's Lexicon* (Boston, 1845–46), 2 parts. ($15.00).

1846

7. 17 July: W. H. Leeds, *The Travellers' Club House* (London, 1839). ($6.00).
8. 23 July: Joseph Gwilt, *An Encyclopaedia of Architecture* (London, 2d ed., 1845); or, less likely, Joseph Guilt, *Rudiments of Architecture* (London, 2d ed., 1839). ($11.00).

9. 7 August: Morrill Wyman, *A Practical Treatise on Ventilation* (Cambridge, Mass., 1846). ($1.75).

10. 18 September: Augustus W. N. Pugin, *Contrasts; or, a Parallel between the Nobel Edifices of the Middle Ages, and Corresponding Buildings of the Present Day* . . . (London, 2d ed., 1841). ($10.00).

11. 23 September: Benjamin R. Haydon, *Lectures on Painting and Design* (London, 1845–46), 2 vols. ($6.50).

12. 19 December: Mrs. Anna Brownell Jameson, *The Heroines of Shakespeare* (New York, 1846), with illustrations by the author. ($3.00).

1851

13. 25 January: Friedrich Overbeck, *Darstellungen aus den Evangelien nach vierzig Originalzeichnungen* (Dusseldorf, [1850–54]). HB purchased one fascicle on this date ($2.50), and another on 29 November 1853. ($2.50).

14. 28 February: Grace Greenwood, *History of My Pets* (Boston, 1851). ($0.50). HB illustrated this for Ticknor, Reed, and Fields.

15. 11 April: Nathaniel Hawthorne, *The House of the Seven Gables* (Boston, 1851). ($1.00).

16. 24 April: John Ruskin, *The Stones of Venice* (London, 1851–53), 3 vols. Also published in New York. HB acquired a volume on this date ($3.50), another on 25 July ($12.60), and volumes 2 and 3 on 1 November 1853 ($22.20).

17. (V2 Wordsworth).

18. 5 July: [Donald G. Mitchell], *The Lorgnette; or, Studies of the Town*, by an Opera Goer. (New York, [ca. 1850]), 2 vols. ($2.50). There are several editions dated 1850 and 1851. HB might have acquired the 2d ed., "set off with Mr. [F. O. C.] Darley's designs."

19. 10 July: (Sheepfolds). Perhaps John Ruskin, *Notes on the Construction of Sheepfolds* (London, 1851).

20. 24 December: ([illegible] Ill'd.). ($4.00).

1852

21. 20 January: ([illegible] Poetry). ($10.00).

22. 19 March: Daniel DeFoe, *The Life and Adventures of Robinson Crusoe* (Boston, 1852). ($1.00). There was also a New York edition of 1852 with two hundred engravings by Grandville, but the price suggests the Boston edition.

23. 13 May: Henry Wadsworth Longfellow, *Poetical Works* (Boston, 1852). ($2.00).

24. 29 May: George W. Kendall, *The War between the United States and Mexico*, with illustrations by Carl Nebel. (New York, 1851). ($35.00).

25. 29 June: J. Burnet, *Turner and His Works.* (London, 1852–59), 2 vols. ($8.00). HB must have acquired only the first volume at this date.

26. 6 July: Gustave Doré, *The Legend of the Wandering Jew: A Series of Twelve Designs* (n.p., n.d.). ($2.50).

27. 13 July: Nathaniel Hawthorne, *The Blithdale Romance* (Boston, 1852). ($0.75).

28. 17 July: W. Williams, *Appletons's New York City Guide* (New York, 1851). ($2.00).

29. 9 August: Mary Roberts, *Ruins and Old Trees, Associated with Memorable Events in English History,* with illustrations by [John] Gilbert, engraved by Folkard (London, 1840?; another ed., [1843]). ($2.00).
30. 26 August: (Chevalier De Fauble [?]). ($3.75).
31. 1 September: (Hasemans Life [?]). ($1.25).
32. 1 October: [John Ruskin], *Modern Painters,* by a graduate of Oxford (London, 3d ed., 1850), 2 vols. HB apparently purchased a volume of the "New Eng[lish] Ed[ition]" on this date ($5.50) and the set on 28 February 1856 ($11.00). On 24 September 1856 he acquired the illustrated vol. 4 ($14.00).

1853

33. 28 January: Walter Scott, *The Lady of the Lake,* illustrated by numerous engravings on wood from drawings by Birket Foster and John Gilbert (Edinburgh, 1853). ($4.00).
34. 11 February: *Household Stories, Collected by the Brothers Grimm,* with two hundred and forty illustrations, by Edward H. Wehnert (London, 1853), 2 vols. ($4.00).
35. 30 April: Leitch Ritchie, *Liber Fluviorum; or, River Scenery of France,* depicted in sixty-one line engravings from drawings by J. M. W. Turner (London, 1853). ($9.00). (On 22 September HB purchased a daguerreotype, otherwise unidentified, for $0.75.)
36. 27 September: John R. Chapman, *Instructions to Young Marksmen . . . as Exhibited in the Improved American Rifle* (New York, 1848). ($1.25).
37. 14 October: Rufus W. Griswold, *The Poets and Poetry of America.* ($4.00). There were many editions after 1842.
38. 16 November: Edmund Spenser, *The Faerie Queen,* illustrated by Edward Corbauld (London, 1853; New York, 1854). ($1.50).
39. 17 November: (Sculpture &c). ($1.50).
40. 28 November: [Sara P. Parton], *Fern Leaves from Fanny's Port-folio,* with original designs by Fred M. Coffin (Auburn, N.Y., 1853). ($1.25). HB could rather have bought the London edition of this year, illustrated by Birket Foster.
41. 17 December: (Boys at Home). ($1.25).

1854

42. 28 October: (Cassells Pictures). ($0.38). Perhaps *Cassell's Illustrated Family Paper,* which began publication in 1853, or any other of Cassell's many books.
43. 14 December: William Cullen Bryant, *Poems.* ($2.00). A Philadelphia edition illustrated by Emanuel Leutze appeared in 1853, while a New York edition of 1854 contained many illustrations by Birket Foster, Harry Fenn, and others.
44. 21 December: (Juveniles). ($0.85).

1855

45. 5 January: (2 Ill[ustrated] Church Catech[is]m[s]). ($0.75).
46. 13 April: William North, *The Slave of the Lamp* (New York, 1855). ($1.00).

47. 20 April: (1 Alphabet). ($0.50).
48. 25 April: *Life of Benjamin Haydon, Historical Painter, from His Autobiography and Journals,* edited . . . by Tom Tayler (London, 1853), 3 vols.; or, (New York, 1853), 2 vols. ($1.75).
49. 18 August: Alfred, Lord Tennyson, *Maud, and Other Poems* (Boston, 1855). ($0.50).
50. 20 August: James J. Jarves, *Art-Hints: Architecture, Sculpture, and Painting* (London, 1855). ($1.25).
51. 10 September: *The Illustrated London Almanac.* ($2.00). On 12 October HB purchased the volumes for 1853–54.
52. 2 October: *The Leisure Hour: An Illustrated Magazine for Home Reading.* ($5.50). HB purchased "No[.] 194" this date, and other copies on 24 December ($0.56), 21 June 1856 ($1.64), and 22 June 1857 ($1.67).
53. 22 October: Thomas Gray, *An Elegy Written in a Country Churchyard,* illustrated (New York, 1855). ($3.00).
54. 29 October: Walter Scott, *Marmion: A Tale of Flodden Field,* illustrated by eighty engravings on wood, from drawings by Birket Foster and John Gilbert (Edinburgh, 1855). ($1.00).
55. 10 December: (Longfellow Ill[ustrated]). Henry Wadsworth Longfellow, *The Poetical Works,* a new edition with upwards of one hundred designs, drawn by John Gilbert, engraved by the brothers Dalziel (London, 1855; Boston, 1856). Another possibility is H. W. Longfellow, *Poems,* illustrated . . . from designs by Jane E. Benham, Birket Foster, etc. (Boston, 1855). ($4.00).
56. 31 December: (Knick Gallery). Perhaps *Sketches Here and There: From the Knickerbocker Magazine* (New York, 1855). ($7.00).

1856

57. 19 June: William Wordsworth, *Poetical Works* (Boston, 1856). ($4.00).

1857

58. 19 August: [Catherine M. Sedgwick], *Married or Single?* by the author of "Hope Leslie" (New York, 1857), 2 vols. ($1.75).
59. 20 August: John Ruskin, *The Elements of Drawing* (New York, 1857). ($1.00).
60. 22 August: John Ruskin, *The Elements of Drawing* (London, 1857). ($1.25).
61. 22 September: (Leonora). Perhaps *Leonora,* by the Honourable Mrs. Maberly (London, 1856), 3 vols. ($3.50).

1858

62. 11 February: John Ruskin, *The Political Economy of Art* (London, 1857). ($0.50).
63. 16 November: (3 Nos[.] Shakespeare). ($8.00).
64. 16 November: William Wordsworth, *Pastoral Poems* (New York, 1858). ($8.00). Illustrated by Birket Foster and others.

In addition to the above purchases HB owned the following volumes:

65. William Dunlap, *History of the Rise and Progress of the Arts of Design in the United States* (New York, 1834). On 27 February 1842 HB wrote to a friend that he had purchased "some little essays on the History of the Arts of Design" (Joanna Andros Collection, Keene, New Hampshire). Unlocated.

66. *Umrisse zu Goethe's Faust* (Stuttgart, 1837) and *Umrisse von Schiller's Lied von der Glocke* (Stuttgart, 1843), both bound into one volume bearing HB's signature and the inscribed date, 1845, on the first free leaf. Outline illustrations by Moritz Retzsch. Author's collection.

67. Henry Wadsworth Longfellow, *Evangeline, A Tale of Acadia* (Boston, 6th ed., 1848). HB's signature on the title page, and a sketch of the "forest primeval" on p. [5]. Special Collections, Clapp Library, Wellesley College.

68. Kate Newell Doggett, *The Grammar of Painting and Engraving Translated from the French of Blanc's Grammaire des Art du Design* (New York, 1874). HB's signature on the title page. This volume came from the library of the Hartford architect George Keller (1842–1935). The Stowe-Day Library of the Harriet Beecher Stowe Center, Hartford.

Appendix B
A Billings Bookshelf

The following chronological short-title list catalogues the books illustrated by HB. It is based on, but contains additions and corrections to, James F. O'Gorman, *A Billings Bookshelf: A Bibliography of Works Illustrated by Hammatt Billings* (Wellesley College, Mass., 3d ed., revised, 1993). The numbering here is new. This list contains only the first appearance of titles that often reappeared (sometimes altered) in later editions. It does not contain titles of works in which appeared second (or later) printings of illustrations by HB. An asterisk before an entry indicates that this title, in the listed edition, is included in the Hammatt Billings Collection in Special Collections in the Clapp Library at Wellesley College (to which additions are always welcome). An entry in parentheses is an undocumented attribution.

1. *Abbott, Jacob. *The Rollo Code of Morals.* Boston: Crocker and Brewster, 1841.
2. Sigourney, L. H. *Pleasant Memories of Pleasant Lands.* Boston: James Munroe, 1842.
3. *Shepard, Isaac F., ed. *The Christian Souvenir.* Boston: Henry B. Williams, 1843.
4. Jarves, James J. *Scenes and Scenery in the Sandwich Islands.* Boston: James Munroe, 1843.
5. (*Easy Nat.* Boston: Redding, 1844).
6. *Chimes, Rhymes, and Jingles; or, Mother Goose's Songs.* Boston: Munroe, 1845.
7. *Frothingham, Richard, Jr. *The History of Charlestown, Massachusetts.* Charlestown: Charles P. Emmons; Boston: Charles C. Little and James Brown, 1845–49.
8. *(Lang, Wm. Bailey). *Views . . . of the Highland Cottages at Roxbury.* Boston: L. H. Bridgham and H. E. Felch, 1845.
9. [Little, George]. *The American Cruiser.* Boston: Waite, Pierce, 1846.
10. Hamilton, Robert, ed. *The Mayflower.* Boston: Saxton and Kelt, 1846.
11. [Livermore, Abiel A.] *The Marriage Offering.* Boston: Crosby, Nichols, 1848.
12. Goodrich, S. G. *A Pictorial History of America.* Hartford: House and Brown, 1848.
13. Poore, Ben: Perley: *The Rise and Fall of Louis Phillipe.* Boston: William D. Ticknor, 1848.
14. [Bumstead, Josiah F.] *Second Reading-Book in the Primary School.* Boston: William D. Ticknor, 1848.
15. [Bumstead, Josiah F.], *Third Reading-Book in the Primary School.* Boston: William D. Ticknor, 1848.
16. "Fanny Fire-Fly." *The Ducks and the Frogs.* Boston: Joseph H. Francis, 1849.
17. *The Gem of the Season.* New York: Leavitt, Trow, 1849.

18. *Shurtleff, J. B. *The Governmental Instructor*. New York: Collins and Brothers, 1849.
19. *Holmes, Oliver Wendell. *Poems*. Boston: Ticknor, 1849.
20. Whittier, John G. *Poems*. Boston: Benjamin B. Mussey, 1849.
21. [Batchelder, Eugene.] *The Romance of the Sea Serpent*. Cambridge: John Bartlett, 1849.
22. *[Fields, James, ed.] *The Boston Book*. Boston: Ticknor, Reed, and Fields, 1850.
23. *Greenwood, Grace [Sara J. C. Lippincott]. *Greenwood Leaves*. Boston: Ticknor, Reed, and Fields, 1850.
24. *Cleveland, Richard J. *A Narrative of Voyages*. Boston: Charles H. Pierce, 1850.
25. *Buckingham, Joseph T. *Specimens of Newspaper Literature*. Boston: Charles C. Little and James Brown, 1850.
26. *Muzzey, A. B. *The Young Maiden*. Boston: Crosby and Nichols, 1850.
27. *The Dramatic Works of William Shakespeare*. Boston: Phillips, Sampson, 1850–51.
28. Longfellow, Henry Wadsworth. *The Golden Legend*. Boston: Ticknor, Reed, and Fields, 1851.
29. *Greenwood, Grace [Sara J. C. Lippincott]. *History of My Pets*. Boston: Ticknor, Reed, and Fields, 1851.
30. Goodrich, S. G. *Poems*. New York: Putnam, 1850.
31. Hawthorne, Nathaniel. *True Stories from History and Biography*. Boston: Ticknor, Reed, and Fields, 1850.
32. [Everett, Edward, ed.] *The Works of Daniel Webster*. Boston: Charles C. Little and James Brown, 1851.
33. *The Boston Almanac*. Boston: B. B. Mussey, from 1852 on.
34. [Gordon, Katharine Parker (Sleeper)]. *Fresh Flowers for Children*. Boston: Munroe, 1852.
35. Wright, Henry C. *A Kiss for a Blow*. Boston: Mussey, 1852.
36. *[Horne, Richard Henry]. *Memoirs of a London Doll*. Boston: Ticknor, Reed, and Fields, 1852.
37. *Quincy, Josiah. *A Municipal History of . . . Boston*. Boston: Little and Brown, 1852.
38. *Greenwood, Grace [Sara J. C. Lippincott]. *Recollections of My Childhood*. Boston: Ticknor, Reed, and Fields, 1852.
39. [Addison, Joseph]. *Sir Roger de Coverly*. Boston: Ticknor, Reed, and Fields, 1852.
40. *Tales from Catland*. Boston: Ticknor, Reed, and Fields, 1852.
41. *Stowe, Harriet Beecher. *Uncle Tom's Cabin*. Boston: John P. Jewett, 1852.
42. Hawthorne, Nathaniel. *A Wonder Book*. Boston: Ticknor, Reed, and Fields, 1852.
43. *[Hildreth, Richard]. *The White Slave*. Boston: Tappan and Whittemore, 1852.
44. *Bailey, Philip James. *Festus*. Boston: Benjamin B. Mussey, 1853.
45. *Clark, Rufus W. *Heaven and the Scriptural Emblems*. Boston: John P. Jewett, 1853.
46. *Homes of American Authors*. New York: Putnam, 1853.
47. *A Memorial of Daniel Webster*. Boston: Little, Brown, 1853.
48. *[Dix, John (Ross)]. *Passages from the History of a Wasted Life*. Boston: Benjamin B. Mussey, 1853.
49. Sargent, Epes, ed. *Selections in Poetry*. Philadelphia: Thomas, Cowperthwait, 1853.
50. Hawthorne, Nathaniel. *Tanglewood Tales*. Boston: Ticknor, Reed, and Fields, 1853.

51. Wellmont, Emma. *Uncle Sam's Palace*. Boston: Benjamin B. Mussey, 1853.
52. *Stowe, Harriet Beecher. *Uncle Tom's Cabin*. (Illustrated edition). Boston: John P. Jewett, 1853.
53. *Sumner, Charles. *White Slavery*. Boston: John P. Jewett, 1853.
54. *Lodge, G. Henry, trans. *The Breughel Brothers*. Boston, Little, Brown, 1854.
55. [Graves, Adelia Cleopatra (Spencer)]. *First Lessons in Gentleness and Truth*. Boston: John P. Jewett, 1854.
56. *The Lady's Almanac*. Boston: John P. Jewett, from 1854 on.
57. Ballou, Maturin M. *The Life Story of Hosea Ballou*. Boston: Tompkins, 1854.
58. *Creyton, Paul [John T. Trowbridge]. *Martin Merrivale*. Boston: Phillips, Sampson, 1854.
59. *[Reynolds, Elhanan W.]. *Records of the Bubbleton Parish*. Boston: Tompkins and Mussey, 1854.
60. *Whittier, John Greenleaf. *A Sabbath Scene*. Boston: John P. Jewett, 1854.
61. Larcom, Lucy. *Similitudes*. Boston: John P. Jewett, 1854.
62. *Stowe, Harriet Beecher. *Sunny Memories of Foreign Lands*. Boston: Phillips, Sampson, 1854.
63. Dix, John Ross. *The Worth of the Worthless*. Boston: Sons of Temperance, 1854.
64. Howitt, William. *A Boy's Adventures in the Wilds of Australia*. Boston: Ticknor and Fields, 1855.
65. Soule, Caroline A. *Home Life*. Boston: Tompkins and Mussey, 1855.
66. Phelps, Phoebe Harris. *Home Stories*. Boston: John P. Jewett, 1855:
    a. *Henry Day Learning to Obey Bible Commands*
    b. *Henry Day's Story Book*
    c. *Mary Day Forming Good Habits*
    d. *Mary Day's Story Book*
67. Follen, Eliza Lee [Cabot]. *Mrs. Follen's Twilight Stories*. Boston: Whittemore, Niles, and Hall, 1855:
    a. *True Stories about Dogs and Cats*
    b. *Made-Up Stories*
    c. *The Pedler of Dust Sticks*
    d. *The Old Garret, Part First*
    e. *The Old Garret, Part Second*
    f. *The Old Garret, Part Third*
68. *Ashton, S. G. *The Mothers of the Bible*. Boston: John P. Jewett, 1855.
69. Sargent, Epes. *Sargent's Standard Series*. [Boston, 1855]:
    a. *The Standard First Reader*
    b. *The Standard Second Reader*
    c. *The Standard Second Reader, Part Two*
70. *The Sunbeam*. Boston: John P. Jewett, 1855.
71. *Curious Stories about Fairies*. Boston: Ticknor and Fields, 1856.
72. [Tappan, Caroline C.]. *The Magician's Show Box*. Boston: Ticknor and Fields, 1856.
73. [Trowbridge, Jerusha J.]. *Our Grandmother's Stories, and Aunt Kate's Fireside Memories*. Boston: Ticknor and Fields, 1856.

74. Carter, Ann Augusta [Gray]. *Rosy Diamond Story Books for Girls*. Boston: Phillips, Sampson [later Lee and Shepard], 1856:
    a. **Great Rosie Diamond*
    b. **Violet*
    c. **Daisy*
    d. *Minnie*
    e. **The Angel Children*
    f. **Little Blossom's Reward*
75. *Jenks, Joseph William, ed. *The Rural Poetry of the English Language*. Boston: John P. Jewett, 1856.
76. Ashton, S. G. *Sabbath Talks with the Little Children about Jesus*. Boston: John P. Jewett, 1856.
77. Ashton, S. G. *Sabbath Talks with the Little Children about the Psalms of David*. Boston: John P. Jewett, 1856.
78. *Midgley, R. L. [David Pulsifer]. *Sights in Boston and Suburbs*. Boston: John P. Jewett, 1856.
79. [Planche, Matilda]. *Sunbeam Stories*. Boston: James Munroe, 1856.
80. Hildrith, Hosea. *A Book for Massachusetts Children*. Boston: John P. Jewett, 1857.
81. *[Guild, Anne E. (Gore)]. *Grandmother Lee's Portfolio*. Boston: Whittemore, Niles, and Hall, 1857.
82. *[Shurtleff, Nathaniel B., ed.]. *Memorial of the Inauguration of the Statue of Franklin*. Boston: City Council, 1857.
83. Baker, Madeline Leslie [Harriette Newell (Woods)]. *Old Moll and Little Agnes*. Boston: Shepard, Clark, 1857.
84. Channing, Barbara H. *The Sisters Abroad*. Boston: Whittemore, Niles, and Hall, 1857.
85. *Greenwood, Grace [Sara J. C. Lippincott]. *Stories and Legends of Travel and History*. Boston: Ticknor and Fields, 1857.
86. Scott, Walter. *Waverley Novels*. Boston: Ticknor and Fields, 1857–59:
    a. *The Black Dwarf* and *Legend of Montrose*
    b. *The Heart of Mid-Lothian*
    c. *Ivanhoe*
    d. **The Monastery*
    e. *The Abbot*
    f. *Kenilworth*
    g. *The Pirate*
    h. *The Fortunes of Nigel*
    i. *Peveril of the Peak*
    j. **Quentin Durward*
    k. **St. Ronan's Well*
87. *"Frank." *Fourteen Pet Goslings*. Boston: J. E. Tilton, [1858].
88. *Goody Right Thirsty*. Boston: Shepard, Clark, and Brown, 1858.
89. *Todd, John. *Lectures to Children*. Northampton: Hopkins, Bridgman, 1858.
90. Talmon, Thrace [Mrs. Eileen Tryphosa Harrington]. *The Strawberry Party*. Boston: E. O. Libby, [1858?].

91. [Hilliard, George S.]. *The First Primary Reader*. Boston: Brewer and Tileston, 1858.
92. [Hilliard, George S.]. *The Second Primary Reader*. Boston: Brewer and Tileston, 1858.
93. [Hilliard, George S.]. *The Third Primary Reader*. Boston: Brewer and Tileston, 1858.
94. *[Haven, C. M.]. *Christmas Hours*. Boston: Ticknor and Fields, 1858.
95. *Dandy Dick, the Celebrated Equestrian Performer*. Boston: J. E. Tilton, 1859.
96. Everett, Edward. *Eulogy on Thomas Dowse*. Boston: Wilson and Son, 1859.
97. Hill, G. C. *Capt. John Smith*. Boston: E. O. Libby, 1859.
98. *Austin, Jane G. *Fairy Dreams*. Boston: J. E. Tilton, 1859.
99. *Harsha, D. A. *The Heavenly Token*. New York: H. Dayton, 1859.
100. *"Uncle Faunus." *The Life and Adventures of Whitenose Woodchuck*. Boston: Brown, Taggard, and Chase, 1859.
101. Franklin, Josephine. *The Martin and Nelly Stories*. Boston: Brown and Taggard, 1859–65:
    a. *Nelly and Her Friends*
    b. *Nelly's First School-Days*
    c. *Nelly and Her Boat*
    d. *Little Bessie*
    e. (*Nelly's Visit*)
    f. (*Zelma* [illustrations by Hyde])
    g. *Martin*
    h. *Cousin Regulus*
    i. *Martin and Nelly*
    j. *Martin on the Mountain*
    k. *Martin and the Miller*
    l. *Trouting*
102. *My Own Little Library*. Boston: Brown, Taggard, and Chase, 1859:
    a. *The Baby Dear*
    b. *Home*
    c. *Shade and Sunshine*
    d. *The Birds of Spring*
    e. *A Song for May*
    f. *The Story of a Bell*
103. [Sleeper, Martha G. (Quincy)]. *Pictures from the History of the Swiss*. Boston: Brown, Taggard, and Chase, 1859.
104. *Dexter, Henry M. *Street Thoughts*. Boston: Crosby, Nichols, 1859.
105. [Guild, Caroline Snowden Whitmarsh]. *The Summer-House Series*. Boston: Brown, Taggard, and Chase, 1859–64:
    a. *Our Summer House*
    b. *Older than Adam*
    c. (*Lives of Familiar Insects*)
    d. (*Wings and Webs*)
    e. (*Aunt Annie's Rainy Day Stories*)
106. *Silsbee, Marianne Cabot [Devereux], ed. *Willie Winkie's Nursery Songs of Scotland*. Boston: Ticknor and Fields, 1859.

107. *[Thayer, William M.]. *The Bobbin Boy*. Boston: J. E. Tilton, 1860.

108. *The Illustrated Pilgrim Almanac*. Boston: A. Williams, 1860.

109. Baker, Madeline Leslie [Harriette Newell (Woods)]. *The Little Frankie Series (Mrs. Leslie's Books for Little Children)*. Boston: Crosby, Nichols, Lee, 1860:
    a. *Little Frankie and His Mother*
    b. *Little Frankie at His Plays*
    c. *Little Frankie and His Cousin*
    d. *Little Frankie and His Father*
    e. *Little Frankie on a Journey*
    f. *Little Frankie at School*

110. *[Whitney, Adeline D. T.]. *Mother Goose for Grown Folks*. New York: Rudd and Carleton, 1860.

111. Baker, Madeline Leslie [Harriette Newell (Woods)]. *The Robin Redbreast Series (Mrs. Leslie's Books for Little Children)*. Boston: Crosby and Nichols, 1860:
    a. *The Robins's Nest*
    b. *Little Robins in the Nest*
    c. *Little Robins Learning to Fly*
    d. *Little Robins in Trouble*
    e. *Little Robins' Friends*
    f. *Little Robins' Love One to Another*

112. *Greenwood, Grace. [Sara J. C. Lippincott]. *Stories from Famous Ballads*. Boston: Ticknor and Fields, 1860.

113. A., H. B. *Stories of Henry and Henrietta*. Boston: T. O. H. P. Burnham, 1860.

114. *Ilsley, Charles P. *The Wrecker's Daughter*. Boston: Albert Colby, 1860.

115. Whitaker, Mary Ann. *Alice's Dream*. Boston: Walker, Wise, 1861.

116. *A Happy Summer-Time*. Boston: Chase, Nichols, and Hall, 1861. (HB may also be the author.)

117. *Hymns for Mothers and Children*. Boston: Walker, Wise, 1861.

118. *The Life and Writings of Bishop Heber*. Boston: Albert Colby, 1861.

119. *[Sleeper, Martha G. (Quincy)]. *Pictures from the History of Spain*. Boston: Brown and Taggard, 1861.

120. Town, Salem. *The Second Reader*. New York: Phinney, Blakeman, and Mason, 1861.

121. *Gleanings from the Poets*. Boston: Crosby and Nichols, 1862.

122. Hanks, S. W. *Light on the Ocean*. Boston: Massachusetts Sabbath School Society, [1862].

123. *The Life of Dandy Dick*. Boston: J. E. Tilton, 1863.

124. Optic, Oliver [William T. Adams]. *Riverdale Story Books*. Boston: Lee and Shepard, 1863:
    a. *The Little Merchant*
    b. *The Young Voyagers*
    c. *Dolly and I*
    d. *Proud and Lazy*
    e. *Careless Kate*
    f. *Robinson Crusoe, Jr.*

125. *Coggeshall, William T. *Stories of Frontier Adventure in the South and West*. New York: Follett, Foster . . . J. Bradburn, 1863.

126. *The Illustrated Pilgrim Memorial*. Boston: National Monument to the Forefathers, 1864.

127. Optic, Oliver [William T. Adams]. *Flora Lee Story Books*. Boston: Lee and Shepard, 1864:
    a. *Christmas Gift*
    b. *Uncle Ben*
    c. *Birthday Party*
    d. *The Picnic Party*
    e. *The Gold Thimble*
    f. *The Do-Somethings*

128. Optic, Oliver [William T. Adams]. *Army and Navy Stories*. Boston: Lee and Shepard, 1864–66:
    a. (*The Soldier Boy*)
    b. (*The Sailor Boy*)
    c. *The Young Lieutenant*
    d. *The Yankee Middy*
    e. *Fighting Joe*
    f. *Brave Old Salt*

129. *Tennyson, Alfred. *Enoch Arden*. Boston: J. E. Tilton, 1865.

130. *Howitt, Mary. *The Favorite Scholar*. New York: James Miller, 1865.

131. *Goodrich, Frank B. *The Tribute Book*. New York: Derby and Miller, 1865.

132. *Ingelow, Jean. *Songs of Seven*. Boston: Roberts Brothers, 1866.

133. *Goldsmith, Oliver. *The Deserted Village*. Boston: J. E. Tilton, 1866.

134. *Poems of Alfred Tennyson*. Boston: J. E. Tilton, 1866.

135. *Ingelow, Jean. *Poems*. Boston: Roberts Brothers, 1867.

136. *Hudson, Charles. *History of the Town of Lexington*. Boston: Wiggin and Lunt, 1868.

137. *Pellico, Silvio. *My Prisons*. Boston: Roberts Brothers, 1868.

138. Baker, George M. *An Old Man's Prayer*. Boston: Lee and Shepard, 1868.

139. Baker, Madeline Leslie [Harriette Newell (Woods)]. *The Woodlawn Series*. Boston: Woolworth, Ainsworth . . . New York: A. S. Barnes, 1868:
    a. *Bertie's Homes*
    b. *Bertie and the Carpenters*
    c. *Bertie and the Masons*
    d. *Bertie and the Plumbers*
    e. *Bertie and the Painters*
    f. *Bertie and the Gardeners*

140. *Alcott, Louisa May. *Little Women . . . Part Two*. Boston: Roberts Brothers, 1869.

141. *Abbott, John S. C. *Lives of the Presidents*. Boston: B. B. Russell, 1869.

142. *Monroe, Lewis B. *Manual of Physical and Vocal Training*. Philadelphia: Cowperthwait, 1869.

143. [*The Nursery Series:*] *The Child's Auction, and Other Stories*. Boston: John L. Shorey . . . Nichols and Hall, 1869.

144. *[The Nursery Series:]* The Great Secret, and Other Stories. Boston: John L. Shorey . . . Nichols and Hall, 1869.

145. *Barnes, William. *Rural Poems*. Boston: Roberts Brothers, 1869.

146. Rosenberg, C. G., ed., *Wonders of the World*. New York: United States Publishing, 1869.

147. [Estes, Dana]. *Echoes from Home*. Boston: Lee and Shepard, 1870.

148. *Morris, William. *The Lovers of Gudrun*. Boston: Roberts Brothers, 1870.

149. [Baker, Harriette Newell (Woods)]. *The Sun-Shine Series*. Boston: Andrew F. Graves, 1870:

    a. *Honeysuckle Cottage*

    b. *The Little Florentine*

    c. *The Load of Chips*

    d. **Tony and His Harp*

    e. *Timmy Top-Boots*

    f. *Sophia and the Gipsies*

150. *Dickens, Charles. *A Child's Dream of a Star*. Boston: Fields, Osgood, 1871.

151. *"Webfoot" [Phelps, William D.]. *Fore and Aft*. Boston: Nichols and Hall, 1871.

152. [Clark, Thomas March]. *John Whopper the Newsboy*. Boston: Roberts Brothers, 1871.

153. Landor, Walter Savage. *Pericles and Aspasia*. Boston: Roberts Brothers, 1871

154. *Stowe, Harriet Beecher. *Pink and White Tyranny*. Boston: Roberts Brothers, 1871.

155. *Lowell, Anna Cabot [Jackson], ed. *Posies for Children*. Boston: Roberts Brothers, 1871.

156. *Conwell, Russell H. *Why and How*. Boston: Lee and Shepard, 1871.

157. *Alcott, Louisa May. *Aunt Jo's Scrap-Bag*. Boston: Roberts Brothers, 1872.

158. [Appleton, Thomas Gold]. *Faded Leaves*. Boston: Private, 1872.

159. *Tennyson, Alfred. *The Last Tournament*. Boston: J. E. Tilton, 1872.

160. Mistral, Frédéric. *Mirèio*. Boston: Roberts Brothers, 1872.

161. *"Carleton" [Charles Carleton Coffin]. *The Story of the Great Fire, Boston*. Boston: Shepard and Gill, 1872.

162. *Hamilton, Gail [Mary A. Dodge]. *Child World*. Boston: Shepard and Gill, 1873.

163. O'Reilly, Mrs. Robert [Eleanor Grace]. *Gile's Minority*. Boston: Roberts Brothers, 1874.

164. [Peabody, Elizabeth Palmer]. *Record of Mr. Alcott's School*. Boston: Roberts Brothers, 1874.

165. *Longfellow, Henry W. (and others). *Laurel Leaves*. Boston: William F. Gill, 1876.

166. **Gems from Tennyson*. Philadelphia: Porter and Coates, 1888.

Appendix C
Billings's Buildings

This is a preliminary chronological list of executed buildings, unrealized architectural projects, and monuments designed by Hammatt Billings (HB) either alone or in partnership with others (as well as a list of buildings by his brother Joseph). It is certainly incomplete. There are many HB drawings for unidentified buildings in the scrapbook at the Stowe-Day Library of the Harriet Beecher Stowe Center in Hartford, and there are probably notices of other works lurking in the pages of the *Boston Evening Transcript* and similar sources. Unless otherwise specified, the design of the following works was by HB alone. Except where noted, executed works remain largely as built.

Buildings

1. Custom House, Boston, 1837. Ammi B. Young, architect; HB, draftsman (1838–41). Altered.
2. Project for the University of Michigan, ca. 1838. Ammi B. Young, architect; HB, draftsman.
3. Boston Museum, Tremont Street, 1845. H. and J. E. Billings. Demolished.
4. Unidentified work for Harvard College, 1846. H. and J. E. Billings.
5. Church of the Saviour (Second Unitarian Church), Boston, 1845. H. (or H. and J. E.) Billings. Demolished.
6. Josiah Quincy House, Wollaston, Massachusetts, 1848. Demolished.
7. Water Arch, Tremont Street, Boston, 1848. Demolished.
8. Project for a library (Stowe Center scrapbook), 1849.
9. Temple Club, West Street, Boston, 1849. H. and J. E. Billings. Altered.
10. Remodeling of entry and stair, Boston Athenaeum, 1850. Demolished.
11. Project for a Perkins house (Stowe Center scrapbook), 1850.
12. Project for an addition to the U.S. Capitol, Washington D.C. (Stowe Center scrapbook), 1850.
13. Grace Episcopal Church, Lawrence, Massachusetts, 1851. H. and J. E. Billings. Some alteration.
14. Richard H. Dana Jr. House, Cambridge, Massachusetts, 1851.
15. Billings-Hall House ("the Eminence"), Auburndale (Newton), Massachusetts, 1852. H. and J. E. Billings.

16. Andrews Norton House, Newport, Rhode Island, 1852. Altered.

17. Project for an Academy of Fine Arts (Stowe Center scrapbook), early 1850s (?).

18. Dwight Foster House, Worcester, Massachusetts, ca. 1854. Unlocated.

19. Canopy over Plymouth Rock, Plymouth, Massachusetts, 1854. Demolished.

20. Unspecified work at Mercantile Wharf, Boston, before 1855. HB with G. J. F. Bryant and Luther Briggs. Demolished?

21. Cottage on Dorr Street, Roxbury (Boston), Massachusetts, before 1857. Unlocated.

22. Commercial Building, 74–6 Franklin Street, Boston, 1857. HB and G. J. F. Bryant. Demolished.

23. Massachusetts Charitable Mechanic Association Building, Bedford and Chauncy Streets, Boston, 1857. HB with N. J. Bradlee and G. J. F. Bryant. Demolished.

24. J. B. Whall Tomb, Mount Auburn Cemetery, Cambridge, Massachusetts, 1858. HB for G. J. F. Bryant. Demolished.

25. Project for building for the Society of Natural History and the Horticultural Society, Boston, 1859. HB with G. J. F. Bryant.

26. Tremont Street Methodist Episcopal Church, Boston, 1860. HB for Woodcock and Meacham.

27. Project for City Hall, Boston, 1860.

28. South Congregational Church, New Britain, Connecticut, 1864. HB for G. F. Meacham.

29. Horatio Harris villa, Roxbury (Boston), Massachusetts, 1865. HB (with G. J. F. Bryant?). Unlocated.

30. Project for Memorial Hall, Harvard University, Cambridge, Massachusetts, 1865. Lost.

31. Cheney Hall, South Manchester, Connecticut, 1866. H. and J. E. Billings.

32. Frank Cheney House, South Manchester, Connecticut, 1866. H. and J. E. Billings.

33. Project for a stable for T. C. Woodridge (Stowe Center scrapbook), 1867.

34. Project for the post office, New York City, 1867.

35. Project for a Dyer house (Stowe Center scrapbook), 1867.

36. Project for Ward Cheney House, South Manchester, Connecticut, 1867.

37. Project for a Gothic building on Tremont Street, Boston (Stowe Center scrapbook), ca. 1867. Perhaps related to the Masonic Temple.

38. Project for a stable for Mr. Appleton (Stowe Center scrapbook), 1868.

39. Library for Mount Holyoke College, South Hadley, Massachusetts, 1868. H. and J. E. Billings. Demolished.

40. Claflin-Ellis House, Newtonville, Massachusetts, 1869. H. and J. E. Billings.

41. Wesleyan Association Building, Boston, 1869. H. (and J. E.?) Billings.

42. Project for a town hall (Stowe Center scrapbook), 1870.

43. Waverley Congregational Church, Belmont, Massachusetts, 1870.

44. Wellesley Congregational Church, Wellesley, Massachusetts, 1870. Destroyed.

45. Project for a railroad station (Stowe Center scrapbook), 1871. Perhaps related to the Park Square Station, Boston.

46. Thayer Library, Braintree, Massachusetts, 1871.

47. Isaac Rich store, Summer Street, Boston, 1872. H. and J. E. Billings. Demolished.
48. Project for the Connecticut State Capitol, Hartford (Stowe Center scrapbook), 1872. H. and J. E. Billings.
49. Project for Haverhill, Massachusetts, public library, 1873.
50. Second Cathedral Building, Boston, 1873. H. (and J. E.?) Billings. Demolished.
51. Project (?) for a house for Dr. Read, Hull, Massachusetts, undated.
52. Project for an insurance company building, Hartford, undated.

Monuments

1. Joseph Tuckerman Monument, Mt. Auburn Cemetery, 1840s.
2. Robert Gould Shaw Monument, Mt. Auburn Cemetery, 1848.
3. Edmund Dwight Monument, Forest Hills Cemetery, 1850s.
4. National Monument to the Forefathers, Plymouth, Massachusetts, 1854.
5. Cushman Monument, Plymouth, Massachusetts, burying ground, 1858. Attribution.
6. Gardner Brewer Monument, Mt. Auburn Cemetery, ca. 1858.
7. Project for a Minute Man Monument, Lexington, Massachusetts, 1859. HB with Thomas Ball and G. J. F. Byrant.
8. Franklin Typographical Society and Boston Printers' Union Monument, Mt. Hope Cemetery, 1860.
9. Jonathan Phillips Monument, Mt. Auburn Cemetery, ca. 1860. HB with G. J. F. Bryant.
10. Soldiers' Monument, Concord, Massachusetts, 1866.
11. Projects for a Soldiers and Sailors' Monument, Boston Common, 1866 and 1870. HB with G. J. F. Bryant.
12. Pedestal for Thomas Ball's statue of George Washington, Public Garden, Boston, 1867.
13. Soldiers' Memorial Tablet, Town Hall, Kennebunk, Maine, 1868. Destroyed?
14. John Damon Monument, Mt. Auburn Cemetery, 1869.
15. Pedestal for the Soldiers' Monument, Braintree, Massachusetts, 1873.

Buildings by Joseph E. Billings alone or with Charles F. Sleeper

1. Church of the Messiah, Boston, 1848.
2. High School, Cambridge, Massachusetts, 1848.
3. Centre Street School, Cambridge, Massachusetts, 1848.
4. Ingraham School, Boston, 1848.
5. Sarah Baxter House, Newton, Massachusetts, 1848.
6. Bragdon Hall, Lasell College, Newton, Massachusetts, 1851. Billings and Sleeper.
7. National Theatre, Boston, 1852. Billings and Sleeper.
8. St. Stephen's Church, Wilkes-Barre, Pennsylvania, 1853. Billings and Sleeper.
9. Boston Navy Yard, various buildings, 1850s and 1860s.
10. Odd Fellows' Hall, Boston, 1871.

Notes

1. "A Rare Man"

1. The National Monument to the Forefathers was designed in 1854 and finally dedicated in 1889 long after Billings's death. In 1974, when the National Park Service added the monument to its Register of Historic Places, it installed a bronze plaque crediting the design to "Hammet" Billings and dating it 1889.

2. As told to me in the 1980s by a member of the curatorial staff of The Pilgrim Society in Plymouth.

3. This is one of more than one hundred personal letters written by Billings to Joanna Emmons, mostly dated between June 1841 and July 1842, now in the possession of Joanna Andros of Keene, New Hampshire.

A later source for the date is Charles F. Read, "Hammatt Billings, Artist and Architect," typescript, 22 December 1920, in the library of the Bostonian Society. Read, an architect who was born in 1850, witnessed Hammatt's signature on a document of 1873 (Pilgrim Society Archives) and Hammatt's brother Joseph's on a document of 1878 (Suffolk County Probate, no. 56345), so he knew them when he was a young professional. It is his note that identifies the photograph of the older Billings in the Pilgrim Society.

See also Richard Stoddard, "Hammatt Billings, Artist and Architect," *Old-Time New England* 62 (January-March 1972): 57, 78 n. 1, and the obituary signed "W.," in Edward Everett Hale's short-lived magazine *Old and New* 2 (March 1875): 355–57 (all citations to *Old and New* are to this obituary). Could "W" be William B. Weedon, a stockholder in and contributor to the journal? See Jean Holloway, *Edward Everett Hale: A Biography* (Austin, Tex., 1956), 173–99.

4. Abraham Hammatt married Lucy Howland, descendant of John Howland of the *Mayflower*, in 1748: William T. Davis, *Genealogical Register of Plymouth Families* (Baltimore, 1985), 124, 148.

5. A. K. Teele, ed., *The History of Milton, Mass.* (Milton, 1887), 171.

6. Letter from Hammatt's brother Henry to Mary H. Hinckley, 10 January 1910 (Milton Historical Society, Milton Public Library). Although much of this seems drawn from the obituary in *Old and New*, the letter supplies the full name of their mother and the fact that she was the daughter of Samuel Janes, M.D., of Watertown, Massachusetts. Henry gives his brother's birth date as 15 June 1818.

7. His siblings were Joseph E., Samuel Janes, Mary R., Hannah L. (Bartlett), and Henry M.: *New England Historic and Genealogical Register* 91 (July 1937): 235–36. Hannah's husband (they were married in 1863) was Nathaniel T. of the Plymouth Bartletts, an

architect and civil engineer, to whom we owe the preservation of many of Hammatt's drawings: *New England Historic and Genealogical Register* 91 (July 1937): 236.

8. *Old and New*; Stoddard, "Hammatt Billings," 57.

9. *Boston Morning Journal*, 17 November 1874, p. 2, col. 1.

10. On 3 May 1842 Thomas Gould stopped by Billings's quarters to talk of life and art according to Billings's letter of that date to Joanna Emmons (Joanna Andros Collection, Keene, New Hampshire).

11. Thomas Ball, *My Three Score Years and Ten* (Boston, 2d ed., 1892), 19–24.

12. *Gleason's Pictorial Line-of-Battle Ship* 1 (6 August 1859): 1. As Billings was more or less the house artist for *Gleason's Pictorial Drawing-Room Companion* (and later *Ballou's*), this is probably a fairly accurate account. The article is unsigned, but may be by Frederic Gleason himself. See also the obituary in *Old and New:* "He began, before leaving Milton, to cut colored paper, first, horses, dogs, and other simple objects, then trees, bridges, deer-hunts, &c., being his own sole instructor."

See also the *Boston Morning Journal* (16 November 1874), p. 3, col. 6.

13. Alice V. L. Carrick, *A History of American Silhouettes* (Rutland, Vt., 1968). Despite this beginning, Billings seems never to have illustrated a book with silhouettes.

14. Paul McPharlin, *The Puppet Theatre in America* (New York, [1949?]), 57, 310.

15. *Old and New*.

16. T[homas] G[old] A[ppleton], *A Sheaf of Papers* (Boston, 1875), 19, and Susan Hale, *Life and Letters of Thomas Gold Appleton* (New York, 1885), 23–29, 56. See also Louise Hall Tharp, *The Appletons of Beacon Hill* (Boston, 1973), 117. Billings was later to provide the frontispiece to Appleton's anonymously and privately published book of poems, *Faded Leaves* (Boston, 1872; see appendix B).

17. Louise Hall Tharp, *The Peabody Sisters of Salem* (Boston, 1950), 45. Extensive observations on Graeter are in Sophia's journal in the Berg Collection, New York Public Library.

18. *Record of a School* (Boston, 2d revised ed., 1836), xxii. This work has as frontispiece a view of the interior of the school by Graeter. For the 3d edition of 1873, Billings is credited with a copy of that view (see appendix B).

When the Temple School closed, Graeter signed on as draftsman with the Maine geological survey; his work illustrates its reports. See Charles T. Jackson, *First Report on the Geology of the State of Maine* (Augusta, 1837), [9].

19. Lydia Maria Child, *The Girls' Own Book* (New York, 1833).

20. *Old and New*.

21. *The National Cyclopaedia of American Biography* 11:350.

22. Drawings for the memorial tablet are in the large Bartlett scrapbook in the Fine Arts Department, Boston Public Library.

23. *Catalogue of the Scholars and Teachers of the English High School, Boston, Mass., from 1821 to 1890* (Boston, 1890), 10.

24. David H. Wallace, *John Rogers: The People's Sculptor* (Middletown, Conn., 1967), 17–27. Rogers attended English from 1844 to 1846.

25. *Old and New*; *Ballou's Pictorial Drawing-Room Companion* 10 (19 April 1856): 252.

26. Letters from Billings to Joanna Emmons (Joanna Andros Collection, Keene,

New Hampshire). In the letter of 16 July, Billings mentioned Plato, Shakespeare, and Spinoza among his reading and suggests that they "be Toujours Fidele to learning." In other letters he commented on authors ranging from Swedenborg to Bulwer-Lytton.

27. Edwin M. Bacon, *King's Dictionary of Boston* (Cambridge, Mass., 1883), 494. Barnard's name appears frequently in the Billings-Emmons correspondence of 1841–42. On 18 August 1841, for example, Billings wrote that he had wanted to show Mr. Barnard a design for a border but could not get it finished on time (Joanna Andros Collection, Keene, New Hampshire).

28. There is a copy of Charles Sumner's *White Slavery in the Barbary States* (1853) illustrated by Billings and inscribed by Dorothea Dix in the Clapp Library at Wellesley College (see appendix B).

29. William H. Whitmore, "Abel Bowen," *Bostonian Society Publications* 1 (1886–88): 35; Ball, *My Three Score Years*, 59–67.

30. *Gleason's* (1859): 1; *Old and New.*

31. Sinclair Hamilton, *Early American Book Illustrators and Wood Engravers, 1670–1870* (Princeton, 1968), 1:xxxiv.

32. *Gleason's* (1859): 1.

33. Letters of 23 June and 20 August 1841, for example, Billings-Emmons correspondence (Joanna Andros Collection, Keene, New Hampshire).

34. Ball, *My Three Score Years*, 65–66.

35. No wood carving has been identified as Billings's. There is one reference to engraving in metal that seems to represent a special case. Sometime between 1852 and 1855 he was asked by Henry I. Bowditch to engrave a motto by Whittier on the face of a sundial. See Vincent Y. Bowditch, *Life and Correspondence of Henry Ingersoll Bowditch* (Boston, 1902), 1:246.

36. *Old and New;* compare the *Boston Morning Journal* (16 November 1874), p. 3, col. 6, where it is written that "the published works of that gentleman [Benjamin] on architecture are filled with illustrations from the hand of Mr. Billings." I can find no evidence to justify this assertion in the books Benjamin published during the 1830s.

37. Jack Quinan, "Asher Benjamin and American Architecture," *Journal of the Society of Architectural Historians* 38 (October 1979): 244–70.

38. Lawrence Wodehouse, "Ammi Burnham Young," *Journal of the Society of Architectural Historians* 25 (December 1966): 268; Wodehouse, "Architectural Projects in the Greek Revival Style by Ammi Burnham Young," *Old-Time New England* 60 (winter 1970): 73–85.

39. Compare the *Boston Morning Journal* (16 November 1874): Billings prepared "a very large portion of the drawings by which this building was constructed."
In a letter to Joanna Emmons of 11 August 1841 Billings wrote that "today is the last day of the ninth month of the third year in which I have served Mr. Young," a statement that would place his entrance into the Young office at the end of 1838 (Joanna Andros Collection, Keene, New Hampshire).

40. *The Second Exhibition of the Massachusetts Charitable Mechanic Association* (Boston, 1839), 25 (no. 1010). Billings again exhibited these or other Custom House drawings a few years later; see *Catalogue of Paintings, of the Third Exhibition of the Boston Artists' Association, of 1844*, nos. 1–5.

41. Bates Lowry, *Building a National Image* (Washington, D.C., 1985), 48–50, 214, plate 29. The drawing bears Young's name, as is proper for whoever drew it. Lowry notes that this is the only known presentation drawing "by" Young.

42. Library of Congress, Copyright Records, Massachusetts, 1850, fol. 269 (copy deposited 20 November 1840).

"New Custom House, Boston." A. B. Young, architect; "Drawn by C. H. Billings; Engraved by G. G. Smith." There is an example in the Boston Athenaeum. There is a second engraved "broadside," also dated 1840, containing plans, section, and east view, also by Billings and Smith, and also in the Boston Athenaeum. See Henry-Russell Hitchcock, *American Architectural Books* (Minneapolis, 1962), no. 1454. What appears to be Billings's drawing for one or the other of these engraved perspectives is in the Prints and Drawings Collection of the American Institute of Architects Foundation, Washington, D.C.

43. See James F. O'Gorman, *On the Boards: Drawings by Nineteenth-Century Boston Architects* (Philadelphia, 1989), 33.

44. This and the following information come from the Billings-Emmons correspondence (Joanna Andros Collection, Keene, New Hampshire).

45. In 1844 Joseph exhibited drawings for designs by Young: *Catalogue of . . . the Third Exhibition of the Boston Artists' Association*, nos. 26 and 28. Joseph does not appear in the directories until 1846; he is frequently described as a civil engineer.

46. Hugh Cabot Papers, Schlesinger Library, Radcliffe College.

47. Suffolk County Deeds, Book 559, fols. 196–97.

48. *Boston Almanac* (Boston, 1854), 59, and *Gleason's* (1859): 1. See also Ednah Dow Cheney's discussion of his "pecuniary necessities" in her *Reminiscences* (Boston, 1902), 132–33.

49. The *New England Historic and Genealogical Register* (91 [1937]: 236) gives 1 April 1841 as the date of the marriage, but the Billings-Emmons correspondence suggests that that cannot be correct.

50. James F. O'Gorman, "H. and J. E. Billings of Boston," *Journal of the Society of Architectural Historians* 42 (March 1983): 61 n. 25.

51. The letter was in the possession of the owner of the house in 1982. It is probably a coincidence that a view of McLean's, then in Somerville, Massachusetts, appeared in *Gleason's Pictorial Drawing-Room Companion* 4 (1853): 305, uncredited but identical to an engraving by Billings in the Boston Athenaeum. The same view had appeared almost a decade earlier as the frontispiece to Richard Frothingham's *The History of Charlestown, Massachusetts* (Boston, 1845–49; see appendix B).

52. Harvard University, Houghton Library, bMS Am 1088 [471].

53. Billings is first listed as residing in Camden Street in 1860. This remained his wife's address through the decade.

Suffolk County Probate, no. 56345 (Hammatt, 1874) and no. 70579 (Phoebe, 1883).

54. Billings-Emmons correspondence (Joanna Andros Collection, Keene, New Hampshire).

55. "Journal of the Proceedings of the Boston Artists' Association," 2 vols., Rare Book Room, Boston Public Library. See also Leah Lipton, "The Boston Artists' Asso-

ciation, 1841–1851," *American Journal of Art* 15 (autumn 1983): 45–57. Hammatt was proposed by the engraver A. C. Warren, as was his brother, who was elected in December. Both signed the original constitution, now, with other material, in the Boston Athenaeum (MS S300).

On 19 June 1842 Billings reported that he was "drawing the figure two hours each day from good studies & casts. I shall also . . . draw same heads from life. . . . I am a designer I must therefore learn my business thoroughly" (Billings-Emmons correspondence, Joanna Emmons Collection, Keene, New Hampshire).

56. *Bulletin of the New England Art Union* (Boston, 1852); Massachusetts Academy of the Fine Arts, *Catalogue of the First Semi-Annual Exhibition* (Boston, 1853); and *Boston Transcript* (26 January 1855), p. 1, col. 4. The Boston Art Club, founded in 1855, succeeded all these, but Hammatt's presence has not been spotted there. See Benjamin Champney, *Sixty Years' Memoirs of Art and Artists* (Worcester, Mass., 1900), 170–72.

Billings was one of the absentee signers of a "memorial" in support of the advancement of art in the United States that was part of the *Proceedings* of the National Convention of Artists, held 20, 22, and 23 March 1858, at the Smithsonian Institution (Washington, D.C., 1858), [17].

57. In the Billings scrapbook at the Stowe-Day Library, Harriet Beecher Stowe Center, Hartford.

58. Countway Library, Harvard University Medical School (B MS b44.3). See Paul R. Baker, *Richard Morris Hunt* (Cambridge, Mass., 1980), 140–41. Hunt attended Rimmer's New York lectures in the same year and left a sketch of the teacher at work.

59. Amelia Peck, ed., *Alexander Jackson Davis, American Architect, 1803–1892* (New York, 1992), 29–31. Davis followed publication of his *Views of the Public Buildings in the City of New York* (1827) with views of Boston "taken" on a trip the next year.

60. Henry T. Bailey, "An Architect of the Old School," *New England Magazine* 25 (1901): 337. The latter, said to have been a commission with G. J. F. Bryant, remains unverified.

61. John H. Thorndike, *Dedication of the Mechanics' Hall* (Boston, 1860); Montgomery Schuyler, "Architecture of American Colleges X: Three Women's Colleges—Vassar, Wellesley, and Smith," *Architectural Record* 31 (May 1912): 532.

62. Cheney, *Reminiscences*, 132.

63. The original photo is in the author's collection; the engraving by George W. Hill appeared in *Ballou's* (1856): 252.

64. *Old and New*. In the scrapbook containing the Billings-Emmons correspondence there are two locks of his hair. One is an almost blond curl labeled "At Birth" and the other is a light brown curl labeled "21 years" (Joanna Andros Collection, Keene, New Hampshire).

65. Ball, *My Three Score Years*, 65.

66. In the collection of the Pilgrim Society, Plymouth, Mass. It is identified by a note signed by Charles F. Read, who knew the architect at the end of his life. It can probably be dated ca. 1870.

67. Neil Harris, *The Artist in American Society* (Chicago, 1982), 224, 237.

68. Harris, *Artist in American Society*, chapter 9.

69. *Old and New; Boston Transcript* (16 November 1874), p. 1, col. 6.; J. J. Jarves, *The Art-Idea*, ed. Benjamin Rowland Jr. (Cambridge, Mass., 1960), 241; *Harper's Weekly* (12 December 1863): 788; Cheney, *Reminiscences;* Thorndike, *Dedication of the Mechanics' Hall;* H. W. Longfellow, "Journal," 11 January 1847 (Houghton Library, Harvard University, MS Am 1340).

70. Billings-Emmons correspondence (Joanna Andros Collection, Keene, New Hampshire).

71. *Old and New;* Cheney, *Reminiscences;* William F. Gill, *Home Recreations, Designed for Home Amusements* (Boston, 1875).

72. *Boston Transcript* (17 January 1884): 4. Several of Billings's clients and patrons are included in this list, as is he.

73. James F. O'Gorman, "The Poet and the Illustrator: Longfellow, Billings, and the 'Disproportion between Their Designs and Their Deeds' in the 1840s," in *Aspects of American Printmaking, 1800–1950*, ed. O'Gorman (Syracuse, N.Y., 1988), 31–51.

74. Ralph W. Emerson, *The Journals and Miscellaneous Notebooks of Ralph Waldo Emerson*, ed. William H. Gilman (Cambridge, Mass., 1960–82), 15:402.

75. *Dwight's Journal of Music* 1 (10 July 1852): 110.

76. John Ross Dix, *The Worth of the Worthless: A Christmas and New Year's Story* (Boston, 3d ed., 1854), 46 (see appendix B).

77. *Rambles about Boston; or, Efforts to Do Good* (Boston, 1856), 91.

78. *Boston Transcript* (24 June 1857).

79. Christopher Crowfield [Harriet Beecher Stowe], *House and Home Papers* (Boston, 1865), 95.

80. Boston Public Library, Rare Book Room, Ms.A. 1.2, vol. 41, fol. 39. See also *William Lloyd Garrison, 1805–1879: The Story of His Life Told by His Children* (New York, 1889), 3:308–9.

81. Billings to James F. Hyde, Mayor of Newton, Massachusetts, 1 February 1854 (Hyde Papers, Jackson Homestead, Newton, Massachusetts).

82. Hans Sperber and Travis Trittshuh, *American Political Terms* (Detroit, 1962), 469, see also 496–97.

83. William Howe Downes, "Boston Painters and Paintings III," *Atlantic Monthly* 62 (September 1888): 387.

Old and New, where we find the anecdote that when he was told a critic had said Washington Allston's angels were equal to Raphael's, he replied, "Allston's angels are all of one family, and Raphael created races."

Gleason's (1859): 1.

84. See appendix A; *Old and New.*

85. Helen M. Knowlton, *Art-Life of William Morris Hunt* (Boston, 1899), 34–35.

That Billings wrote about art in articles both published and unpublished is suggested by his obituary in the *Boston Morning Journal* (16 November 1874): 3. Other than an article on Mount Auburn Cemetery, none of this literature has come to light.

86. There is a tiny sketchbook in the Prints and Drawings Department, Museum of Fine Arts, Boston (M28144), with a Bedford Square, London, address and drawings dated during the summer months. In the Rare Book Room of the Boston Public Library

is a letter from Billings to "Townsend," dated 10 August 1865. The contents reveal it was written in London. A Yorkshire watercolor is in the author's collection.

87. Joseph E. Morris, *The North Riding of Yorkshire* (London, 2d ed., 1920), 150.

88. Elizabeth H. Denio, *Catalogue of Works of Art Belonging to Wellesley College* (Boston, 1883), 18.

89. *Boston Post* (16 November 1874), p. 3, col. 2.; Suffolk County Probate, no. 56345.

2. "Unrivalled Skill in This Branch of Art"

1. This chapter draws upon and revises James F. O'Gorman, "War, Slavery, and Intemperance in the Book Illustrations of Hammatt Billings," *Imprint* 10 (1985): 2–10. Any discussion of American book illustration depends heavily upon Sinclair Hamilton's pioneering catalogue *Early American Book Illustrators and Wood Engravers, 1670–1870* (Princeton, 1968).

2. Frank Weitenkamp, "The Emergence of the American Illustrator," *Art Quarterly* 18 (winter 1955): 394–402. This author wrote that they appeared "almost overnight," but it was not quite so easy.

Boston Almanac (Boston, 1854), [2]. The *Almanac* was published by John P. Jewett, for whom Billings had illustrated *Uncle Tom's Cabin* about the time this testimonial was written.

3. J. J. Jarves, *The Art-Idea*, ed. Benjamin Rowland (Cambridge, Mass., 1960), 196–97.

4. See James F. O'Gorman, "Hammatt Billings," and John Neal Hoover, "Felix Darley," in *Private Library* 7 (1994): 102–13 and 115–29, respectively.

5. *Umrisse zu Goethe's Faust* (Stuttgart, 1837) and *Umrisse zu Schiller's Lied von der Glocke* (Stuttgart, 1843), bound together. The volume, in the author's collection, is signed and dated "1845" by Billings (see appendix A).

6. For these titles see appendix B.

7. "Engraving," *The Crayon* 4 (October 1857): 316–17.

8. Bertha E. Mahony and others, *Illustrators of Children's Books, 1744–1945* (Boston, 1961), 90.

9. John C. Eckel, *The First Editions of the Writings of Charles Dickens* (New York, 1932), 187.

10. The typography of *A Happy Summer-Time*'s title page suggests that Billings might have been the author of the text as well as the artist of its "six elegant designs."

11. *Old and New; The Letters of John Greenleaf Whittier*, ed. J. B. Packard, 3 vols. (Cambridge, Mass., 1875), 2:240.

12. Although he was celebrated for his illustrations to Keats, no volume of work by the English poet has surfaced with Billings's embellishments. There did once exist a drawing for "The Eve of St. Agnes," however (Elizabeth Denio, *Catalogue of Works of Art Belonging to Wellesley College* [Boston, 1883], 18).

13. James L. Yarnall, "Tennyson Illustration in Boston, 1864–1872," *Imprint* 7 (autumn 1982): 10–16.

14. See L. Perry Curtis, *Apes and Angels; The Irishman in Victorian Caricature* (Washington, D.C., 1971).

15. Hamilton, *Early American Book Illustrators*, 1:76–77.

16. Compare Emerson's journal entry for May 1837 (or 1839) in which are linked the "philanthropic enterprises of Universal Temperance, Peace, and Abolition of Slavery" (quoted in David S. Reynolds, *Beneath the American Renaissance* [New York, 1988], 93; see the whole of his chapter 2 for the reform impulse).

17. See Lowell's *Bigelow Papers*, first series, 1846–48 (Martin Duberman, *James Russell Lowell* [Boston, 1966], 102).

18. The drawings are 5″ x 7″ graphite, ink, and wash, on wove paper. The *Palo Alto* is in the author's collection; the other two are in a private collection in New York. Loose examples of the engravings are in the Prints and Drawings Collection of the Library of Congress and in the Archives of American Art (microfilm reel NY59–11, frames 652–54).

19. John S. C. Abbott, *Lives of the Presidents of the United States of America from Washington to the Present Time* (Boston, 1869), opp. p. 319 (see appendix B).

20. S. G. Goodrich, *A Pictorial History of America; Embracing Both the Northern and Southern Portions of the New World* (Hartford, 1849), 794 (see appendix B). This is a profusely illustrated volume issued in many editions. The frontispiece and engraved title page are credited to Billings; he may have also been responsible for many of the smaller vignettes in the section on the Mexican War.

21. Ben Huseman has suggested Nebel as the source of this as well as other Billings views of the battles, but here the connection was with the later rather than the earlier version: Martha A. Sandweiss, Rick Stewart, and Ben W. Huseman, *Eyewitness to War: Prints and Daguerreotypes of the Mexican War, 1846–1848* (Fort Worth, Tex., 1989), 163–64 and 326–27 (for the view of Chapultepec). In fact, Billings might have looked at Nebel's own source for his *Buena Vista*; the 1848 view by Joseph H. Eaton as lithographed by Henry R. Robinson or Jose Severo Rocha.

22. *Ballou's Pictorial Drawing-Room Companion* 10 (1 March 1856): 168–69, see also 173. The same issue also contains his view of Chapultepec.

23. See Arthur Bernon Tourtellot, "Harold Murdock's 'The Nineteenth of April 1775,'" *American Heritage* 10 (August 1959): 60–84, and David Hackett Fischer, *Paul Revere's Ride* (New York, 1994), 329.

24. "Cost Book A," Roberts Brothers (Little, Brown archives, now in Houghton Library, Harvard University), fol. 93. See James F. O'Gorman, *A Billings Bookshelf: An Annotated Bibliography of Works Illustrated by Hammatt Billings* (Wellesley, Mass., 3d ed., 1993), 77, and David Tatham, *Winslow Homer and the Illustrated Book* (Philadelphia, 1992).

25. *Literary World*, 1 January 1871; William Dean Howells, *Atlantic Monthly*, "Recent Literature," (February 1871): 269–70.

26. W. J. Linton, *The History of Wood-Engraving in America* (London, 1882), 16.

27. Frank Jewett Mather Jr. and others, *The American Spirit in Art* (New Haven, 1927), 285. (On the same page they call Darley "the first great American illustrator.")

28. John Harthan, *The History of the Illustrated Book* (London, 1981), 204; Percy Muir, *Victorian Illustrated Books* (New York, 1971).

Mahony and others, *Illustrators of Children's Books*, 90.

29. Hamilton, *Early American Book Illustrators*, 1:xxxix, 74–77; supplement, 46–49.

The author's *Billings Bookshelf* has added a great many titles to Hamilton's preliminary gathering (see appendix B).

3. "The Power of the Pencil Adds Much to the Power of the Pen"

1. For a more detailed treatment of and documentation for this section, see James F. O'Gorman, "The Poet and the Illustrator: Longfellow, Billings, and the 'Disproportion between Their Designs and Their Deeds' in the 1840s," in *Aspects of American Printmaking, 1800–1950*, ed. O'Gorman (Syracuse, N.Y., 1988), 31–51.

2. Andrew Hilen, ed., *The Letters of Henry Wadsworth Longfellow* (Cambridge, Mass., 1966–82), 3:80 (28 June 1845); 3:57 (2 March 1845); 3:80 n. 2 (21 July 1845); 3:89 (18 October 1845).

3. Hilen, *Letters*, 3:48 (3 December 1844) and 3:59 (17 March 1845).

4. H. W. Longfellow, "Journal," 9 January 1847 (Houghton Library, Harvard University, MS Am 1340). It is characteristic of the depths to which Billings's reputation had fallen in the years after his death that all references to him but one were omitted from the journal excerpts published in Samuel Longfellow, *Life of Henry Wadsworth Longfellow* (Boston, 1886).

5. Longfellow, "Journal," 11 January 1847, 18 January 1847.

6. Hammatt Billings Collection, Special Collections, Clapp Library, Wellesley College.

7. Hilen, *Letters*, 3:226 (18 November 1849).

8. Longfellow, "Journal," 28 January 1850.

9. Raymond L. Kilgour, *Messrs. Roberts Brothers, Publishers* (Ann Arbor, Mich., 1952), 37–38.

10. This section is based upon James F. O'Gorman, "Billings, Cruikshank, and *Uncle Tom's Cabin*," *Imprint* 13 (spring 1988): 13–21.

11. E. Bruce Kirkham, *The Building of Uncle Tom's Cabin* (Knoxville, 1977), 66.

12. For Billings's illustrations to other works by Stowe, see appendix B.

13. Rare Book Room, Boston Public Library, MS A 1.2, vol. 41, fol. 39.

14. *The Letters of John Greenleaf Whittier*, ed. J. B. Packard, 3 vols. (Cambridge, Mass., 1875), 2:240.

Bernard F. Reilly Jr., "The Art of the Antislavery Movement," in *Courage and Conscience: Black and White Abolitionists in Boston*, ed. Donald M. Jacobs (Indianapolis, 1993), 49.

15. Reilly in *Courage and Conscience*, 48, 62.

16. Ellwood Parry, *The Image of the Indian and the Black Man in American Art, 1590–1900* (New York, 1974), 48, and Reilly in *Courage and Conscience*, 62–63, 141.

17. Illustrated editions by C. H. Clarke and Co. (London, 1852), for example, repeat Billings's scene line for line. It seems oddly intrusive amid other illustrations by another hand. The *Slave Auction* in Bohn's shilling edition (London, 1853) clearly stems from Billings's archetype, but the engraver took the liberty of moving figures into new poses. The painting is illustrated and briefly discussed (without recognition of its origin in Billings's work) in James E. Fox, "Iconography of the Black in American Art (1710–1900)," Ph.D. diss., University of North Carolina, 1979, 186, 460.

18. See David H. Wallace, *John Rogers: The People's Sculptor* (Middletown, Conn., 1967).

19. Parry, *The Image and the Indian,* 99.

20. Christine Hult, "*Uncle Tom's Cabin:* Popular Images of Uncle Tom and Little Eva, 1852–1892," *Nineteenth Century* 15 (1995): 3–8.

21. Elizabeth Ammons, "Heroines in *Uncle Tom's Cabin,*" in Ammons, *Critical Essays on Harriet Beecher Stowe* (Boston, 1980), 152–65. Not everyone agrees with Ammons's reading. See Cynthia Griffin Wolff, " 'Masculinity' in *Uncle Tom's Cabin,*" *American Quarterly* 47 (December 1995): 595–618. Billings's illustrations support Ammons's interpretation.

22. *Norton's Literary Advertiser,* n.s. 1 (1 June 1854): 175.

23. All four illustrations are usually credited to Abigail May, but only the frontispiece and Meg before the mirror seem to be in her hand. The scenes of skating and the return of the father are certainly by someone more skillful (or they have been significantly reworked by the engraver), but that someone was not Billings.

24. *Nation* 7 (22 October 1868): 335.

25. Houghton Library, Harvard University, bMS AM 1130.8 (16 June 1868).

26. Joel Meyerson and Daniel Shealy, eds., *The Selected Letters of Louisa May Alcott* (Boston, 1987), 100–101 (24 January 1864). Alcott probably refers to a version of *The Rose Family: A Fairy Tale* published by Redpath in 1864. Greene was to illustrate her *Morning Glories* of 1868, and she was probably the "Miss Green" who designed the cuts for *Little Men* of 1871 according to "Cost Book A" in the archives of Little, Brown (now at Houghton Library, Harvard University). Sinclair Hamilton's suggestion (*Early American Book Illustrators and Wood Engravers, 1670–1870* [Princeton, 1968], no. 206 [3]) that Billings is the illustrator of the latter book must be rejected.

27. Myerson and Shealy, *Selected Letters,* 125–26. See also Hamilton, *Early American Book Illustrators,* 1:48, 2:49, and figs. 14–15.

28. Myerson and Shealy (*Selected Letters,* 126) tentatively identify Tito as Tito Melema, a character in George Eliot's *Romola* of 1863, and Will as William Batchelder Greene.

29. Martha Saxton, *Louisa May* (Boston, 1977), 305–6; Myerson and Shealy, *Selected Letters,* 126.

30. Houghton Library, Harvard University, bMS AM 1130.8 (4 April 1869).

Merrill, who was born in 1848, was a whole generation younger than Billings, and his work would naturally appear more au courant. For Alcott's opinion of Merrill see Valerie Alderson's introduction to the World's Classics edition of *Little Women* (Oxford University Press, 1994), xii.

4. "His Pencil Has Been in Constant Demand"

1. Frank Luther Mott, *A History of American Magazines,* 5 vols. (Cambridge, Mass., 1938–68), 2:409–12, and Sally Pierce, "Gleason's Pictorial: Elevating and Celebrating American Life," *Ephemera Journal* 5 (1992): 12–24. It was *Ballou's* from 1855; the editor was Maturin M. Ballou. Billings illustrated his biography of his father, *The Life-Story of Hosea Ballou, for the Young* (Boston, 1854); see appendix B.

2. Mott, *A History of American Magazines*, 2:452–65, 469–87.

3. "Illustrated Literature," *Ballou's Pictorial Drawing-Room Companion* 8 (1855): 297. This eventually turns into a pitch for the magazine, whose designing and engraving "is executed by native artists, such as Billings, [Samuel W.] Rowse, and others, who are mostly Bostonians."

4. Mott, *A History of American Magazines*, 1:718–20.

5. See *Boston Miscellany of Literature and Fashion* 2 (1842): 187, 280–81. The *Boston Common* was reengraved for T. S. Arthur's *Ladies Magazine*.

6. (James R. Osgood), *Boston Illustrated* (Boston, 1875), 17.

7. *Pictorial National Library* (1848) 1:5–6.

8. Boston Athenaeum, *Change and Continuity: A Pictorial History of the Boston Athenaeum* (Boston, 1976), 22. Athena/Minerva does not appear in the photograph.

9. *Bulletin of the New England Art Union*, 1:52. The view of the federal Custom House in Boston (1:12) is probably after Billings. The *Pictorial National Library* does not appear in Mott's *History of American Magazines*.

10. See James F. O'Gorman, "The Poet and the Illustrator: Longfellow, Billings, and the 'Disproportion between Their Designs and Their Deeds' in the 1840s," in *Aspects of American Printmaking, 1800–1950*, ed. O'Gorman (Syracuse, N.Y., 1988), 31–51.

11. Mott, *A History of American Magazines*, 2:43–44.

12. Mott, *A History of American Magazines*, 2:262–74.

13. *Youth's Companion* 31 (1 January 1957): 4.

14. *Harper's* 10 (15 September 1866): 581, 588.

15. *Harper's* 10 (15 September 1866): 588; (6 January 1866): 12 (cf. *Ballou's* 12 [10 January 1857]: 17); and (13 January 1866): 28 (cf. *Ballou's* 12 [16 May 1857]: 305).

16. Mott, *A History of American Magazines*, 3:176.

17. Mott, *A History of American Magazines*, 3:176. Billings is listed, for example, on the inside rear cover of the issue of 10 July 1869 (see also 4 [8 August 1868]: 512). It should be noted, too, that Billings's works that appeared as book illustrations might reappear in any of the juvenile illustrated magazines of the day, often without credit given or artist mentioned. For example, his illustration *Amy's Dream*, from Caroline Guild's *Our Summer House, and What Was Said and Done in It* of 1859 (see appendix B) reappears on p. 108 of *Merry's Museum and Woodworth's Cabinet* for April 1860.

18. Mott, *A History of American Magazines*, 3:357–60. See *Saturday* n.s. 1 (3 December 1870): 771, 792.

19. *Gleason's Pictorial Line-of-Battle Ship*, published in Boston in 1858–59, reused some of Billings's illustrations from *Gleason's / Ballou's*.

20. Pierce, "Gleason's Pictorial," 12–13.

21. Related to the iconography of Progress in this and other engraved works by Billings is a pair of large (16½" x 6¾"), unfinished, ink-over-pencil drawings, unsigned but convincingly attributed on the basis of both style and content to Billings, apparently prepared in anticipation of the centennial year, 1876. They are in the author's collection. One depicts a classical arch, dated 1776, inscribed "Westward the Star of Empire Makes Its Way" and surmounted by an Indian, a pioneer, a yeoman, a goodwife, and Agricul-

ture. Within this frame is the figure of Liberty, a youth wearing a Phrygian cap and carrying a bow and quiver, overlooking a landscape in which Indians watch the approach of a wagon train. On the plinth are "Industries of 1776," two circular scenes, one depicting a "Hand Press," the other, a "Hand Loom." In the other drawing, of similar format, allegorical figures of the Arts and Learning surmount an arch dated 1876. Victory, a young woman carrying a laurel wreath, and Liberty, now a mature female with fasces, palm branch, shield, and sword, overlook a highly industrialized harbor scene. The plinth depicts "Industries of 1876": a "Power Press," and a "Power Loom."

22. *Dodge's Literary Museum* 6 (8 January 1853): 77; *Ballou's* (1856): 252.

23. See appendix A for books illustrated by Gilbert that Billings apparently owned.

24. S. Houfe, *Dictionary of British Book Illustrators* (London, 1978), 67.

25. He also followed Gilbert in other book and periodical illustrations. According to a note on fol. 94 of the Dearborn scrapbook of nineteenth-century wood engravings and drawings assembled by the illustrator John R. Chapin, and now in the American Antiquarian Society, "The Am[erica]n Tract Soc[iet]y used to send to England and have him [John Gilbert] make the drawings on the wood which were engraved in this country, until they discovered Hammatt Billings of Boston, who was a servile imitator of Gilbert." This harsh judgment is one of the few derogatory criticisms of Billings stemming from his own time.

26. This wording comes from the text accompanying the reprint of the 1853 engraving in *Gleason's Pictorial Line-of-Battle Ship* 1 (25 December 1858): 1.

27. The quotations are from David S. Reynolds, *Walt Whitman's America* (New York, 1995), 336.

"Song of Myself" appeared in the first edition of *Leaves of Grass* published on 4 July 1855; the first of Billings's emblematic visions of the states had appeared in *Ballou's* in January.

28. William H. Gerdts and Mark Thistlethwaite, *Grand Illusions: History Painting in America* (Fort Worth, Tex., 1988), 7 and 47 for this section.

29. Gerdts and Thistlethwaite, *Grand Illusions*, 7, 10, 85, and 132. The Boston exhibition was of paintings from New York's Düsseldorf Gallery. See also Louisa Tuthill, *Success in Life: The Artist* (New York, 1854).

30. At about the same time he purchased a life of the English history painter Benjamin R. Haydon, although this may also have been due to Haydon's association with Keats, whose work Billings is said to have illustrated especially well. He already owned Haydon's *Lectures* of 1845–46 (see appendix A). Not all the scenes of history published in *Ballou's* were created by Billings. For example, J. H. Hill drew *Bunker Hill* (13 June 1857).

31. "The Use of Engravings," *Ballou's* 11 (20 December 1856): 397.

32. Pierce, "Gleason's Pictorial," 22.

33. His *Battle of New Orleans* appeared in *Ballou's* as a two-page spread (pp. 8–9) on 5 January 1856 (see also p. 13); his depiction of the naval battle between the *Constitution* and the *Guerriere* appeared on 16 February on pp. 104–5 (see also p. 109). The *Battle of New Orleans* reappeared at a fraction of its original size and on steel by O. Pelton in John

Abbott's *Lives of the Presidents* of 1869, for which it is said to have been "expressly engraved" (if not expressly drawn!).

34. Prints and Drawings Department, Museum of Fine Arts, Boston (M28144).

35. There is a drawing in the London sketchbook of the rear of a figure carrying a pot of flowers on her head that seems based on—although reversed from—that to the right of Giulio Romano's *Fire in the Borgo* in the Vatican. The reversal suggests an intermittent print source.

36. Ann Uhry Abrams, "Visions of Columbus: The 'Discovery' Legend in Antebellum American Paintings and Prints," *American Art Journal* 25 (1993): 75–101. It is characteristic that Billings's work is unmentioned in this article.

37. *Ballou's* (1856): 397.

5. "Draws So Many Things So Well"

1. Christopher Crowfield [Harriet Beecher Stowe], *House and Home Papers* (Boston, 1865), 95 (these chapters first appeared in *Atlantic Monthly* in 1864).

2. *Boston Morning Journal* (16 November 1874).

3. Elizabeth Denio, *Catalogue of Works of Art Belonging to Wellesley College* (Boston, 1883), 18. Neither can now be located.

4. *Ballou's Pictorial Drawing-Room Companion* 10 (19 April 1856): 252.

5. "Journal of the Proceedings of the Boston Artists' Association," 2 vols., Rare Book Room, Boston Public Library. See also Leah Lipton, "The Boston Artists' Association, 1841–1851," *American Journal of Art* 15 (autumn 1983): 45–57.

6. "Rimmer—Lecture Drawings," Countway Library, Harvard University Medical Library, B MS b44.3, a scrapbook of graphite and ink sketches dated February-March 1864.

7. *Ballou's* (1856): 252.

8. One is in the author's collection, another in the American Antiquarian Society, and a third, undated and perhaps later, in the Special Collections Library at Wellesley College. A group of them dated 1841–42 are in a scrapbook now in a private collection in New York City.

9. Billings's name appears along the lower curve of the portrait; it remains to be determined if he designed the entire racist cover. Lithography by E. W. Bouvé of Boston, a firm for whom Billings worked according to Edith A. Wright and Josephine A. McDevitt, "Early American Sheet-Music Lithography," *The Magazine Antiques* 23 (March 1933): 101. Other Billings covers for Bouvé exist.

10. *Pictorial National Library* 1 (July 1848): frontispiece and 52.

11. Leah Lipton, *A Truthful Likeness* (Washington, D.C., 1978), 116, 185–86, and H. Pfister, *Facing the Light* (Washington, D.C., 1978), cat. 76. Compare the large Tappan and Bradford lithograph ca. 1849 (a copy is in the Boston Athenaeum).

12. Joseph T. Buckingham, *Specimens of Newspaper Literature* (Boston, 1850). The plate survives at the American Antiquarian Society. See E. M. Barton, "Report of the Librarian," *Proceedings of the American Antiquarian Society*, n.s. 12 (1898): 341; n.s. 14 (1900): 61; and C. L. Nichols, "The Portraits of Isaiah Thomas," *Proceedings*, n.s. 30 (1921): 255, 261–

(1921): 255, 261–62 (where Billings's first name is given as Henry). The Thomas portrait was engraved by S. A. Schoff, who also cut the portrait of Benjamin Russell that forms the frontispiece to the second volume, but the delineator of that is not named.

13. *Boston Transcript* (17 November 1859). Examples were for sale at the Washington Statue Fair held in Boston.

14. The participants in this venture are all named on the engraving or on the label affixed to the frame. Information about the profit sharing comes by letter from the archivist at Mount Vernon, who also notes that the wood was sold to Cruchett by John Augustine Washington Jr., the last private owner of the estate: John P. Riley to author, 21 December 1989. Examples of this trinket abound, some in round and some in square frames.

15. Paul Revere Frothingham, *Edward Everett: Orator and Statesman* (Boston, 1925), 377–404.

16. These are assigned to Billings without comment by Richard Stoddard, "Hammatt Billings, Artist and Architect," *Old-Time New England* 62 (January-March 1972): 76. The Smith portrait came to the Hood from John Field (Dartmouth '14); the Phelps was the gift of Edward W. Stoughton. Hammatt Billings's name appears in black paint on the reverse of each. Nevertheless, the possibility remains that these are not the work of Hammatt but of Edwin (or Edward) T. Billings, a workaday New England portraitist. See George C. Groce and David H. Wallace, *The New-York Historical Society's Dictionary of Artists in America* (New York, 1957), 49.

17. Denio, *Catalogue of Works of Art*, 18. She gave no dates.

18. *Artists' Sale: Catalogue of Choice Pictures, by Celebrated American Artists*, Samuel Hatch auction, Boston, n.d. A copy is in the Boston Public Library.

19. William Russell to Billings, 28 June 1855, Pilgrim Society, Plymouth, Massachusetts. No such painting is now identifiable.

20. "Engravings of People," 1 (Massachusetts Historical Society).

21. It is possible this composition was inspired by Darley's *Scenes in Indian Life: A Series of Original Designs Portraying Events in the Life of an Indian Chief; Drawn and Etched on Stone by Felix O. C. Darley* (Philadelphia, 1843). Billings's technique is closer to Retzsch, however.

22. *National Union Catalogue*, which reproduces the old catalogue card of the library. Each drawing is listed as 2½" x 3½", mounted.

23. Each is 5" x 7". See Brandywine River Museum, *A Child's Garden of Dreams: An Exhibition of Children's Books and Their Original Illustrations . . . from the Betsy B. Shirley Collection* (Chadd's Ford, Pa., 1990), [8]. The main essay in this catalogue was written by Justin B. Schiller, the New York bookseller, who, in a letter to the author dated 11 December 1983, wrote that the drawings are unsigned "but attested to by Goodspeeds [the Boston antiquarian dealers, now defunct] who had previously sold them to another collector . . . in the 1930s or early '40s."

24. Denio, *Catalogue of Works of Art*, 18.

25. Author's collection. The sketch is on wove paper, 4" x 6"; the watercolor is on heavy wove paper, 6½" x 11". Many sketches of Egyptian subjects are in the collection.

26. "Records of Wellesley College" (Trustees' Minutes), 1, fol. 66 (3 June 1880). See also Denio, *Catalogue of Works of Art*, 43–44.

27. *Old and New* 2 (March 1875): 355–57. (Unless otherwise noted, hereafter *Old and New*.)

28. Fine Arts Department, Boston Public Library.

29. Denio, *Catalogue of Works of Art*, no. 29. According to Billings's obituary in *Old and New*, the originals were 15″ x 20″, brushed with black and white on a middle tint and, although "exquisite" as drawings, were "usually greatly injured by imperfect engraving." This sounds as if more than one were engraved.

30. Although the edition of Priest is dated 1839 the engraving is tipped in and must be later. The caption refers to Albert Barnes's *Notes, Explanatory and Practical, on the Book of Revelation*, which was copyrighted in 1851. Compare, too, the drawings as preserved in the photographs with Billings's illustrations in Rufus Clark, *Heaven and the Scriptural Emblems* (Boston, 1853 [ca. 1852]). Billings's obituarist in *Old and New* suggests a dating of about 1867 ("executed . . . about eight years ago"), but that seems too late.

31. Denio, *Catalogue of Works of Art*, 18; J. J. Jarves, *The Art-Idea*, ed. Benjamin Rowland Jr. (Cambridge, Mass., 1960), 206; Robert F. Perkins Jr. and William J. Gavin III, *The Boston Athenaeum Art Exhibition Index, 1827–1874* (Boston, 1980).

32. Jarves, *Art-Idea*, 206. Billings had illustrated Jarves's *Scenes and Scenery in the Sandwich Islands* of 1843, so his work had been well known to the author for some time.

33. Library of Congress, Copyright Records, Massachusetts, 1849, 195 (13 June 1849). Billings is styled the "author."

34. Library of Congress, Copyright Records, Massachusetts, 1858, 574. There is no notation of a deposit. Martin Farquhar Tupper, *Proverbial Philosophy: A Book of Thoughts and Arguments, Originally Treated* (Boston, 1859), 143–45. A drawing for this print is mentioned in *Old and New*.

35. David S. Reynolds, *Walt Whitman's America* (New York, 1995), 315.

36. Billings seems not to have worked for the Boston house of Prang, which would have been the most likely producer of such a work. The story reappeared, unillustrated, in Hale, *His Level Best, and Other Stories* (Boston, 1973), 281–93.

37. E. E. Hale, "Confidence," *Old and New* 6 (December 1872): 669–74.

38. The ad is signed by George A. Coolidge, business agent for Roberts Brothers, the publishers.

39. Georgia Barnhill of the American Antiquarian Society in conversation with the author.

40. Denio, *Catalogue of Works of Art*, 18.

41. David E. Smith, "Illustrations of American Editions of *The Pilgrim's Progress* to 1870," *Princeton University Library Chronicle* 26 (1964–65): 16–26. See also the *Bulletin of the American Art Union* (August and December 1850).

42. Library of Congress, Copyright Records, Massachusetts, 1853, 249. Also mentioned are J. Andrews and H. Billings.

43. In the early 1850s Billings had his office in the newly erected Liberty Tree Building. It remains to be seen whether he designed it. It still stands, sadly neglected, on Washington Street and Boylston.
Billings had illustrated *Uncle Tom's Cabin* in the previous year for Jewett.

44. *Dwight's Journal of Music* 3 (18 June 1853): 84. The engraving was to be published

"soon" according to this announcement, which goes on to say that it will portray "no less than the whole of John Bunyan's Allegory, with all its scenes and characters," including 280 figures. The same journal announced publication in its issue of 22 October, p. 21; see also p. 24.

45. Nancy Carlson Schrock lists another Billings/Bunyon item: a small (3⅞" x 3¼") engraving by A. C. Warren and J. Andrews after a design by H. Billings: "Joseph Andrews, Engraver and Swedenborgian Spokesman," master's thesis, University of Delaware, 1977, 90 (cat. 178). Ednah Dow Cheney (*Reminiscences* [Boston, 1902], 132—33) mentions "a series of illustrations for 'Pilgrim's Progress,'" by Billings, which she thought had not been published. Perhaps she conflated his Book of Revelation drawings with his Pilgrim.

46. Elwood C. Perry III, *The Art of Thomas Cole* (Newark, N.J., 1988), 349.

47. *Dodge's Literary Museum* 7 (27 August 1853): 189. The critic was astonished by published praises of the plate, "which were evidently written to order."

48. An example is in the collection of the City Museum of New York; it is 6⅞" x 9½".

49. 11½" x 23". A number of variations occur in several versions examined by the author. For example, there are two at the Boston Athenaeum in each of which a different stone and a different ink were used for the second color.

50. Edwin M. Bacon, *King's Dictionary of Boston* (Cambridge, Mass., 1883), 407. Another hotel delineated by Billings and engraved by George G. Smith was the American House in Hanover Street. It is shown before its rebuilding in 1851 (Bacon, *King's Dictionary*, 15).

51. Moses King, *King's Handbook of Boston* (Cambridge, Mass., 1878, and many later editions). In the 7th ed. it appears on p. 69 as a small woodcut vignette.

52. Examples are in the collections of the Boston Public Library, the Winterthur Museum, and the Boston Athenaeum.

53. The McLean Asylum: Richard Frothingham Jr., *The History of Charlestown, Massachusetts* (Boston, 1845—49); Faneuil Hall Market: Josiah Quincy, *Municipal History of Boston* (Boston, 1852); see also Christopher P. Monkhouse, *Faneuil Hall Market: An Account of Its Many Likenesses* (Boston, 1969); Boston Common: *Boston Miscellany of Literature and Fashion* 2 (1842). Examples of most of these can be found in the print collection at the Boston Athenaeum.

54. *The Third Exhibition of the Massachusetts Charitable Mechanic Association* (Boston, 1841), no. 866 (the artist is here called "C. H. H. Billings").

55. Billings-Emmons correspondence, 29 November 1841 (Joanna Andros Collection, Keene, New Hampshire).

56. On wove paper, 3½" x 5"; author's collection.

57. The collection also contains slightly larger studies of these side groups. A palm tree locates the right-hand scene in the tropics, or perhaps the Holy Land, but that does little to clarify the matter.

58. *The Eighth Exhibition of the Massachusetts Charitable Mechanic Association* (Boston, 1856), [viii].

59. Other examples of this diploma are in the collections of the Society for the

Preservation of New England Antiquities in Boston and the Pennsylvania Academy of the Fine Arts in Philadelphia. The Academy's came with a silver medal awarded in 1878 to Thomas Eakins for watercolor painting.

60. Lithography by N. D. Gould. The Society for the Preservation of New England Antiquities owns an example.

61. The Antiquarian Society copy bears an inscribed date of 5867 (i.e., 1867 [many nineteenth-century people believed the world was 4,000 years at Christ's birth]). Billings's design must predate that.

62. For other certificates see chapter 9.

63. The date inscribed on the example in the author's collection is 1850.

64. There are annotations in Williams's hand on proofs of these views in a scrapbook, information about which comes from Eric Rudd in a 1975 letter to David Tatham. There is a view of the interior of a jewelry store after Billings in the Dearborn scrapbook at the American Antiquarian Society (John R. Chapin, "Specimen Collection of Wood Engravings and Drawings," fol. 52).

6. "Has Shown Himself a Master"

1. *Boston Morning Journal* (16 November 1874): 3.

2. *Ceremonies at the Dedication of the Soldiers' Monument in Concord, Mass.* (Concord, 1867), 13, 30. Emerson was a member of the building committee.

3. Harold Kirker and James Kirker, *Bulfinch's Boston, 1787–1817* (New York, 1964).

4. James F. O'Gorman, *H. H. Richardson: Architectural Forms for an American Society* (Chicago, 1987).

5. This chapter draws heavily upon, but adds to and revises, James F. O'Gorman, "H. and J. E. Billings of Boston: From Classicism to the Picturesque," *Journal of the Society of Architectural Historians* 42 (March 1983): 54–73.

6. James R. Osgood, *Boston Illustrated* (Boston, 1875), 8, and the lists of architects in the *Boston Almanac* (Boston, 1845 and 1874).

7. For a historical survey of Boston architecture, see Douglass Shand Tucci, *Built in Boston: City and Suburb* (Boston, 1978).

8. S. N. Dickinson, *Boston Almanac* (Boston, 1845), 49. The list is current as of 1 November 1844; it includes A. Benjamin, C. H. H. Billings, R. Bond, G. J. F. Bryant, A. Gilman, G. W. Gray, C. G. Hall, Howard and Briggs, C. Roath, I. Rogers, E. Shaw, W. Sparrell, D. Sullivan, J. Thorndike, T. Voelckers, S. Washburn, and A. B. Young.

9. *The Second Exhibition of the Massachusetts Charitable Mechanic Association* (Boston, 1839), 25 (no. 1010); and *The Third Exhibition of the Massachusetts Charitable Mechanic Association* (Boston, 1841), 94 (no. 866). The Michigan drawing cannot now be located; A. J. Davis also submitted a project (John Donoghue, "Alexander Jackson Davis," Ph.D. diss., New York University, 1977); neither was built. See also University of Michigan, *Regents' Proceedings, 1837–64* (Ann Arbor, 1915), 81–83.

10. Some of Billings's views for Lang were reused by L. C. Tuthill in her *History of Architecture* (Philadelphia, 1848). For the history of architectural graphics and especially perspective presentation in Boston see James F. O'Gorman, *On the Boards: Drawings by*

Nineteenth-Century Boston Architects (Philadelphia, 1989), and O'Gorman, *The Perspective of Anglo-American Architecture* (Philadelphia, 1995).

11. "Architects and Architecture," *Christian Examiner* 49 (September 1850): 278–79.

12. See the preface to Edward Shaw, *Modern Architect* (Boston, 1854).

13. Obituary, *Journal of the American Institute of Architects* 8 (1920): 140. The precise year is given in a preserved excerpt from his destroyed diary (17 March 1851) kindly sent to me by Susan Maycock. Hammatt's impact on other architects extended beyond immediate contact. The scrapbook compiled after 1847 by Thomas Tefft of Providence (1826–59), now in the Rhode Island Historical Society, contains cuttings from *Ballou's* depicting Billings and his work.

14. John A. Chewning, "William Robert Ware and the Beginnings of Architectural Education in the United States," Ph.D. diss., MIT, 1986, 451.

15. See Margaret Henderson Floyd, *Architectural Education in Boston* (Boston, 1989), chapter 1.

16. He did not, however, sign the agreement in June: Walter Whitehill, "A Centennial Sketch," in *Boston Society of Architects*, ed. M. E. Goody and R. P. Walsh (Boston, 1967), 19.

17. There is mention of a "plan [of the] Fed[eral] St[reet] Ch[urch]" for which the publisher and bookseller William D. Ticknor paid Hammatt twenty-five dollars on 22 October 1845 (Houghton Library, Harvard University, fMS AM 1185.14(1), fol. 120). This remains unexplained. Could it relate to the congregation's plan to abandon Bulfinch's church fifteen years later?

18. The brothers were paid for unknown work at Harvard College in May 1846 (Harvard University Archives, Harvard College Papers, Second Series, vol. 13, 1845–46, 307, "H & J. E. Billings' bill . . . [$]328.00").

19. [Jane S. Knowles], *Change and Continuity: A Pictorial History of the Boston Athenaeum* (Boston, 1976).

20. Billings's design of this project remains unknown, but see below in the text.

21. Selected bibliography: *Catalogue of the Paintings . . . in the Collection of the Boston Museum* (Boston, 1847), 29–30; Josiah Quincy, *The History of the Boston Athenaeum* (Cambridge, Mass., 1851), 164–66, 198–99; *History of the Boston Museum* (Boston, 1873); *Boston Museum . . . Present Structure Erected 1846. Remodeled 1868, 1872, and 1876, and the Auditorium Entirely Rebuilt 1880* (Boston, 1880); and Howard M. Ticknor, "The Passing of the Boston Museum," *New England Magazine* n.s. 28 (June 1903): 378–96.

22. William Chambers, *Things As They Are in America* (London, 1854), 214.

23. *Catalogue of the Paintings*, 29–30. This makes no mention of the globes for gas light, which were an outstanding feature of the facade (*Ballou's Pictorial Drawing-Room Companion* 16 [26 March 1859]: 193), nor do they appear in the earliest view of the building ("Favorite Melodies from the Grand Chinese Spectacle of Aladdin or His Wonderful Lamp, As Produced at the Boston Museum. Bufford Lith., 1847" [sheet music cover]). They were, however, in place by October 1848.

24. Chambers, *Things As They Are*, 215.

25. Mary Van Meter, "A New Asher Benjamin Church in Boston," *Journal of the Society of Architectural Historians* 38 (October 1979): 262–66.

26. *Boston Post* (3 August 1846): 1; (8 August): 1; (14 August): 1; (15 August): 2 (Gilman's letter); *Boston Courier* (22 August): 2; (26 August): 2.

27. *Christian Examiner*, 284.

28. He also bought (on 23 July) Joseph Gwilt's *Encyclopaedia of Architecture*, probably in the second edition of 1845, a work illustrating north and central Italian palazzi. See appendix A.

29. *Articles of Association of the Proprietors of the Temple Club House* (Boston, 1849); *Ballou's* 9 (4 August 1855): 76. The building remains, but the facade is gone and the interiors transformed.

30. In a letter to the historian Charles Deane dated 17 October 1849, Eliza S. Quincy mentions "my brother's house" and "Billings, the architect of the house" (Massachusetts Historical Society). According to Hobart Holly of the Quincy Historical Society, it was erected the previous year and leveled in 1970.

31. Robert E. Lucid, ed., *The Journal of Richard Henry Dana, Jr.* (Cambridge, Mass., 1968), 3 vols., (22 July 1851): "agreed with Billings on a place for the house"; (21 March 1852): took possession. See B. Bunting and R. H. Nylander, *Survey of Architectural History in Cambridge, Report Four: Old Cambridge* (Cambridge, Mass., 1973), 98 and fig. 75.

32. The letter is in the James Hyde Papers at the Jackson Homestead, Newton, Massachusetts. I have not searched for a Foster house in Worcester.

33. Charles Francis Adams, *Richard Henry Dana, A Biography* (Boston, 1890), 213–15.

34. See appendix B.

35. Letters from C. E. Norton to the builder, Andrew McGregor, 1852–53, are in the Charles Eliot Norton Papers at the Houghton Library, Harvard University.

36. See chapter 1.

37. Billings scrapbook, Stowe-Day Library, Harriet Beecher Stowe Center, Hartford, between fols. 35 and 36.

38. Billings-Emmons correspondence, 3 August 1841 (Joanna Andros Collection, Keene, New Hampshire).

39. Billings-Emmons correspondence, 29 May 1842 (Joanna Andros Collection, Keene, New Hampshire).

40. *Boston Transcript* (8 November 1847): 2; (9 November): 2; (10 November): 2; (11 November): 2. Both churches are noted in Tuthill's *History of Architecture*, 258 (a work containing some illustrations by Hammatt; see appendix B), where the brothers are collapsed into one person: "Two beautiful Gothic churches, of freestone, were built [in Boston] in 1847. Billings, architect."

41. *Christian Examiner*, 285–86.

42. Suffolk County Registry of Deeds, book 550, fols. 58–59.

43. Suffolk County Deeds, book 559, fols. 196–97. Joseph is not mentioned in this document, probably because he did not join in the agreement to erect the building. He is usually given credit in contemporary accounts along with his brother for the church as built: *Boston Almanac* (Boston, 1854), 59, and *Rambles about Boston; or, Efforts to Do Good* (Boston, 1856), 91.

44. *Boston Almanac* (Boston, 1854), 59 (a publication with which Billings was associated), and *Gleason's Pictorial Line-of-Battle Ship* 1 (6 August 1859): 1.

45. *Merrimack Courier* (17 October 1846): 2 ("J. & A. Billings"); M. B. Dorgan, *History of Lawrence* ([Cambridge, Mass.], 1924), 127; and Edith Saunders, *The First Hundred Years of Grace Church* (Lawrence, 1946), 8.

46. A. H. Amory and William Lawrence, *Sermons Preached at the Fiftieth Anniversary of Grace Church* (Cambridge, Mass., 1896), 5–6.

47. William H. Pierson Jr., *American Buildings and Their Architects: Technology and the Picturesque, the Corporate and Early Gothic Styles* (Garden City, N.Y., 1978), 190; for the board-and-batten church, see 432.

48. "Church of the Messiah, Florence St., Boston. J. E. Billings, Architect. J. H. Bufford's Lith." Undated lithograph in the author's collection.

J. E. received sixty-five dollars for the plan of the Centre Street School and eighty-five dollars for the design of the second high school: *Annual Documents of the City of Cambridge* (1848), 42–43; (1849), 26–27.

Boston Transcript (22 May 1847): 2; (3 April 1848): 4. The notice of the dedication names only Ingraham as designer, but the *Boston Almanac* (Boston, 1849), 82, says "Mr. Billings was the architect" working under Ingraham's direction. J. E. is listed as drafts-man for the building in Henry Barnard, *School Architecture* (New York, 2d ed., 1849), 190.

49. "Mr. Billings of the firm of Billings & Sleeper, Boston, is the Architect & Superintendent": letter of Edward Lasell, founder of the school, 26 May 1851 (Lasell Junior College).

Boston Transcript (22 April 1852): 2; (2 November): 2. A contract between owner and builder of the National Theatre in which the architect is not mentioned is in the Rare Book Room of the Boston Public Library (MS Th. 11 [6]).

George Gates Raddin Jr., *The Wilderness and the City: The Story of a Parish, 1817–1967* (Wilkes-Barre, 1968), 656.

50. *Boston Transcript* (12 July 1853): 2; George H. Preble, "History of the Boston Navy Yard, 1797–1874," (1875), 322 (ms. in the National Archives; a copy in the Curator's Office, Boston Navy Yard, National Park Service); and Bettina A. Norton, *The Boston Naval Shipyard, 1800–1974* (Boston, 1975, reprinted from the Proceedings of the Bostonian Society [1974]).

51. Quincy, *History of the Boston Athenaeum*, 232–37; Ralph W. Emerson, *Journals*, 10:250 (June 1868). There are Billings sketches at the Stowe-Day Library of the Harriet Beecher Stowe Center in Hartford and at the Athenaeum.

Dwight's Journal of Music 23 (31 October 1863): 126; (12 December): 147. The Music Hall organ survives in the Memorial Music Hall in Methuen, Massachusetts. See chapter 10.

52. These drawings are in the Billings scrapbook, Stowe-Day Library.

53. Lithographs of Billings's "City-hall Extension" project are in the Massachusetts Historical Society; *Report of the Committee on Public Buildings upon an Enlargement of the City Hall* (City Document no. 44) (Boston, 1860); and George L. Wrenn III, "The Boston City Hall," *Journal of the Society of Architectural Historians* 21 (March 1962): 188–92.

54. J. J. Jarves, *The Art-Idea*, ed. Benjamin Rowland Jr. (Cambridge, Mass., 1960), 196–97; Ednah Dow Cheney, *Reminiscences* (Boston, 1902), 132–33; Charles F. Read, "Hammatt Billings, Artist and Architect," typescript of an address given to the Bostonian Society in 1920 and preserved in its library.

55. "View of the New Jail for Suffolk County . . . 1848. H. Billings, del. G. J. F. Bryant, Architect. J. H. Bufford's Lith." (Boston Athenaeum).

56. *Boston Transcript* (11 August 1855).

57. "Improvement of Franklin St.," *Boston Almanac* (Boston, 1859), 51–52.

58. The plan may be that preserved in the Bradlee Papers at the Boston Athenaeum, vol. 20, 113; *Dedication of the Mechanics' Hall*, 6–7.

59. *Proceedings on the Occasion of Laying the Corner Stone of a Building for the Use of the Mass. Charitable Mechanic Association, September 30, 1857* (Boston, 1857); *Dedication of the Mechanics' Hall*.

60. *Ballou's* 15 (27 November 1858): 337.

61. Jean Ames Follett-Thompson, "The Business of Architecture: William Gibbons Preston and Architectural Professionalism," Ph.D. diss., Boston University, 1986, 48.

62. Stoddard, "Hammatt Billings," 61; *Frank Leslie's Illustrated Newspaper* (7 August 1869): 327, 333.

63. *Boston Morning Journal* (17 November 1874): 2.

64. John Buchanan-Brown, *The Book Illustrations of George Cruikshank* (North Pomfret, Vt., 1980), fig. 1.

65. Edward Stanwood, *Boston Illustrated* (Boston, 1872), 86.

66. "Methodist Episcopal Church. Hammatt Billings, Arch. J. H. Bufford's Lith. Boston" (Boston Athenaeum).

67. *[New Britain] True Citizen* (25 August 1865): 2; *New Britain Record* (17 January 1868): 2; [David N. Camp], *A Half Century of the South Congregational Church* (New Britain, 1893); and Kate Brooks, *A History of the South Congregational Church* (New Britain, 1938), 16–17.

68. Several sketches in the Stowe-Day scrapbook seem related to Merrill Wheelock's Gothic seven-story Masonic Temple on Tremont at Boylston Street, Boston, dedicated in 1867: fols. 9, 11, and 54, the latter with a "Tremont St." notation (Harriet Beecher Stowe Center, Hartford).

69. R. B. Shaffer, "Ruskin, Norton, and Memorial Hall," *Harvard Library Bulletin* 3 (1949): 213–31. There is apparently no record of this in the Harvard University Archives.

70. *New York Times* (7 June 1867): 2, for brief descriptions of fifty-one entries; National Archives, RG 121, Public Buildings Service, General Correspondence, Letters Received, 1843–1910, box 306, entry no. 22, for Billings's description of his own. See also I. N. Phelps Stokes, *The Iconography of Manhattan Island* (New York, 1926), 5:1929.

71. "An Industrial Experiment at South Manchester," *Harper's New Monthly Magazine* 45 (November 1872): 836–44, and Edward Loomis Nelson, "The Cheney's Village at South Manchester, Connecticut," *Harper's Weekly* 34 (1 February 1890): 87–88. See also John Stilgoe, *Borderlands* (New Haven, 1988), 252–54.

72. Mathias Spiess and Percy W. Bidwell, *History of Manchester, Connecticut* (Manchester, Conn., 1924), 94–102; William E. Buckley, *A New England Pattern: The History of Manchester, Connecticut* (Chester, Conn., 1973), 87, 150; and Ellsworth S. Grant, "The Silken Cheneys," *Connecticut Historical Society Bulletin* 44 (July 1979): 65–79; 44 (October 1979): 106–16.

73. John S. Garner, *The Model Company Town: Urban Design through Private Enterprise in Nineteenth-Century New England* (Amherst, Mass., 1984), 30–35 (where, however, the remarks on Cheney Hall are wildly inaccurate).

74. Microfilms of working drawings are on file in the Manchester Town Planning Office; prints are in the author's collection. A sheaf of original drawings is on deposit at the Society for the Preservation of New England Antiquities. See Anderson Notter Feingold, Inc., *Preservation and Development Plan for Cheney Brothers National Historic Landmark District* (Boston, 1980).

75. Copies of these drawings are in the author's collection. See Alice Farley Williams, *Silk and Guns: The Life of a Connecticut Yankee, Frank Cheney, 1817–1904* (Manchester, Conn., 1996), 102–13.

76. Billings scrapbook, Stowe-Day Library, Harriet Beecher Stowe Center, Hartford, fols. 24–35, 65–67, and 74.

77. Vincent J. Scully Jr., *The Shingle Style* (New Haven, 1955).

78. Henry-Russell Hitchcock, *The Architecture of H. H. Richardson and His Times* (Cambridge, Mass., 1966), 161–67.

79. A copy of "General Description and Specifications to Accompany Design for State Capitol," signed H. and J. E. Billings, is also in the Stowe-Day Library, Harriet Beecher Stowe Center, Hartford. The project was overlooked by David P. Curry and Patricia D. Pierce, eds., *Monument: The Connecticut State Capitol* (Hartford, 1979), but is mentioned in David P. Ranson, *Geo. Keller, Architect* (Hartford, 1978), 71. There was some connection between Keller and Hammatt: the Stowe-Day Library owns a copy of Kate N. Doggett, trans., *The Grammar of Painting and Engraving* (New York, 1874), once owned by Keller, with Hammatt's signature on the title page (see appendix A).

80. The Second Empire competitive design is preserved in a photograph in the smaller Bartlett scrapbook, Fine Arts Department, Boston Public Library.

A photograph of an undated design for an unnamed insurance company building for Hartford is also in the smaller Bartlett scrapbook in the Boston Public Library.

81. Edwin M. Bacon, *King's Dictionary of Boston* (Cambridge, Mass., 1883), 297; and Moses King, *King's Handbook of Boston* (Boston, 7th ed., 1885), 202; Cyr Hanton, Amy Semmes, and Roger Spears, "The Wesleyan Association Building," 1980 (paper written for Eduard Sekler, Harvard University, Carpenter Center).

"Odd Fellows Hall. Architect J. E. Billings. Crosby and Co. Lith., Boston" (Boston Athenaeum).

Two projects in the Stowe-Day scrapbook should also be mentioned: "Design for a Town Hall to be built of rubble stone with granite dressings" dated 1870, and variant designs for a large railway station dated 1871 (Harriet Beecher Stowe Center, Hartford). Neither is further identified (the latter might relate to Boston's Park Square station of 1872).

82. Nancy Lurie Salzman, *Building and Builders: An Architectural History of Boston University* (Boston, 1985), 25–27.

83. Claflin Collection, Rutherford B. Hayes Presidential Center, Fremont, Ohio. Hartwell had trained in the Billings office.

84. Keating, Lane and Co., wholesale clothing, first occupied the building at 81 Franklin in 1864 according to the *Boston Directory*. See Jane Holz Kay, *Lost Boston* (Boston, 1980), 87.

85. *The Rich Men of Massachusetts* (Boston, 2d ed., 1852), 57.

86. E. M. Bacon, *Boston Illustrated*, (Boston, [ca. 1886]), 96–97; *Report of the Commissioners Appointed to Investigate the Cause . . . of the Great Fire* (Boston, 1873).

87. Several as yet unidentified references to Billings projects are in Henry T. Bailey's "Complete Catalogue of Plans . . . [etc.] The Property of Gridley J. F. Bryant" (1890), now in the library of the University of Oregon. See also Bailey's article on Bryant, "An Architect of the Old School," *New England Magazine* 25 (1901).

88. *Boston Mercantile Journal* (10 November 1873): 1.

89. *Belmont, Massachusetts: The Architecture and Development of the Town of Homes* (1984), 100.

90. Edward Herrick Chandler, *The History of the Wellesley Congregational Church* (Boston, 1898), 89; E. M. Hinchliffe, *Five Pounds Currency, Three Pounds Corn: Wellesley's Centennial Story* (Wellesley, 1981), 64. Some documents, drawings, and draft specifications are in the church archives. In the Stowe-Day scrapbook is an undated design for a decorative fresco "for church at Wellesley" (Harriet Beecher Stowe Center, Hartford).

91. Mary B. Claflin, *Under the Old Elms* (New York, 1895). The house has been somewhat altered and added to.

92. *Norfolk County Gazette* (6 June 1874).

93. See James F. O'Gorman, *On the Boards: Drawings by Nineteenth-Century Boston Architects* (Philadelphia, 1989), 69–70.

94. *Architectural Heritage of Haverhill* (Haverhill, Mass., 1976), 20.

7. "A Rare Achievement of Architectural Skill"

1. Edward Abbott, "Wellesley College," *Harper's New Monthly Magazine* 315 (August 1876): 321–32 (unless otherwise noted, quotations in this chapter that refer specifically to the building are from this excellent early account). Abbott, a clergyman and author, was the son of Jacob Abbott, author of the popular Rollo books for children, at least one of which Billings illustrated.

2. The basic publication on the history of the college is Jean Glasscock, ed., *Wellesley College, 1875–1975: A Century of Women* (Wellesley, 1975). Additional information and documents are in the College Archives, Clapp Library.

3. Samuel Longfellow, *Life of Henry Wadsworth Longfellow* (Boston, 1886), 3:255.

4. Unless otherwise noted, information about the Durants and Wellesley College is based on information available in the archives of the college. Some is available in Glasscock, *Wellesley College*.

5. See Andrew Jackson Downing, *A Treatise on the Practice of Landscape Gardening*, ed. Henry A. Sargent (New York, 6th ed., 1859), 427.

6. Bertha E. Blakely, "The Library of Mount Holyoke College," 1952, typescript, Mount Holyoke Archives.

7. Blakely, "The Library of Mount Holyoke"; Mary O. Nutting, *Historical Sketch of Mount Holyoke Seminary* (Washington, D.C., 1876), 6, 12; and S. D. Stow, *History of Mount Holyoke Seminary* (South Hadley, Mass., 1887), 221, 226–27, 270.

8. Helen Lefkowitz Horowitz, *Alma Mater: Design and Experience in the Women's Colleges from their Nineteenth-Century Beginnings to the 1930s* (New York, 1984), 43 (and chap. 3). My discussion of Wellesley and its context owes much to this fine work.

9. Horowitz, *Alma Mater,* chapter 1. For the broader context of architectural planning for higher education in the United States, see Paul Venable Turner, *Campus, An American Planning Tradition* (Cambridge, Mass., 1984).

10. *Historical Sketch of Vassar College* (New York, 1876), 10–19.

11. Horowitz, *Alma Mater,* chapter 2.

12. Horowitz, *Alma Mater,* 42.

13. Billings scrapbook, Stowe-Day Library, Harriet Beecher Stowe Center, Hartford. This drawing was first brought to my attention by the late Lee Ann Clements. See her "A New Light on College Hall," *Wellesley Alumnae Magazine* 62 (spring 1978): 4–7.

14. Wellesley College, Trustees' Minutes, 1:viii–ix.

15. Gates and gatehouses are also in several projects in the Stowe-Day scrapbook (Harriet Beecher Stowe Center, Hartford).

16. For some particulars see also the *Boston Journal* (26 June 1875 [or 1876]).

17. Vedder's painting was removed to the college's Farnsworth Art Museum after 1889. It is now in the Detroit Art Institute, having been deaccessioned in the 1950s, when understanding of American painting was at low ebb.

18. See note 16 this chapter. Wilhelm Zahn, *Ornamente aller klassischen Kunst-epochen nach den originalien in ihren eigenthümlichen Farben* (Berlin, 1849; 3d ed., 1870).

19. See also the *College Calendar* for 1877–78 (quoted in Frances Gotkowitz's undergraduate thesis, "The Development of a Master Plan for Wellesley College," 1980, available in the college archives).

20. Montgomery Schuyler, "Architecture of American Colleges X: Three Women's Colleges—Vassar, Wellesley, and Smith," *Architectural Record* 31 (May 1912): 512–37.

21. *Zion's Herald* (2 October 1873). The *Herald* was published in Billings's Wesleyan Association Building in Bromfield Street, Boston.

22. Billings had owned *Stones of Venice* since its publication in 1851. See appendix A.

23. *Boston Daily Advertiser* (12 June 1873).

24. Horowitz, *Alma Mater,* chapter 5.

25. [Martha Hale Shackford and Edith Harriet Moore,] *College Hall* [Boston, 1914]. This is a memorial gathering of photographs of the building with a brief descriptive text produced immediately after the fire.

8. "Some Lasting Memento of Their Worth"

1. Howard Colvin, *Architecture and the After-Life* (New Haven, 1991), ix.

2. "Essay on Architectural Monuments," *Analectic Magazine* (April 1820): 278.

3. Paul R. Baker, *Richard Morris Hunt* (Cambridge, Mass., 1980), chapter 18.

4. This is the larger of the two scrapbooks of Billings's drawings in the Print Room of the Boston Public Library. According to an inscription, it was compiled by Hammatt's brother-in-law, N. T. Bartlett, and is dated July 1879. There are some fifty-nine pages of tipped-in drawings.

5. Quoted from J. Jay Smith, *Designs for Monuments and Mural Tablets: Adapted to Rural Cemeteries, Church Yards, Churches, and Chapels* (New York, 1846), 6.

6. James S. Curl, *Victorian Celebrations of Death* (Detroit, 1972), and Edmund V. Gillon Jr., *Victorian Cemetery Art* (New York, 1972).

7. For an overview of the cemetery movement, see Davis P. Schuyler, "Public Landscapes and American Urban Culture, 1800–1870: Rural Cemeteries, Urban Parks, and Suburbs," Ph.D. diss., Columbia University, 1979.

8. John C. Loudon, *On the Layingout . . . of Cemeteries* (London 1843), quoted in James S. Curl, *A Celebration of Death* (New York, 1980), 249.

9. Smith, *Designs,* 6. The title page clearly credits Loudon as the "basis" of Smith's remarks.

10. An example is Nathaniel S. Dearborn's *Guide through Mount Auburn*. It is profusely illustrated with wood engravings and reached its eleventh edition by 1857. See Blanche Linden-Ward, "Strange but Genteel Pleasure Grounds: Tourist and Leisure Uses of Nineteenth-Century Rural Cemeteries," in *Cemeteries and Gravemarkers,* ed. Richard E. Meyer (Ann Arbor, Mich., 1989), 293–328.

11. For an overview of commemorative monuments see Peggy McDowell and Richard E. Meyer, *The Revival Styles in American Memorial Art* (Bowling Green, Ohio, 1994).

12. The portfolio was issued in London by M. Taylor. Bond bequeathed his architectural library of seventy-five volumes to Amherst College where it is now preserved in Special Collections.

13. Smith, *Designs,* 28–30.

14. Schulze obtained copyrights for designs in 1851 and 1853 (Library of Congress, Copyright Records, Massachusetts, 1851, p. 50; 1853, p. 8). His *Original Designs in Monumental Art* (Boston, 1851), containing forty-eight lithographic plates (in the copy in the Boston Public Library), went through four editions to 1860. His *Designs for Monuments by Paul Schulze, Architect, New York* appeared in 1858. It contained six lithographic plates, all signed and dated 1858, plus title page. In 1860 he issued another collection of thirty-six lithographic plates (including title page) under the same name. None of these titles appears in Henry-Russell Hitchcock's *American Architectural Books* (Minneapolis, 1962).

15. Blanche Linden-Ward, *Silent City on a Hill: Landscapes of Memory and Boston's Mount Auburn Cemetery* (Columbus, Ohio, 1989).

16. Frederic A. Scharf, "The Garden Cemetery and American Sculpture: Mount Auburn," *Art Quarterly* 24 (September 1961): 83.

17. Hammatt Billings, "Sketches at Mount Auburn," *Boston Almanac* (Boston, 1857), 49–60. That Billings wrote other articles is suggested by his obituary in the *Boston Morning Journal* (16 November 1874): 3: "As a writer on art his many articles—published and unpublished—will be remembered by those whose good fortune it was to peruse them." This body of work has yet to be recovered.

For information on these monuments see Dearborn's *Guide through Mount Auburn,* 11th ed., 1857.

18. See Gillon, *Victorian Cemetery Art.*

19. *The Rich Men of Massachusetts* (Boston, 2d ed., 1852), 61, 223.

20. *Boston Transcript* (4 May 1853): 2, and (21 May): 2, and Francis George Shaw, "Robert Gould Shaw," in *Memorial Biographies of the New England Historic and Genealogical Society* (Boston, 1881), 2:38–61.

21. Cornelius C. Vermeule III, "Greek Sculpture, Roman Sculpture, and American Taste: The Mirror of Mount Auburn," *Sweet Auburn* [newsletter of the Friends of Mount Auburn] (fall 1990).

22. Dearborn, *Guide through Mount Auburn* (Boston, 1857), 17. Billings's drawing is in the large Bartlett scrapbook in the Fine Arts Department, Boston Public Library, fol. 4.

23. An inscription on the matt in what appears to be Billings's hand identifies the design and gives it to him. The whereabouts of the model are unknown.

24. *Rich Men of Massachusetts*, 52; Hamilton Andrews Hill, "Hon. Jonathan Phillips," in *Memorial Biographies of the New England Historic and Genealogical Society* (Boston, 1885), 4:93–117.

25. The Phillips lot is number 2404 on Lawn Avenue. In the scrapbook of Billings's architectural sketches is a small design (fol. 63) for a sarcophigal monument with Egyptian Revival details (Stowe-Day Library, Harriet Beecher Stowe Center, Hartford).

26. Daniel T. McColgan, *Joseph Tuckerman* (Washington, D.C., 1940). Joseph was the uncle of Henry T. Tuckerman (1813–71), author of *Book of the Artists* (New York, 1867), among other works. The monument is on Oak Avenue just off Willow.

27. *Mt. Auburn Memorial* 1 (9 November 1859): 173. The tomb fell into disrepair and was demolished in 1940.

28. Also buried in the plot are Amorys and Pennimans, proper Bostonians all. The Brewers are buried beneath individual Gothic stones behind the monument. These are presumably also by Billings.

29. *Rich Men of Massachusetts*, 17.

30. For a contemporary view of the monument, see the lithograph in Wilson Flagg, *Mount Auburn: Its Scenes, Its Beauties, and Its Lessons* (Boston, 1861).

31. The Damon lot is number 3615 on Mound Avenue.

32. *The National Cyclopaedia of American Biography* 12:341; *Rich Men of Massachusetts*, 26. [William A. Crafts], *Forest Hills Cemetery* (Boston, 1858), 106–7, with illustration.

33. Members of the Parkman, Wells, Mills, and Cook families are interred within the plot. According to cemetery records Dwight was not buried until 1853. Only one of the original headstones remains.

34. *Rich Men of Massachusetts*, 71.

35. Vincent Y. Bowditch, *Life and Correspondence of Henry Ingersoll Bowditch* (Boston, 1902), 1:239–47. A view of the face is given between pp. 246 and 247. This is the one reference that has yet come to light of Billings's practicing the art of engraving he presumably learned as an apprentice in Abel Bowen's shop.

36. For Sherwin, see *The National Cyclopaedia of American Biography* 11:360.

37. *Dedication of the Monument on Boston Common Erected to the Memory of the Men of Boston Who Died in the Civil War* (Boston, 1877), 13–15, 35.

38. The Corcoran Gallery of Art (51.39). Gridley J. F. Bryant and Hammatt Billings, *Specifications for Stone-Cutter's Materials and Work for Memorial Monument* (Boston, [1866]).

39. See Bryant and Billings, *Specifications*.

40. Peggy McDowell, "Martin Milmore's Soldiers and Sailors' Monument on the Boston Common: Formulating Conventionalism in Design and Symbolism," *Journal of American Culture* 11 (spring 1988): 63–85. This was written before Billings's second design came to light.

41. *The New England Historic and Genealogical Register* (Boston, 1867), 21:282.

42. *Ceremonies at the Dedication of the Soldiers' Monument in Concord, Mass.* (Concord, 1867), 13, 30.

43. In the next year, 1868, H. and J. E. Billings provided the design for another minor commission, a wall-mounted inscription "in memory of the soldiers from Kennebunk, [Maine.]" It was placed in the town hall in 1869. This was demolished ca. 1920, so the tablet probably does not survive. What little we know of this comes from documents now in the Brick Store Museum in Kennebunk.

44. George A. Thayer, *The Braintree Soldiers' Memorial* (Boston, 1877), 49.

45. R. L. Rusk, *The Letters of Ralph Waldo Emerson* (New York 1939), 4:461 (28 and 30 August 1854).

46. Jackson Homestead, Newton, Massachusetts.

47. *Ballou's Pictorial Drawing-Room Companion* 11 (11 October 1856): 232–33, and (25 October): 268.

48. Thomas Ball, *My Three Score Years and Ten* (Boston, 2d ed., 1892), 366–79. Billings was a member of the committee organized in 1859 to undertake the erection of the work. He resigned when he was given the commission for the design of the base.

49. Ball, *My Three Score Years*, 212–13, 366–79.

50. *Frank Leslie's Illustrated Newspaper* (17 July 1869): 277 and 281; see also (31 July 1869): 307.

Quoted in Justin Winsor, ed., *The Memorial History of Boston* (Boston, 1881), 4:413.

9. "Well Calculated to Promote Fraternal Feeling"

1. This chapter is drawn from and somewhat revises James F. O'Gorman, "Colossus of Plymouth," *Journal of the Society of Architectural Historians* 54 (September 1995): 278–301.

2. Early descriptions of the existing monument abound. See, for example, that printed on the reverse of an undated (but ca. 1890) souvenir photograph published by C. H. Rogers of Plymouth (there is one in the files of the Pilgrim Society, Plymouth), or *The Proceedings at the Celebration by the Pilgrim Society at Plymouth, August 1st, 1889 of the Completion of the National Monument to the Forefathers* (Plymouth, 1889), 21–22.

3. Rose T. Briggs, *Plymouth Rock: History and Significance* (Boston, 1968) provides a convenient summary of the facts. I am grateful for permission to read parts of John Seelye's major iconographic study of Plymouth Rock, now in preparation.

4. Peter J. Gomes, ed., *The Pilgrim Society, 1820–1970* (Plymouth, 1971), 7.

5. William S. Russell, *Pilgrim Memorials, and Guide to Plymouth* (Boston, 2d ed., 1855), 118.

6. *Boston Weekly Museum* (11 January 1851): 244.
Boston Transcript (25 March 1852): 2.

7. Trustees' Minutes, June 1853, in the Pilgrim Society, Plymouth. Unless otherwise noted, all quotations from documents come from the records of the society, especially the Trustees' Committee Minutes and the papers relating to the national monument to be found in boxes 3, 4, 6, 9, 9a, and 9b. A call for designs that were due in November appeared in the *Boston Transcript* (4 August 1854): 2.

8. Bainbridge Bunting and Margaret Henderson Floyd, *Harvard: An Architectural History* (Cambridge, Mass., 1985), 44–45, 55–56, 290–91 n. 18, 46–49. Bond, as noted in chapter 8, owned George Maliphant's *Designs for Sepulchral Monuments* of 1835.

9. Douglass Shand Tucci, *Built in Boston: City and Suburb* (Boston, 1978), 23, 43.

10. *The National Cyclopaedia of American Biography.*

11. Also described as "Hungarian" in the Trustees' Minutes, Zucker is mentioned in Manhattan sources for 1855: Dennis Steadman Francis, *Architects in Practice: New York City, 1840–1900* (New York, 1980).

12. Jackson Homestead, Newton, Massachusetts.

13. Frances Boott Greenough, ed., *Letters of Horatio Greenough to His Brother, Henry Greenough* (Boston, 1887), 128–29.

14. "On the Proposed National Monument at Edinburgh," *Blackwood's* 5 (1819), 377–87; reprinted (as "National Monuments") in Alison's *Miscellaneous Essays* of 1845 (ed. Philadelphia, 1853), 73–84.

15. Massachusetts Academy of Fine Arts, *Catalogue of the First Semi-Annual Exhibition of Paintings* (Boston, 1853).

16. A descendant of *Mayflower* passenger John Howland married Abraham Hammatt in 1748. See William T. Davis, *Genealogical Register of Plymouth Families* (Baltimore, 1985), 124, 148.

17. Billings to James F. Hyde, mayor of Newton, Massachusetts, 1 February 1854 (Hyde Papers, Jackson Homestead, Newton, Massachusetts). See chapter 1.

18. No bronze medal is known to the author.

19. Printed solicitation in the author's collection. All statuettes known to the author are the smallest version (and measure approximately twenty-two and one-half inches high), and those that are dated were cast in 1867. For published examples see Jennifer A. Gordon, *Cast in the Shadow: Models for Public Sculpture in America* (Williamstown, Mass., 1985), 18–20; it should be noted, however, the statuette is not a maquette for the monument), and Christie's catalogue "Nineteenth- and Twentieth-Century American Paintings . . . and Sculpture" (31 May 1990), no. 253. The arrangement of the ancillary figures differs in these two statuettes: that at Vassar (which agrees with one in the author's collection) has Law to Charity's right; on that sold at Christie's Law is replaced by Freedom.

20. *Ballou's Pictorial Drawing-Room Companion* 9 (1 November 1856): 284.

21. The idea of awarding them dates from late summer 1855, as we know from the printed solicitation copyrighted 1 September in the author's collection. One of these bronze statuettes was exhibited at the Washington Statue Fair in November 1859: *Boston Transcript* (17 November 1859).

22. There are in fact three engraved views copyrighted 1 September 1855: a broadside, the solicitation for funds, and a certification of contribution (copies in the author's collection). These agree with each other, but not in all particulars with the statue or the (later) version in the *Illustrated Magazine*. The drapery clasp centered at *Faith*'s throat is, however, common to all except the magazine version, where it is placed asymmetrically above her left breast. It is the latter version that appears in the *Illustrated Pilgrim Memorial* of 1866.

The last quote ("Looking downward . . .") comes from a description given by Billings himself, published in Russell, *Pilgrim Memorials*, 193–95. There are slight discrepancies with the magazine account.

23. William Chambers, *Things As They Are in America* (London, 1854), 214–15, and Francis Dillon, *The Pilgrims* (New York, 1975), 166.

24. In this the proposal improved upon one of Billings's possible sources of inspiration, Crespi's figure of San Carlo Borromeo, whose viewing platform, as shown clearly in the engraving after Billings's sketch, was reached by a tall, rickety ladder propped against its flank (see fig. 88).

25. This detail appears in an engraved view copyrighted 1859 (author's collection).

26. Russell, *Pilgrim Memorials*, 194.

27. William W. Wheildon, *Memoir of Solomon Willard* ([Boston], 1865), 58.

28. *History of the Siege of Boston* (Boston, 1849; 2d ed., 1851), 337–47. Billings worked on the frontispiece to Richard Frothingham's *History of Charlestown, Massachusetts* (Boston, 1845–49).

29. In Seelye's forthcoming study of Plymouth Rock.

30. Pamela Scott, "Robert Mills and American Monuments," in *Robert Mills, Architect*, ed. John M. Bryan (Washington, D.C., 1989), 143–77.

31. Neil Harris, *The Artist in American Society* (Chicago, 1982), 188–92.

32. Peter A. Clayton and Martin J. Price, *The Seven Wonders of the Ancient World* (London, 1988); E. Lesbazeilles, *Les Colosses anciens et moderns* (Paris, 1876); Virginia L. Bush, *Colossal Sculpture of the Cinquecento* (New York, 1976); Marvin Trachtenberg, *The Statue of Liberty* (New York, 1977); and Karal Ann Marling, *The Colossus of Roads* (Minneapolis, 1984). Trachtenberg's chapter 4, "The Colossal Vision," is fundamental to this section.

33. Trachtenberg, *Statue of Liberty*, 84.

34. Lesbazeilles, *Colosses*, 3. Billings could have known of other European proposals for colossal statues that appeared in the American illustrated press during these years, such as the twenty-five-foot figure of the American Republic in the *Illustrated News* 2 (29 October 1853): 1, or Pompeo Marchesi's monument to the Austrian emperor, a fifty-foot figure on a pedestal surrounded by lesser figures, published in *Ballou's* 6 (17 June 1854).

35. Scott, "Robert Mills," 158.

Jacob Landy, "The Washington Monument Project in New York," *Journal of the Society of Architectural Historians* 28 (1969): 291–97. See also Lauretta Dimmick, "'An Altar Erected to Heroic Virtue Itself': Thomas Crawford and His *Virginia Washington Monument*," *American Art Journal* 23 (1991): 4–73.

36. *Letters on the Internal Improvements and Commerce of the West* (Boston, 1839), 22–23 (letter dated 24 November 1838). See John Seelye, *Beautiful Machine* (New York, 1991).

37. Henry A. S. Dearborn, *Sketch of the Life of the Apostle Eliot, Preparatory to a Subscription for Erecting a Monument to His Memory* (Roxbury, Mass., 1850). This includes a lithographic view of the design but not, alas, the name of the designer. It does resemble, somewhat, the monuments shown in Paul Schulze's plates of the following years.

38. See Vivien Green Fryd, *Art and Empire: The Politics of Ethnicity in the United States Capitol, 1815–1860* (New Haven, 1992), 192. For the problems surrounding the use of the cap as an emblem of liberty in a slave-holding republic, see also Jean Fagin Yellin, "Caps and Chains: Hiram Powers' Statue of 'Liberty,'" *American Quarterly* 38 (1986): 798–826.

39. John H. Thorndike, *Dedication of the Mechanics' Hall* (Boston, 1860), 6–7.

40. Hammatt Billings, "Sketches at Mount Auburn," *Boston Almanac* (Boston, 1857),

49–60. For the Athenaeum see Emerson, *Journals*, 10:250 (June 1868), and Josiah Quincy, *The History of the Boston Athenaeum* (Cambridge, Mass., 1851), 232, 234–35.

41. *A Memorial of Daniel Webster from the City of Boston* (Boston, 1853), 53, 78.

42. *Boston Transcript*, 4 (26 February 1853): 137 and 143. Other proposals for a Webster monument appear in the *Boston Daily Journal* (29 August 1853): 2 (Doric column), and *Dodge's Literary Museum* 7 (10 September 1853) (bronze statue of Webster addressing the Senate).

43. For Billings's rendering of the battle of 19 April 1775 created for the Lexington Monument Association see chapter 2.

44. This brief and tantalizing notice of 10 April 1860 also suggests a falling out between Ball and Billings. According to this, the commission went to Ball, but Billings was appealing through Edward Everett to the board for "restitution of certain rights claimed by him." The editors, as always champions of Billings and his work, go on to write that "it would be palpably unjust to deprive him of any of the results of his genius." A serious split seems unlikely, given the fact that Billings and Ball were still collaborating in 1867 on the Washington monument in the Public Garden.

45. Charles Hudson, *History of the Town of Lexington* (Boston, 1868), 218–19. By the time this history was published, the hope of actually erecting the monument was effectively dead. Thomas Ball (*My Three Score Years and Ten* [Boston, 2d ed., 1892], 215–16) wrote that a small model was paid for and a contract drawn up for a fifteen-foot figure (far short of that envisioned in Billings's view of the monument on the engraved certificate), but that the project foundered at the Civil War.

46. Michael Richman, *Daniel Chester French* (Washington, D.C., 1976), 39–47.

47. Massachusetts Academy, *Catalogue*.

48. Jean V. Matthews, *Rufus Choate: The Law and Civic Virtue* (Philadelphia, 1980), 48–49.

49. See, for example, Arthur Quinn, *A New World: An Epic of Colonial America from the Founding of Jamestown to the Fall of Quebec* (Boston, 1994), 80–116.

50. Edward Everett, ed., *The Works of Daniel Webster* (Boston, 4th ed., 1853), 7–8, 11, 48–49.

51. *An Account of the Pilgrim Celebration at Plymouth, August 1, 1853* (Boston, 1853), [1]. Everett's speech, from which I quote, is printed here, 62–77, and reprinted in Edward Everett, *Orations and Speeches on Various Occasions* (Boston, 1859), 3:232.

52. For the expression of similar sentiments, see Lyman Beecher, *The Memory of Our Fathers* (Boston, 1828), esp. 22–23, and Rufus Choate, "The Age of the Pilgrims: The Heroic Period of Our History," in *The Works of Rufus Choate*, ed. Samuel Gilman Brown (Boston, 1862), 1:371.

53. Felicia Hemans, "The Landing of the Pilgrims in New England," in *The Poetical Works of Felicia Hemans* (Philadelphia, 1853), 495.

54. Trachtenberg, *Statue of Liberty*, 70–71.

55. This drawing is in the large Bartlett scrapbook in the Fine Arts Department, Boston Public Library.

56. See Yellin, "Caps and Chains," for other examples.

57. Edward A. Maser, ed., *Cesare Ripa: Baroque and Rococo Pictorial Imagery, the 1758–60*

Hertel Edition (New York, 1971), no. 66, for example, or H.-F. Gravelot and C.-N. Cochin, *Iconologie par figures* (Geneva, 1972).

58. This is a "syncretistic process" that Trachtenberg calls "synthomorphosis" (*Statue of Liberty*, 65; see also Fryd, *Art and Empire*, 193). I doubt that Billings thought in such terms.

59. Bo Wennberg, *French and Scandinavian Sculpture in the Nineteenth Century* (Stockholm, 1978), 166–67, and H. W. Janson, *Nineteenth-Century Sculpture* (New York, 1985), 185–86.

60. Wendy Greenhouse, "The Landing of the Fathers," in *Picturing History: American Painting, 1770–1930*, ed. William Ayres (New York, 1993), 45–63.

61. Carl L. Crossman and Charles R. Strickland, "Early Depictions of the Landing of the Pilgrims," *Antiques* 98 (1970): 777–81; *The History of the Pilgrims; or, a Grandfather's Story of the First Settlers of New England* (Boston, 1831 [4th ed., 1848]), frontispiece; and J. W. Barber, *United States Book; or, Interesting Events in the History of the United States* (New Haven, 1833), opp. p. 37, where it shares the page with the *Settlement of Jamestown*.

62. Greenhouse, "Landing of the Fathers," 50–51.

63. Fryd, *Art and Empire*, 25–28.

64. Ashbel Steele, *Chief of the Pilgrims; or, the Life and Time of William Brewster* (Philadelphia, 1857); it is described on 214–15 n. 5. See also Fryd, *Art and Empire*, 51–54.

65. Barber, *United States Book*, opp. p. 60, for example.

66. Fryd, *Art and Empire*, 28–32.

67. Harris, *Artist in American Society*, 193.

68. Angela Miller, *The Empire of the Eye* (Ithaca, N.Y., 1993), 16 (and chap. 6).

69. Wesley Frank Craven, *The Legend of the Founding Fathers* (New York, 1956), 9–10, 17, 37–38. See also Lawrence Buell, *New England Literary Culture* (Cambridge, Mass., 1986), 33, 45, 201.

70. Harris, *Artist in American Society*, 194.

71. Blanche Linden-Ward, *Silent City on a Hill: Landscapes of Memory and Boston's Mount Auburn Cemetery* (Columbus, Ohio, 1989), 118.

72. The letter (of either 13 October or 13 December 1855) goes on to say the monument "is worthy of the taste of the period and of the genius that conceived it." But Quincy is also bothered by the potential cost, and he reminds Billings of the histories of the Bunker Hill and Washington Monuments. The architect had designed a house for the Quincys in Wollaston, Massachusetts, in 1848.

73. Paul Revere Frothingham, *Edward Everett: Orator and Statesman* (Boston, 1925), 379.

74. The original, which I quote, is dated 21 November 1855. It was published in the *American Congregational Year-Book* (New York, 1859), 6:iii, with other letters linking the past with the present and the future.

75. Wise was Everett's daughter's father-in-law.

76. *Illustrated Pilgrim Memorial* (Boston, 1864), 32–39, and *Proceedings at the Celebration by the Pilgrim Society*, 12–16. See also *Architects' and Mechanics' Journal* 1 (1859): 11.

77. At the evening ball after Daniel Webster's stirring speech in 1820, a scallop shell was hung around his neck. This, according to Gomes (*Pilgrim Society*, 8), was the first use of this medieval emblem in relation to the American Pilgrims. The shells survive as landscape ornaments on Allerton Hill (see fig. 83).

78. Herbert B. Adams, "Plymouth Rock Restored," *Magazine of American History* 8 (1882): 46.

79. A scrapbook at the Countway Library of the Harvard University Medical School contains sketches by Billings and others after blackboard drawings by Rimmer made during February and March 1864. For Rimmer's work on *Faith*, see Truman H. Bartlett, *The Art Life of William Rimmer* (Boston, 1882), 87, and Jeffrey Weidman, "William Rimmer: Critical Catalogue Raisonne," Ph.D. diss., Indiana University, 1982, 1:382–86. The plaster figure seems not to have survived.

80. See the stereocard published in William C. Darrah, *The World of Stereographs* (Gettysburg, Pa., 1977), 189 (fig. 293).

81. T. H. Bartlett, "Early Settler Memorials—III," *American Architect and Building News* 20 (1886): 215–18.

82. Four sketches, one for ancillary figures on the chairs, and others for the *Compact*, were exhibited at the Pilgrim Society in 1989, although they cannot at present be located. In 1983 Barbara A. Murek, then an assistant editor for the National Trust of the papers of Daniel Chester French in the Library of Congress, wrote the author of Billings's correspondence with French regarding these reliefs, but Sarah Allaback has been unable recently to locate such letters.

83. Trachtenberg, *Statue of Liberty*.

10. "From the Pencil of Billings"

1. *Boston Transcript* (24 and 26 October 1848).

2. Charles Coleman Sellers, *Charles Willson Peale* (New York, 1969), 181–99; Paul R. Baker, *Stanny: The Gilded Life of Stanford White* (New York, 1989), 167–69.

3. *Boston Transcript* (27 July 1850): 2. The *Transcript* for 6, 14, 16, and 17 August carries notices of the parade and the funeral car. The following information and quotations are gleaned from these issues.

4. Holman Hamilton, *Zachary Taylor: Soldier in the White House* (Indianapolis, 1951).

5. Samuel Longfellow, *Life of Henry Wadsworth Longfellow* (Boston, 1886), 2:186–87. The poet added that he would "stay quietly at home" in his summer residence at Nahant.

6. Henry T. Bailey, "An Architect of the Old School," *New England Magazine* 25 (1901); *Harper's Weekly* (18 and 27 October 1860); *New-York Illustrated News* 2 (3 November 1860).

7. See *Boston Transcript* (14–25 November 1859) for various accounts of the decorations and proceedings. The following information and quotations are gleaned from these issues.

8. [George Spencer Phillips], *Local Loiterings, and Visits in the Vicinity of Boston* (Boston, 1845), 65.

9. Billings-Emmons correspondence, 5 July 1841 (Joanna Andros Collection, Keene, New Hampshire).

10. *Boston Transcript* (9 July 1851): 2, and *Gleason's Pictorial Drawing-Room Companion* [deluxe edition] 1 (19 July 1851): 192, from which the following quotations are con-

flated. Although displays apparently occurred every year during this period, Hovey only occasionally operated them, and Billings's name appears in accounts only for 1851 and 1853.

11. *Gleason's* 5 (9 July 1853): 32.

12. *Gleason's* 4 (26 February 1853): 137 and 143. All this preceded the official Public Garden Act of 1859. See chapter 9.

13. Billings scrapbook, fols. 23–25 (Stowe-Day Library, Harriet Beecher Stowe Center, Hartford).

14. *Boston Transcript* (6 November 1849): 2. This notice reports that "a wood-cut of the design will be prepared by Billings as a final . . . acknowledgement of the subscriptions," but none has come to the author's attention. See also *Transcript* (9 November 1849): 4.

15. Compare Billings's allegorical representation of "the State of Massachusetts" in *Ballou's* for 9 February 1856.

16. "Scrapbook—Criticisms, 1839–50," Henry Wadsworth Longfellow Papers (Houghton Library, Harvard University, MS Am 1340 [221], fol. 229 [unidentified]).

17. Jane Holz Kay, *Lost Boston* (Boston, 1980), 161. For a view of the hall before the installation of the Wackler-Billings-Herter organ see *Gleason's* 3 (18 December 1852): 385.

18. *Dwight's Journal of Music* 15 (30 July 1859): 143. See also the issue of 19 November, p. 271.

19. *Dwight's* 21 (21 June 1862): 95–96 and 23 (2 May 1863): 21–22.

20. *Dwight's* 23 (23 October 1863): 126. For the firm see Katherine S. Howe and others, *Herter Brothers: Furniture and Interiors for a Gilded Age* (New York, 1994). The omission of this commission in Howe's publication was rectified by Catherine Hoover Voorsanger in her "Gustave Herter, Cabinetmaker and Decorator," *The Magazine Antiques* 147 (May 1995): 740–51. Voorsanger, however, unaccountably fails to mention Billings's work on the design. Though Gustave and Christian Herter worked together in 1863, the name "Herter Brothers" dates only from the next year.

21. *Dwight's* 23 (12 December 1863): 147. See also *Harper's Weekly* 12 (December 1863): 788: Billings "with characteristic frankness and unselfishness, [pronounced Herters's design] superior to his own." The *Harper's* account is repeated in *The Great Organ in the Boston Music Hall* (Boston, 1865): 22–23.

22. *Old and New* 2 (March 1875): 355–57.

23. For the history of the organ see *The Great Organ in Serlo Hall, Methuen, Mass.* (1909); William King Covell, "The Old Boston Music Hall Organ," *Old-Time New England* 18 (April 1928): 182–89; Covell, *The Boston Music Hall Organ* (London, 1931); and Edward W. Flint, *The Great Organ in the Methuen Memorial Music Hall* (Methuen, 1954).

24. Quoted here from Voorsanger, "Gustave Herter," 745.

25. J. J. Jarves, *The Art-Idea*, ed. Benjamin Rowland Jr. (Cambridge, Mass., 1960), 241. Henry James, *The Bostonians* (1885), chapter 20. For contemporary views of the music hall with the Wackler-Billings-Herter organ in situ, see *Frank Leslie's Illustrated Newspaper* (23 May 1868): 151 and 153, or (5 June 1869): 188.

26. In the following descriptions, the quotations are taken from the drawings.

27. These might be related to Billings's Massachusetts Charitable Mechanic Association building of this date.

28. There is also a design for another fireplace, much simpler than these two.

29. See the Hudson River Museum catalogue, *Eastlake-Influenced American Furniture, 1870–1890* (Yonkers, N.Y., 1974).

30. Roy Morris Jr., *Ambrose Bierce* (New York, 1995).

31. *Eastlake-Influenced American Furniture*, [6].

Index